AA

GUIDE TO
NATIONAL
TRUST
PROPERTIES & IN BRITAIN

Shalford Mill, on the river Tillingbourne

Produced by the Publications
Division of the
Automobile Association

EDITOR:
Richard Powell
ART EDITOR:
Mike Preedy MSAID

TEXT CONTRIBUTORS:
Richard Powell
(The West Country,
South and South East England),
Roger Thomas
(Wales and the Marcher Lands,
Central and Eastern England,
The North Country),
Valerie Wenham
(Northern Ireland),
Donna Wood
(Scotland)

Maps produced by the
Cartographic Department of the
Automobile Association

The contents of this book are
believed correct at the time of
printing. Nevertheless, the publisher
cannot accept any responsibility
for errors or omissions, or for
changes in details given

ISBN 0 86145 198 8
AA ref 52634

Filmsetting by
Vantage Photosetting Co Ltd,
Eastleigh and London, England
Printed and bound by
Jarrold & Sons Ltd, Norwich,
England

Published by the
Automobile Association,
Fanum House, Basingstoke,
Hampshire RG21 2EA

Soar Mill Cove, Salcombe, Devon   Sheffield Park Garden, East Sussex   St Elvis, St Bride's Bay, Dyfed

CONTENTS

Tattershall Castle, Lincolnshire

Wasdale, Cumbria

Glenfinnan Monument, Highland

White Park Bay, Co. Antrim

*Lanhydrock —
reached via an avenue of beeches and sycamores*

INTRODUCTION

Like bus drivers, telephone operators, nurses and many others, theatre folk work while others are playing. We are nocturnal animals. As others arrive home we are setting out for the theatre. During my forty years as an actor I have many times travelled the length and breadth of the British Isles filling some of my happiest daytime leisure hours exploring National Trust properties.

I first joined the Trust some thirty years ago and now cannot envisage life without it. I have to admit that I am parsimonious – not mean; merely frugal. I need only visit seven properties to recoup my annual subscription. So the first thing I do each year is to dash off to seven of the Trust's holdings – and from then on I am in credit. (Don't tell them – they may put up my subscription.)

Of course, I have many favourites – from the minute priest's house at Alfriston in Sussex to the seven courtyards, fifty-two staircases and three hundred and sixty-five rooms that make up the great house of Knole (and while in Kent don't miss Ellen Terry's gem of a house at Smallhythe). From the rolling grassland on Ditchling Beacon in Sussex to the thousands of acres of craggy beauty in the Lake District. From Gray's simple monument at Stoke Poges to the bleak silent stretches of Hadrian's Wall in Northumberland.

Dr Johnson said of the Giant's Causeway, 'Worth seeing but not worth going to see'; this guide collects together all the properties owned by the Trust which *are* worth a special visit. It has been produced by the Automobile Association, lavishly illustrated by specially commissioned photographs and enlivened by anecdotes of history and legend, for all those interested in Britain and the conservation of her heritage.

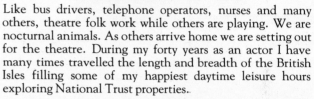

Donald Sinden

KEY TO MAP PAGES

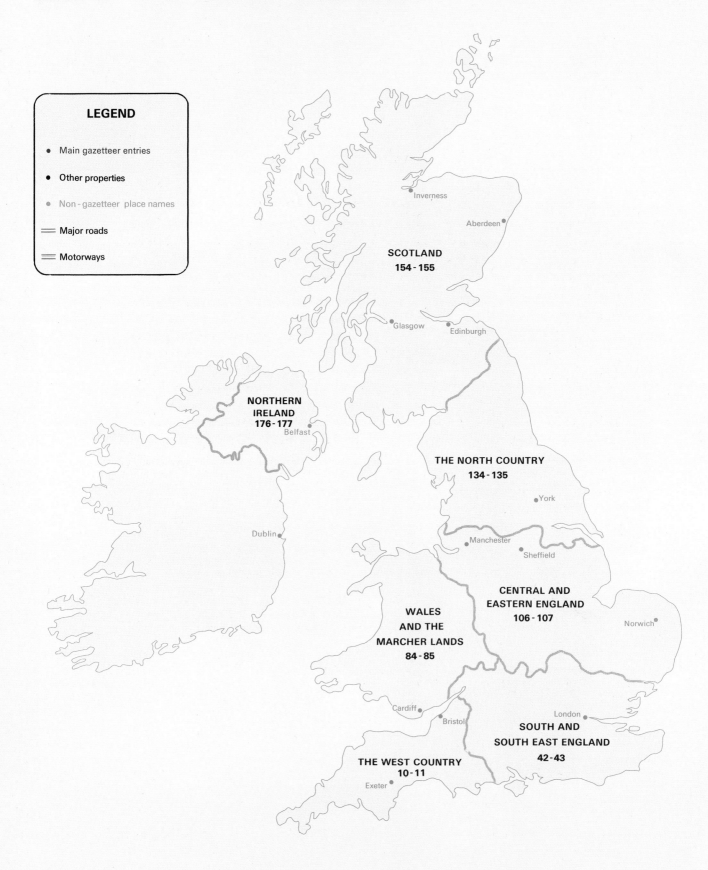

LEGEND

- Main gazetteer entries
- Other properties
- Non-gazetteer place names
══ Major roads
≡ Motorways

Inverness

Aberdeen

**SCOTLAND
154 - 155**

Glasgow

Edinburgh

**NORTHERN
IRELAND
176 - 177**

Belfast

**THE NORTH COUNTRY
134 - 135**

York

Dublin

Manchester

Sheffield

**CENTRAL AND
EASTERN ENGLAND
106 - 107**

Norwich

**WALES
AND THE
MARCHER LANDS
84 - 85**

Cardiff

London

Bristol

**SOUTH AND
SOUTH EAST ENGLAND
42 - 43**

**THE WEST COUNTRY
10 - 11**

Exeter

ABOUT THE BOOK

The book is divided into seven regions, as shown on the map opposite. Within each region the places described are listed in alphabetical order. Where relevant, map references and information about opening times, admission charges, facilities for the disabled, refreshments and location accompany each entry. Where parking is an important consideration, e.g. at large country houses, we say whether it is free or charged. If a property is only open for three days or less in a week, this is indicated as 'limited opening'.

The map reference applies to the regional map at the beginning of the section in which the entry falls. The map can also be used to plan visits to other properties in the same area. The National Grid reference number can be used with Ordnance Survey maps and AA road atlases.

At the end of each section is a list of 'Other Properties'. These are mostly smaller sites owned by the National Trust which do not justify a full description. These are marked on the regional maps in black, while the main gazetteer entries are marked in red.

The opening times given are intended as guidelines only, since specific hours of admission may change at short notice. We therefore advise visitors to telephone the appropriate National Trust Information Office in advance to avoid disappointment. The addresses and telephone numbers, along with the counties they cover, are listed at the beginning of each section.

THE WEST COUNTRY

Soar Mill Cove —
an idyllic corner of south Devon

ANTONY HOUSE

Cornwall   SX45

A grey stone building, approached across a velvet lawn flanked on either side by a brick wing, Antony House has an attractive, unassuming elegance. It is the work of an architect still untraced, who built the house for the Carew family, owners of the estate since the 15th century, between 1710 and 1721.

Unlike many country houses, Antony was spared a complete Victorian modernisation. Some of the rooms in the house retain their original panelling of Dutch oak, and still have furniture which was made for them in the 1720s. Family relics and the collection of family portraits illustrate how history affected the family through their changing tastes and lifestyle.

The Carew family were extremely fond of travel, and this is illustrated nowhere better than in the delightful terraced garden of 25 acres. For example, from the Far East there are a Burmese bell temple and two Japanese stone lanterns, a loquat tree from eastern Asia and a maidenhair tree from China; from the United States a large hickory tree and many *magnolia grandiflora*. Very English, however, are a topiary and some yew hedges. Mr Pole Carew, who largely redesigned the garden himself in about 1800, was no doubt greatly helped by the natural beauty of the site, which slopes gently down to the river Lynher and commands an ancient ferry point over the river Tamar marking the boundary between the counties of Cornwall and Devon.

Open April to end Oct. Admission charged. Free parking. 5m W Plymouth on A374 (via Torpoint car ferry).

ARLINGTON COURT

Devon   SS64

Pillars at each corner and a porch over the front door are the only ornament on this plain, beautifully proportioned white house of about 1820. It is a little spoiled, however, by a new wing added later in the century.

The Chichester family built this house, on land which they had owned for 500 years, but it was the enterprising Miss Rosalie Chichester, born in 1865 and the last of her line, who gave the house its unusual character. She filled the rooms with collections of pewter, shells, musical instruments and model ships.

Most of the rooms are shown to visitors. The servants' quarters and kitchens are hidden in the basement, so the whole of the ground floor is

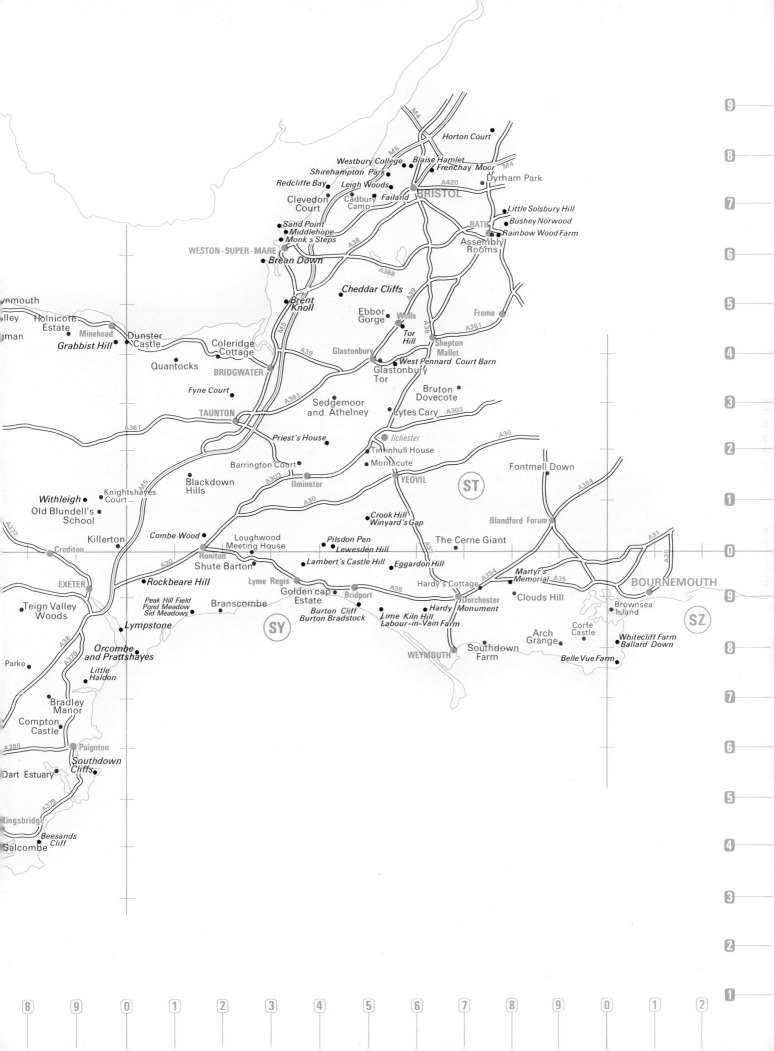

devoted to living rooms. The furniture in all of the rooms is mainly Regency and Victorian. An unexpectedly grand staircase leads to the bedrooms. These are totally 19th-century in character and, like downstairs, are unlikely to have changed since Miss Chichester's birth.

Miss Chichester was a great nature-lover, and characteristically she turned the 2,700-acre estate into a nature reserve, ringing it with an eight-mile-long iron fence. Within this boundary the pastures, lakes and woods are as she left them. A nature trail leads through the woods to the lakeside, and the stables, built in 1864, now contain a good museum of horse-drawn carriages.

Open April to end Oct. Admission charged. Free parking. Wheelchairs available. Restaurant. 8m NE Barnstaple off A39.

BARRINGTON COURT

Somerset   *ST31*

This E-shaped 16th-century mansion is built of warm Ham Hill stone and, externally at least, appears not to have changed since the day building was completed. Who the builder was is uncertain; it was either Henry Daubeney, whose family had owned the estate since the reign of the Norman kings, or William Clifton, a wealthy merchant to whom Daubeney sold the estate to support his expensive lifestyle at court. Whoever built it, it is a traditional building of the times – apart from the flamboyant array of twisted finials and spiralled chimneys which enliven the roofline.

Barrington Court became derelict by the end of the 19th century and passed to the Trust in 1907, by which time the great hall was being used as a cider cellar, and the house had been stripped of all its original interior features – apart from two overmantels. The linenfold panelling in the hall, the roof of the staircase and the spectacular early 16th-century screen and carved ceilings in the small dining room were collected and installed, along with all the other furnishings, by Colonel A. A. Lyle, to whom the house was leased by the Trust in 1920.

The stable block dominates the garden which was created by the imaginative designer Gertrude Jekyll, and in her usual style it is laid out as a series of small gardens and formal designs, each with a distinctive character and subtle colouring.

Open April to end Sept. Admission charged. Free parking. Wheelchair access to garden only. 3m NE Ilminster, off B3168.

BATH ASSEMBLY ROOMS

Avon   *ST76*

In these upper rooms in Alfred Street, the high society of Georgian England gathered for balls and grand occasions where the wealthy flaunted their riches and their young vied for marriage

partners. This was the age Jane Austen wrote about, and scenes from *Persuasion* and *Northanger Abbey* endure in these rooms. They occupy the upper floors of an imposing Bath stone building designed in 1771 by John Wood the younger; he and his father are responsible for Bath's particular style of elegant architecture. Wood restricted the splendid decorative plasterwork to the high ceilings and window surrounds of the main rooms, which are two storeys high, because, sensibly, he felt decoration any nearer eye-level would become lost when placed in competition with the elegance of the crowds. In the basement there is a Museum of Costumes (not NT).

Open all year. Admission charged. Wheelchair access, lift to Costume Museum in basement. Alfred Street, Bath, E of the Circus.

BLACKDOWN HILLS

Somerset   *ST11*

From these 1,000ft-high hills there are views over the Vale of Taunton, to Exmoor, to the Quantocks, and as far afield as the Welsh mountains on the north side of the Bristol Channel. The Trust owns just 61 acres here, but they are typical of the whole range.

The slopes of the hills are thickly wooded, and threaded by well-trodden footpaths leading from the National Trust car park. The lower parts of the hills are on clay, and are often waterlogged, but a profusion of wild plants, birds and butterflies lends an air of magic to lazy summer days.

Half a mile west of the National Trust property is the Wellington Monument, a slender 175ft-high obelisk of stone, at the top of which is a small chamber reached by steps. From this vantage point the views are extraordinary – although the wind can be ferocious. The monument was built in 1817 by local gentry wishing to honour the Iron Duke, who took his title from the little town at the foot of the Blackdown Hills.

2m S of Wellington, ½m E of A38.

The east front of Bradley Manor, a delightful relic of 15th-century Devon in the Lemon valley

THE FIRST BALL
In Jane Austen's day the Assembly Rooms were known as the Upper Rooms; in this passage the heroine of *Northanger Abbey* is preparing for her first ball.

'. . . our heroine's entrée into life could not take place till after three or four days had been spent in learning what was mostly worn . . . when all these matters were arranged, the important evening came which was to usher her into the Upper Rooms. Her hair was cut and dressed by the best hand, her clothes put on with care, and both Mrs Allen and her maid declared she looked quite as she should do.'

BODRUGAN'S LEAP

Cornwall   *SX04*

Between Gorran Haven and Mevagissey, on Cornwall's south coast, the Trust owns a three-acre site, a high cliff otherwise unremarkable but for the legend attached to it. In about 1490 Sir Henry Trenowth of Bodrugan, a keen supporter of Richard III, was chased to this spot by Sir Richard Edgecumbe of Cotehele, a supporter of Henry VII and the Tudor cause. (Richard III lost his life and his kingdom to Henry at Bosworth in 1485.) Here Sir Henry leapt from the cliff into a waiting boat below, and escaped to France – a feat remembered through the name of this place for more than four and a half centuries.

1½m S of Mevagissey.

BOSCASTLE HARBOUR

Cornwall   *SX09*

Along the 40 miles of inhospitable coastline between Hartland and Padstow, Boscastle Harbour offers the only protected anchorage. It is like a small fjord, entered from the open sea through a narrow gorge-like way between the cliffs of Penally Point and Willapark, which turns through two right angles before reaching the harbour.

The curving jetty which heralds the calm waters of Boscastle Harbour itself was rebuilt by Sir Richard Grenville in 1584. It is hollow to absorb the battering of the sea, and is still as effective as it was 400 years ago. The outer breakwater, which was added in the 19th century when Boscastle was busy shipping slate, was blown up by a German mine in 1941, but has been rebuilt by the National Trust. The Palace Stables, also dating from the period of

The history of Boscastle Harbour stretches back to the 14th century when the Duchy of Cornwall Harbour Master is known to have let it at £1 per annum. Corn, slate and manganese ore were the port's 19th-century exports; hardware, pottery, coal and manure, its imports

the slate boom, are now let as a youth hostel. The ponies which hauled the slate to the ships were housed here. Altogether the Trust owns 340 acres in and around Boscastle, including 100 acres of cliff with fine views.

3½m NE of Tintagel, on the B3263.

BRADLEY MANOR

Devon   *SX87*

Just on the edge of Newton Abbot, this limewashed medieval manor lies snugly in the wooded valley of the river Lemon, and presents to the visitor a delightful jumble of gables and oriel windows. The gatehouse and some lesser buildings have been destroyed, but the manor itself remains remarkably unaltered. It was begun in 1419 by the Yarde family, and the hall is essentially from that date. In 1427 the chapel to the right of the hall was built. Its wooden waggon roof is especially interesting for the carved bosses. Then, in 1495, the present gabled front was added.

Many of the original windows and much of the interior decoration belong to the 15th and 16th centuries. A notable later addition is the attractive plasterwork in one of the upstairs rooms, which dates from the late 17th century.

Limited opening April to end Sept. Admission charged. Wedge Newton Abbot, W of A381.

BRANSCOMBE AND SALCOMBE REGIS

Devon   *SY28, 18*

The Trust owns about 500 acres of the south Devon coastline between Branscombe Mouth and Salcombe Mouth, to the west. Along this four-mile stretch is Branscombe Beach, a popular spot with holidaymakers, set at the end of a green valley at the top of which is Branscombe village. The cliffs along here are riddled with caves, popular in the 18th century with smugglers.

Branscombe village is a charming collection of whitewashed stone and thatched cottages. Also to be found here are an old forge, and a bakery – which still produces delicious bread from ovens fired by faggots.

S of Salcombe Regis.

BROWNSEA ISLAND

Dorset   *SZ08*

Although this 500-acre island lies in busy Poole Harbour and is visited by thousands of people each year, it remains surprisingly unspoilt. It is an island of woods and heathland, marshland and beaches, its only community huddled around the old quay, which is overlooked by a castle. Half the island is a nature reserve, and is one of the last strongholds of the red squirrel.

The Dorset Naturalists' Trust run 1½-hour tours of the nature reserve, which has limited access. Otherwise the miles of woodland and heathland paths, and a quiet bathing beach, can be freely enjoyed by visitors to this haven on the busy south coast.

Open April to end Sept. Admission charged. Wheelchairs available. Cafeteria near Quay. Ferries from Poole and Sandbanks.

BRUTON DOVECOTE

Somerset   *ST63*

On a hillock outside the Somerset village of Bruton stands a dovecote and the remains of an old wall – all that is left of an Augustinian abbey. The dovecote, now roofless, is a square tower, three storeys high with mullioned windows and four gables. It probably dates from the 16th century, when hundreds of pigeons would have roosted and nested within the shelter of its walls and fed off the crops of the local peasantry, to provide the monks with a constant source of fresh meat.

½m S of Bruton across railway, ¼m W of B3081.

BUCKLAND ABBEY

Devon   *SX46*

This austere house, set in a remote site deep in the Devon countryside, is famed – curiously enough – for its maritime connections. It is, however, just 11 miles from Plymouth, and here two of Britain's most famous seafarers – Sir Richard Grenville of the *Revenge* (see Lundy entry, page 28), and Sir Francis Drake, the first man to circumnavigate the world – found it convenient to live.

The massive central square tower at the heart of the house betrays its origin. The building was originally a Cistercian abbey, founded in 1278, a simple but massively solid structure erected by monks renowned for their agricultural expertise. The order continued to live and work at Buckland for 260 years until 1539, when Henry VIII had them evicted in his purge of the monasteries and the abbey was sold to Sir Richard Grenville's grandfather. He did little with the land, but his grandson, the famous captain, converted the buildings into a country house. The church dominates the feel of the house, for everywhere there remain the lines and forms of ecclesiastical architecture.

Sir Francis Drake bought the house from Grenville in 1581 and his family remained there almost continuously until about 1813. The only significant changes made by the Drakes were the addition of a Georgian chamber and a main staircase in about 1770. Otherwise the house is unchanged since Grenville's day.

The house today contains a Drake, Naval, and West Country Folk Museum, Drake's famous drum among the exhibits. In the beautiful 14th-century tithe barn to the east of the house there is a collection of several old wagons, coaches and carts.

Open April to end Sept. Admission charged. Free parking. Refreshments. 11m N of Plymouth.

CADBURY CAMP

Avon   *ST47*

The dramatic and beautiful site of Cadbury Camp is well worth a visit. It is a perfectly preserved Iron Age hill-fort which lies on high ground between Bristol and the coast at Clevedon, offering splendid views of the Bristol Channel and the mouth of the Severn with the Welsh coast and the shadow of mountains beyond Cardiff. To the north is the lush green and curiously named Gordano Valley, and to the south the Mendips rise above a coastal plain

Castle Drogo's grand site was chosen on the occasion of a family picnic in the summer of 1910. Sir Edwin Lutyens and Adrian Drewe, eldest son of the Drewe family, imagined a long drive along a hilltop road culminating in the sight of the castle, a splendid edifice of granite crowning the pinnacle of the hill

Dovecotes

The National Trust and the National Trust for Scotland between them own about 20 dovecotes, or 'doocots' as they are called north of the Border. These 20 represent only a small proportion of a huge number of dovecotes that, from Norman times until the 17th century, provided an important source of fresh meat. Dovecotes are often built of local materials, and provide an architectural record in miniature – for example, those in the Cotswolds are built of the famous local limestone, while in Worcestershire they are half-timbered, with wattle and daub walls.

Before root crops were widely grown for use as winter fodder, most livestock had to be slaughtered and the meat salted down for the winter. Salt was often scarce in those days, and much of the available meat would go bad before it could be eaten. However, the Romans had handed down to the Normans the knowledge that birds could be kept as a source of meat, and that the pigeon was conveniently a bird of habit, often roosting regularly in the same place. Suitable houses were built and the birds encouraged to roost and nest in them. Therefore a self-perpetuating source of meat could be easily kept, especially as the birds fed off the crops of the serfs. In Norman times this practice spread right across the country, and indeed became so popular that it became necessary to limit the number of dovecotes to one for each manor, in order to save the crops of the common people from total devastation. There was, however, no limit to size, and some dovecotes are known to have housed 1,000–2,000 birds.

CASTLE DROGO

Devon   SX79

This is perhaps the last great country house ever built in Britain. It was designed by Sir Edwin Lutyens in 1910–13 for Sir Julius Drewe, a businessman whose chain of Home and Colonial Stores enabled him to retire an extremely wealthy man at the age of 33.

He built this extraordinary mock-Gothic castle in Devon on the strength of a discovery that a baron called Drogo de Teigne, who had owned land in the county in Norman times, was his ancestor. The setting where Drewe decided to found his ancestral home is as dramatic as he or Lutyens could have wished for. The castle is perched on the edge of a 900ft-high cliff above the Teign gorge. All about it are spectacular views of Dartmoor National Park.

The foundation stone was laid on 4 April 1911 – Sir Julius' 55th birthday. The original plans were for a much larger house, illustrated by the model Lutyens made which is on exhibition in the gun room, but Sir Julius and his wife decided the rooms were too large for comfort, and made a last-minute revision in 1912.

Castle Drogo took twenty years to build. Every block of granite was specially quarried, and tirelessly laid by two masons. This colossal project has given posterity a magnificent piece of architecture, an extravagant salute to a more romantic age.

The interior is equally reminiscent of a medieval castle – the walls, apart from some hangings and tapestries, are to a great extent left unplastered – and not overly luxurious or comfortable. It is dramatic, though, with many changes in level, cavernous passages and rooms, and a splendid staircase.

Open April to end Oct. Admission charged. Free parking. Wheelchair available. Restaurant. 4m NE of Chagford, 6m S of A30.

MEMORIES AT CASTLE DROGO

Wealth and privilege could not protect the owners of Castle Drogo from the tragedies brought to so many thousands of families by the slaughter of World War I. Adrian Drewe, the eldest son, who had helped his father and the architect choose the site of the great castle that he was to have inherited, was killed in Flanders in 1917.

His mother created a shrine to his memory in a small room within the castle, and it can still be seen today, a rare survivor of a practice once common in upper-class families who wished to remember their dead. In the room are all the trophies and mementoes collected by Adrian during his years at school, at university and in the army. It is a poignant place where memories are almost as real as the thick granite walls.

cut by the threads of streams and dykes. To the east, the buildings of Bristol climb the hillsides from the city's river front.

Footpath up hill N from Middletown on the B3130, or from minor road to the N.

CADSONBURY

Cornwall   SX36

This is an enchanting, mysterious site: an unexcavated early Iron Age hill-fort on the summit of a steep hill which stands alone in the valley of the river Lynher. Our ancestors of possibly the fifth to third centuries BC built this stronghold, which archaeologists call univallate, that is, with one line of rampart-and-ditch defences. This spot is 425ft above the valley floor, and standing here it is easy to imagine why it was chosen for fortification, since it commands all the valley to the south.

Car park beside river. Signposted path at southern end of hill. Near New Bridge, 2m SW of Callington.

Drake's Drum

In the great hall of Buckland Abbey Drake planned his voyage to Cadiz in 1587 to 'Singe the King of Spain's Beard', and a year later planned the tactics which defeated Spain's great Armada. So the hall is a fitting home for Drake's Drum, one of our nation's most famous heirlooms.

Legend and mystery surround the age-worn drum, which accompanied Drake on his circumnavigation of the globe. His coat of arms is painted on one side, while a pattern of studded nails decorates the other. The drum is said to sound should England ever be in danger. Its beat was heard, it is told, over the calm Devon seas on the day war was declared in 1914. Four years later sailors related how they heard its loud beat of victory when the German fleet surrendered and was scuttled.

The drum was treasured by Drake, and it was with him when he died at sea off Puerto Bello in January 1596.

CERNE GIANT

Dorset ST60

This extraordinary figure has survived for more than 1,500 years; a 180ft-high man carved in outline on the chalk of the Downs, delineated by chalk-filled trenches about two feet wide and two feet deep. Facial features, nipples, ribs and the erect phallus are all shown – yet he has never in all that time been censored. The figure wields an enormous club. He is probably a Romano-British representation of Hercules, whose cult was revived by the Emperor Commodus in the second century. He is also obviously a figure of fertility, and Hercules appears to have been mixed with a local British god who had a more earthy tradition.

His influence must have overridden that of the parish priest and that of nearby Cerne Abbas Abbey. His survival is due to the local people, who must have tended him, and prevented him from becoming overgrown.

On Giant Hill, N of Cerne Abbas, 8m N of Dorchester, just off A352.

The Cerne giant, unique in Britain

CHAPEL CARN BREA

Cornwall SW32

The 657ft-high summit of Chapel Carn Brea overlooks the last few remaining miles of country before Land's End, and is said to have the widest sea views in England. On top of the rounded hill is a huge round Neolithic cairn, 62ft in diameter and probably originally 15ft high. It was badly damaged in World War II, but a slab coffin can still be seen on the south side. Stone-built chambers once lay at the centre.

Access on foot from lane skirting NE of hill which connects the A30 with the B3306.

CHAPEL PORTH

Cornwall SW64

Just south of St Agnes Head the National Trust owns 367 acres of cliff and moorland, including the narrow valley of Chapel Coombe, which leads to Chapel Porth and the sea. These high cliffs and now desolate moorlands were once the scene of great activity because of the rich deposits of tin and copper found here. Testament to this are the remains of the engine houses now in the care of the Trust.

The Wheal Coates tin mine, a very old mine, is right on the cliff edge. The pumping-engine house of the Towanroath shaft, built in the 1860s, perches precariously 200ft above the sea, and higher up the steep cliff still are the remains of the winding engine houses. This mine stopped production on 17 March 1914.

Chapel Porth – a huge expanse of beach two miles long – is revealed at low tide. From inside a sea cave in the cliffs below Wheal Coates it is possible to look up a mine shaft beneath the pump house.

Car park. Refreshments. 1½m SW of St Agnes, 1m N of Porthtowan.

THE CHURCH HOUSE

Devon SX77

At the centre of Widecombe-in-the-Moor, an attractive but highly commercialised Devonshire village at the heart of Dartmoor, is the Church House. A 16th-century granite building, it stands in a pleasant square, a colonnade along its front providing a covered walkway. Although the 15th-century church is the village's most famous building, the Church House has been described as one of the best of its kind in Devon. The house plays a full role in village life as it has done for centuries. It was the village school, and before that a brewhouse dating back to 1537. The part of the house known as Sexton's Cottage is a National Trust information centre, cottage and shop; the rest is leased as a village hall.

Open May to end Sept. Admission free. Wheelchair available. 6m NW of Ashburton in the village square.

The west front of Clevedon Court, which in the 16th century had a new west wing built on to it by John Wake. His family had inherited the estate a century before, and they remained Lords of the Manor of Clevedon until 1630. John Wakes' west wing was rebuilt three times during subsequent centuries and was finally demolished in the 20th century. The rest of the house, however, remains as John Wake knew it in 1570. The Wake emblem – a bear clasping a shield – can be seen perched on the gable on the left of the picture. The family motto was 'Wake and pray'

Behind the Church House in Widecombe-in-the-Moor rises the 16th-century tower of the 14th-century church, named the 'cathedral of the moors' because of its size and grandeur. The tower and the Church House were probably built with money donated by wealthy tinsmiths

CLEVEDON COURT

Avon   *ST47*

This is one of those houses which appears to have grown rather than to have been built. A rare and complete survival from the 14th century, it stands near the foot of hills which stretch to the Avon Gorge, and overlooks Clevedon Moor.

The house was built by Sir John de Clevedon in about 1320. He fashioned it around earlier buildings – the mid-13th-century tower and old hall. It follows the typical medieval plan – great hall flanked by living quarters for the lord and lady on one side, and the storerooms and kitchens on the other. The exception is the unusual chapel, notable for its long, rectangular south window filled with stone tracery perhaps depicting the fishing net of St Peter, the saint to whom the chapel is dedicated. The imposing two-storeyed porch, rather like an entrance to a church, leads into a passage to the left of which is the great hall, unchanged but for the addition of an 18th-century ceiling and an Elizabethan doorway. A window from the first-floor chapel overlooks the hall, so the servants could listen to the service, and the lady of the manor could keep an eye on her household.

In 1709 Clevedon passed into the hands of Abraham Elton, a Bristol merchant. His family remained at the Court until 1961. The two most famous Eltons are Sir Charles, born in 1778, and Sir Edmund Harry Elton, who inherited the property in 1883. Sir Charles was a formidable scholar and proficient writer, and guests at the Court in his time included literary figures John Clare, Charles Lamb, Robert Southey, Coleridge, Tennyson and Thackeray. But perhaps Sir Edmund was the more extraordinary. He became an internationally famous potter, an unusual occupation for a lord. Examples of his work are kept in the Museum Room in the old tower. In the Justice Room, to the right of the porch, is a collection of exquisite Nailsea glass.

COLERIDGE AT NETHER STOWEY

A regular visitor to Coleridge's cottage at Nether Stowey was John Thelwall, an ardent radical. There is nothing radical, however, about this letter Coleridge sent to Thelwall on 6 February 1797.

'. . . I never go to Bristol. From seven till half past eight I work in my garden, from breakfast till twelve I read and compose, then read again, feed the pigs, poultry, etc. till two o'clock; after dinner work again till tea; from tea till supper, review. So jogs the day, and I am happy. I have society – my friend T. Poole, and as many acquaintances as I can dispense with.

. . . We are very happy, and my little David Hartley grows a sweet boy and has high health; he laughs at us till he makes us weep for very fondness. You would smile to see my eye rolling up to the ceiling in a lyric fury, and on my knee a diaper pinned to warm . . .'

David Hartley was Coleridge's eldest son, and T. Poole was a local tanner with a love of literature, who lived adjacent to Coleridge and became a close friend.

CLOUDS HILL

Dorset   *SY89*

Aircraftsman Shaw, stationed at nearby Bovington Camp, rented this small, very ordinary cottage, in 1923. The name Shaw was a pseudonym for T. E. Lawrence, or Lawrence of Arabia. He disguised himself as Shaw to avoid publicity after his return from North Africa.

After first renting the cottage he later bought it; it became his 'earthly paradise', where he spent his evenings away from the camp reading, writing or listening to his gramophone. Here he wrote *Seven Pillars of Wisdom*, published in 1926. He was returning to the cottage on his motorcycle one evening in 1935 when he crashed and was killed. The cottage is kept much as he left it, sparsely furnished with sombre, utilitarian furniture, some of which he made himself. His gramophone and 78 r.p.m. records of Beethoven and Mozart remain, as well as photographs of his legendary Arabian Campaign.

Open April to Sept, limited opening Oct to March. Admission charged. 1m N of Bovington Camp, 9m E of Dorchester.

COLERIDGE COTTAGE

Somerset   *ST13*

Samuel Taylor Coleridge, his wife Sarah and infant son, David Hartley, moved to this little cottage in Nether Stowey in December 1796. In those days it was smaller, and had a roof of thatch rather than tile. Here Coleridge wrote some of his finest verse, including *The Ancient Mariner* and the first part of *Christabel*. The poet Wordsworth and his sister Dorothy moved to nearby Alfoxden six months later and the four friends met regularly. The two great literary men often went on nocturnal walks together, with notebooks and camp stools. This eccentric behaviour (as the locals thought it), combined with the strangers' northern accents and Dorothy Wordsworth's brown complexion, soon gave rise to the rumour that they were French spies. An investigator from the Home Office duly arrived at the local inn (now Globe House), where servants gave reports of conversations they had overheard between Coleridge and his friends. The investigator decided, however, that the poets were merely harmless cranks.

Coleridge left Nether Stowey after three years, but it was here in this small cottage that he was most inspired as a poet.

Open April to end Sept. Admission charged. Refreshments and parking in village. At W end of Nether Stowey, 8m W of Bridgwater.

Open April to end Sept. Admission charged (children under 17 must be accompanied by an adult). Free parking. Refreshments. 1½m E of Clevedon, on Bristol road (B3130).

COMPTON CASTLE

Devon   *SX86*

The towers, battlements and buttresses of a stronghold of the past greet the visitor to Compton. This medieval house has strong vertical lines and an up-and-down roofline of chimneys and little steep-pitched roofs. Its façade was perhaps imposing and forbidding in the violent age in which it was built, but to the modern eye it is pleasantly quaint and romantic, set in a delightful Devonshire coombe.

The earliest part of the castle is the great hall, around which the rest has grown. This was built in about 1340 with a buttery (wine store), pantry and a solar. The buildings at the west end were rebuilt and a tower added between 1450 and 1475. Further changes came about in the first half of the 16th century, among them the extension of the house, the addition of four towers, and the enclosure of all by the 24ft-high Court Wall. These defences were against the frequent raids along the coast made by the French, and mark the final phase in the development of the house.

Compton was sold by the Gilberts, owners for 600 years, in 1800, and it became derelict. In 1930, however, Commander Walter Raleigh Gilbert bought back the house and painstakingly restored it, a task completed by the Trust after it was given in 1951.

Open April to end Oct. Admission charged. Free parking. Wheelchair available. 4m W of Torquay, 1m N of Marldon.

CORFE CASTLE

Dorset   *SY98*

Few castles in England can rival the dramatic setting of Corfe's ruins. They tower above the pretty village from their hilltop site, guarding a natural passageway through the ridge of the Purbeck Hills. It is not surprising that such a fine strategic site was first fortified many centuries ago, and the castle built here by William the Conqueror (and recorded in *Domesday Book*) was probably not the first. It is thought that it was first fortified by King Alfred against the Danes; and Edward, the Saxon king, was murdered here in AD 978. However, the ruined tower-keep that dominates the hilltop today dates from late Norman times. The castle's defences were gradually improved by the addition of outer walls, mural towers and a deep ditch. By the late 13th century Corfe Castle was considered to be virtually impregnable – a reputation it kept for several centuries, for in the Civil War it became the last Royalist stronghold between London and Devon, resisting all Parliamentarian attacks until one of the garrison turned traitor and let the besieging enemy in. Like many castles, Corfe was 'slighted' by Cromwell after the war, though a good deal of its sturdy masonry withstood his attempts to blow it up. Some of the handsome Purbeck stone was used to build houses in the village, leaving the castle a majestic ruin that is among the finest sights in Dorset.

Open March to Oct. Admission charged. Refreshments in village. 5m NW of Swanage on A351 Wareham-Swanage road.

CORNISH BEAM ENGINES

Cornwall   *SW 64*

A familiar sight in the Cornish landscape are the tall narrow buildings marking the sites of old mines. These are the engine houses in which the massive steam-driven beam engines were kept to pump water from the shafts and galleries and to wind miners and tin, copper, lead or silver from the mine. These engines were used for 250 years in the West Country.

Four of these engines are cared for by the Trust. Those open to the public at East Pool,

NEAR TRAGEDY AT EAST POOL
J. W. Trounson of Redruth tells this story, which happened some time at the turn of the century.

'On one occasion the driver was hoisting men up the shaft, the engine going at full speed, when he suddenly realised with horror that the cage was likely to go right through the top of the head frame. He just could not have been watching his indicator that clearly showed where the cage was in relation to the shaft. There was simply no time to shut off steam and apply the brake, for the cage

The Elizabethan Spirit

The family responsible for Compton were the Gilberts, who lived there for 600 years from about 1334. The most famous of the Gilberts were the three brothers, John, Humphry and Adrian – half-brothers of Sir Walter Raleigh. They were at the heart of a movement which led England's naval defence against the Spaniards and the country's imperial ambitions towards America. Sir Humphry played a decisive part in exploring Newfoundland, but on his return in 1583 his little ship *Squirrel*, just eight tons, went down in bad weather off the Azores. Sir Humphry was last seen sitting abaft with a book in his hand shouting 'We are as near to heaven by seas as by land'.

Adrian, his brother, continued the effort at home to seek out the north-west passage (the ambition of all adventurers of the time), by organising sponsorship and support for expeditions. His other brother, John, inherited Compton, and he played a major part in the defence of the country against the Spaniards and the defeat of the Armada through both his skill as a naval commander and his logistical expertise. These brothers embodied the spirit of the Elizabethan age, a spirit continued by Sir Humphry's youngest son Raleigh, who founded the first Plymouth settlement in America in 1607. He abandoned the project a year later to return and inherit Compton, but the first steps had been taken, and the colony was revived in 1608.

was too near the top and even a few seconds delay would have meant it going over the wheel and the men thrown out. With considerable presence of mind, the driver slammed in the reversing lever with the result that the engine stopped almost instantaneously, sheering the great crankshaft in two and doing a vast amount of damage. The cage was in fact within a few feet of the winding wheel when it stopped; to be followed by a very short prayer meeting up there and then a rush of miners into the engine house where blasphemy broke all records'

Camborne, are superb examples of the use of high-pressure steam patented by Richard Trevithick in 1802. He was the Cornish engineer largely responsible for the development of beam engines. The East Pool winding engine was built in 1887, and continued in service until 1920 when the mine was closed. It is now restored and operated by electric power.

The largest and newest engine in Cornwall is the East Pool pumping engine, which lies on the other side of the road from the winding engine. It began life in 1892 at the Carn Brea mine, but was moved to East Pool and re-started in 1925. It was used for a further 30 years. It represents the pinnacle of development in Cornish beam engines – the pumping rod descended 1,700ft down the shaft, and pumped 27,000 gallons of water an hour.

Open April to end Oct. Admission charged. At Pool, 2m E of Camborne on either side of A3047.

The East Pool Whim, or winding engine, was built in 1887 at Holman's Foundry, Camborne. It operated at East Pool Mine from 1887 to 1920, when the mine closed, and was the last rotative beam winding engine to be made in Cornwall. Its cylinder diameter is 30 ins and the length of its stroke about 9 ft

COTEHELE

Cornwall   SX46

The medieval age is kept alive at Cotehele, a knightly manor of silvery-grey granite. The Edgcumbe family owned the estate, gaining it first through marriage, from 1353 until 1947, when it was handed to the Trust.

The original house was small and compact, and it was not until it was inherited by Richard Edgcumbe in 1468 that it began to grow. He was a supporter of Henry Tudor, and declared against the then reigning monarch, Richard III. As a result, the King's agent, Sir Henry Trenowth of Bodrugan (see page 13), set about capturing him. The chase ended beside the river Tamar, where Richard found himself cornered. Putting a stone into his cap he cast it into the river. Trenowth's soldiers heard the splash, and running to the spot, saw only the cap drifting downstream. Assuming their quarry was drowned, they gave up the search. Richard survived to fight for Henry Tudor at Bosworth in 1488, and as a reward was knighted when his

lord became Henry VII. He returned to Cotehele and began to enlarge the old house, adding the gateway and gate tower, and making other improvements. He died in Brittany in 1489, but his son, Piers, married a rich wife and was able to continue the work. His greatest achievement was the glorious great hall. Cotehele has not changed since, apart from the addition of the north-west tower in 1627.

The Cotehele estate was self-contained, and the Tamar powered four mills here. One watermill remains, restored to complete working order, with attendant blacksmith's, carpenter's, saddler's and wheelwright's shops and a cider mill. The mill, an 18th-century building, stands on a riverside quay, also owned by the Trust. In dock here is the *Shamrock*, a Tamar ketch-rigged barge built in 1899, which sailed this river for 70 years. The quay also houses a small branch of the National Maritime Museum, where models of ships are displayed.

Open April to end Oct, garden also open Nov to end March. Admission charged. Free parking. Wheelchairs available. Restaurant. On W bank of Tamar, 2m E of St Dominick.

CRACKINGTON HAVEN

Cornwall   SX19

Most of this land, three miles of some of the finest cliff-walking scenery in England, was given to the Trust in memory of air crews killed in the Battle of Britain. The highest cliffland in Cornwall is here, at High Cliff – 731ft high – described in a dramatic scene in Thomas Hardy's novel *A Pair of Blue Eyes*. The few houses at Crackington Haven are hidden away in a cleft. It is a sheltered little bay where in the 19th century small schooners beached to load with local slate.

Car park at farm. 6m NE of Boscastle.

CREECH: GRANGE ARCH

Dorset   SY98

Local landowner Denis Bond, following the popular trend of the time, built this arch of Portland stone in 1746. It sits on a brow of the Purbeck Hills; his house sits in the wooded valley below. The reason for the arch is that Denis Bond wished to have something eye-catching to see from the house – so he built this folly. Although the building is of no practical use, it is a magnificent viewpoint.

3m W of Corfe Castle, 4m E of Worbarrow Bay.

CUBERT AND GANNEL

Cornwall   SW76

The Gannel is a 2½-mile-long sea inlet on the north coast of Cornwall. Just south of Newquay, the mouth of the estuary is guarded by two rugged headlands, Pentire Point West, and Pentire Point East. The western headland and the southern coast of the inlet, as far as the hamlet of Penpol, are Trust-owned, and include the superb bathing beaches of Crantock, accessible down a path beside Crantock Church to Yugga Cove. Around Pentire Point West is Porth Joke, above which is an unspoilt, wild little valley noted for its variety of wild plants. Marsh and bog flora grow beside the little stream, but up on the cliffs lime-loving plants flourish – although it is acid soil here. These plants thrive because of the windblown sand found on the cliffs, made from broken sea shells over thousands of years.

At the head of the valley is Cubert Common, still grazed by commoners' animals and one of the few remaining enclosed commons in England. Further westwards still, across Kelsey Head with its cliff castle and attendant islet, the Chick (where seals breed), is another glorious beach at Holywell Bay.

4m W of Newquay.

DART ESTUARY

Devon   *SX85*

Just south of Dartmouth Castle, which overlooks the mouth of the estuary and guards the passage to the historic naval port of Dartmouth, the Trust owns some 200 acres along 1½ miles of cliffland. The principal Trust property stretches from wooded and sheltered Gallants Bower to exposed Warren Point, a headland off which there are treacherous rocks known as the Dancing Beggars. The views from the coastal footpath are magnificent, taking in Start Bay and the approach to Dartmouth.

Car park at Little Dartmouth, 1½m S of Dartmouth.

DODMAN POINT

Cornwall   *SX03*

The rocks of Percunning Cove, shot with veins of coloured minerals – white, green, pink and brown – have created a pebble beach of astonishingly colourful stones, reached through a rock arch from Hemmick Beach north-west of the Dodman. A path from Hemmick runs right round Dodman Point. The Dodman itself is an Iron Age cliff castle, cut off by a deep ditch called the Balk. On the top is a granite cross, erected in 1896 to guide fishermen. Behind it is a tiny coastguard's watch-house, shaped like a stone pulpit. In the days of sail Dodman Point was notoriously perilous, claiming many ships which overran Falmouth in the dark or in bad weather. In 1897 the Royal Navy destroyers *Thrasher* and *Lynn* went aground in thick fog; and more recently the pleasure boat *Darlwin* foundered here, with the loss of all on board.

Access from car park in Penare hamlet, ¾m N.

DUNSTER CASTLE

Somerset   *ST94*

Dunster is a perfect setting for the romantic ideal of a castle. The pretty village nestles at the foot of the spur from which the castle rises and to the south lies an uncluttered valley of fields and trees, with the sun-catching waters of the Bristol Channel beyond.

The Domesday Book reveals that in the time of Edward the Confessor a fortified tower stood here. After the Norman invasion William de Mohun built a castle in its place. The Mohuns sold to the Luttrells in 1376 and they settled here for 600 years.

A new house was designed in 1617, and built within the castle bailey, with a symmetrical brick front but irregular south side, incorporating part of the old curtain wall. During the Commonwealth the old fortifications were swept away, but the Jacobean mansion house was left untouched. To this the famous Victorian architect Antony Salvin made many improvements, and added the two great towers, castellated and battlemented, and the tower at the centre of the south side, which today gives the house the romantic appearance so suited to its site. Salvin also modernised much of the interior, but the oak staircase, wonderfully carved in the 1680s, and the oak-panelled dining room, with its remarkable plaster ceiling, were both untouched.

The garden is terraced, and even on this windy site semi-tropical shrubs are grown in sheltered corners – these include a lemon tree, established in 1842, which still fruits regularly. The river Avill flows around the base of the tor on which the castle stands – and the garden stretches down to its banks. Beside the river, on a site where there has been a mill since at least 1080, is a restored 18th-century mill. It now grinds flour for sale.

Open April to Sept. Admission charged. Free parking. Wheelchair access to grounds and park only. 3m SE of Minehead.

The dining room at Dunster Castle. Like many of the castle's rooms, this one was restored by Colonel Francis Luttrell in the late 17th century

A tremendous variety of wild flowers, plants and trees grow in Ebbor Gorge, on the north-western edge of the Mendips Hills

DYRHAM PARK

THE VANISHED GARDENS OF DYRHAM

On the bare hillside in front of Dyrham Park's east front stands a lone statue of Neptune. At one time he overlooked formal gardens which were first laid out at the end of the 17th century and remained unsurpassed in England for a hundred years. Only Neptune and two fish ponds on the opposite side of the house remain of this former glory. John Povey, nephew of William Blathwayt, the creator of the gardens, wrote in 1700, 'Before you are on top of the Hill (where Neptune stands) a Cataract abt. 50 foot High another throwing a good Body of Water abt. 20 foot high and under is a large Cataract of water descending the whole hill and coming underground to the Parterre.' The water flowed under the stables to feed the fish ponds, and this vast supply, which fed numerous fountains, ponds and basins, still troubles Dyrham from time to time – a typical example of the problems the National Trust has to overcome – problems only dreamt about in the worst nightmares by ordinary homeowners.

Avon   *ST77*

Dyrham is barely glimpsed in its vale from the entrance gate, and disappears altogether as the drive descends a steep hillside of rough pasture dotted with trees before it turns along the valley floor to the house. The east front, which then greets the visitor, is a great wall of Bath stone blocking the valley with neat rows of tall, narrow many-paned windows.

The present shape of Dyrham is due entirely to William Blathwayt, a civil servant who 'raised himself by his industry from very moderate circumstances' to become Secretary of State to William III. He married Mary Wynter, the heiress to Dyrham, in 1686. At that time the house was a traditional Tudor mansion, but after Mary's death five years later William began rebuilding. Little of the old house remains, apart from the great hall.

The interior is laid out as apartments, late 17th-century rooms of sensible and sober taste, influenced by the Dutch – William often went to the Netherlands on business. The furniture, paintings and pottery he collected are all still part of the house.

A Dutch-style garden of parterres, terraces and detailed formal designs surrounded Dyrham until about 1800, when it fell to the 'modern' taste for landscaped gardens – the style of 'Capability' Brown, which survives today.

House open April to end Oct. Park open all year. Admission charged. Free parking. Wheelchair available. Refreshments. 7m N of Bath off A46.

EBBOR GORGE

Somerset   *ST54*

The National Trust has leased this delightful, unspoilt corner of the Mendips to the Nature Conservancy Council, who manage it as a nature reserve – so visitors must keep to the footpaths. In this spectacular wooded gorge, reached only by footpath, grow ash, oak, wych elm and numerous other species. Beneath their green canopy mosses, fungi and ferns live in the damp shade. There are two nature walks here, one designed for the disabled.

This area was densely populated by men of the New Stone Age in about 3000 BC, and bones, tools and ornaments have been found in the caves in the gorge. The most spectacular find, a beautiful polished green stone axe, from Bridge Pot Shelter at the head of the gorge, is kept in Wells Museum. Remains of bears, reindeer and even of lemmings have also been found.

3m NW of Wells.

FONTMELL DOWN

Dorset   *ST81*

This is a ridge of chalk downland, exceptional because it is unimproved – that is, the rich soils have not been turned to arable farming – and is therefore a rare habitat. The sheep which graze the downs keep the turf short and eat the coarse vegetation; this allows many unusual and often strangely named plants such as salad burnet, squinancywort, purging flax, hoary plantain and harebell to thrive. In places where the sheep cannot reach, taller plants, including orchids like the remarkable bee orchid, may be found – as well as the butterflies which the flowers attract. From Fontmell Down there are fine views across Blackmore Vale and the Wessex of Thomas Hardy.

Between Shaftesbury and Blandford.

FOWEY

Cornwall   *SX15*

Opposite the ancient seaport of Fowey, still guarded by Henry VIII's St Catherine's Castle, is Pont Pill Creek. Although almost part of Fowey harbour itself, the creek is today a quiet, apparently forgotten backwater. A mile from the mouth it narrows to the little hamlet of Pont. In the 19th century this hamlet was an extension of Fowey. Grain, timber, coal and sand were shipped from here. The once busy quays and foot-bridge have been restored by the Trust, who own land on both sides of the creek. All the Trust property can be seen by following the three-mile Hall Walk. This begins at Bodinnick ferry, across the harbour from Fowey, and leads first down to a granite memorial to Sir Arthur Quiller-Couch, author of delightfully humorous novels about Cornish life which he wrote under the pseudonym 'Q'. He died at Fowey in 1944. It was along this Walk that Charles I almost lost his head to a Parliamentary cannonball shot from Fowey by the besieged Earl of Essex during the Civil War. The walk continues up Bodinnick's steep street and along the north bank of the creek, wooded with oak, sycamore, chestnut and hazel, to Pont. It then returns along the south bank, with views over the harbour, to the ferry at Polruan. Further splendid views are from the Trust's land at St Catherine's Point, above the town and castle at the mouth of the harbour.

Pont Pill Creek, opposite Fowey

GLASTONBURY TOR

Somerset   *ST53*

Although only 552ft above sea level, Glastonbury Tor is one of the West Country's most compelling landmarks. It can be seen from many miles away, and its finger shape, crowned by a tower, is quite unmistakable. The tower is all that remains of a 15th-century church which originally stood here. As is so often the case on hilltop sites, the church was dedicated to St Michael, Captain of the Heavenly Host. Views from the Tor's summit are widespread, but most visitors come to savour the atmosphere of ancient mystery which clings to the Tor and to stand on ground steeped in legend.

E of Glastonbury on N side of A361.

GLENDURGAN GARDEN

Cornwall   *SW72*

Glendurgan is a delightful garden set above the Helford River in one of three valleys that spill their streams into the river at Durgan.

In 1820 Alfred Fox bought the valley, and set about creating this informal garden. Many paths thread their way through the valley, which is

planted with beautiful trees and shrubs from all over the world. These include Japanese loquat, Mexican cypress and tree ferns from New Zealand. The valley also shelters a variety of rhododendrons.

Open March to end Oct. Admission charged. Free parking. House not open. 4m SW of Falmouth, ½m SW of Mawnan Smith, on road to Helford Passage.

GODREVY TO PORTREATH

Cornwall   *SW64*

The Cornwall Coast Path, open to the public as part of a long-distance footpath, wends its way for six miles through National Trust land between Godrevy Point and Portreath. From Portreath the path follows the high clifftops to the precipitous cleft called Ralph's Cupboard. Offshore is Samphire Island, where samphire – once used for pickling – grows. At the foot of a narrow valley is Porthcadjack Cove, where there is good swimming off the rocks. Nearby is Basset's Cove (the Bassets once owned all the land along the coast), one of several good small beaches along this stretch. Above the cove are the remains of Crane Castle, an Iron Age hillfort. To continue towards Godrevy the path runs along the top of 250ft-high cliffs, and skirts the terrible chasm aptly known as Hell's Mouth.

This is a fine coast for wild flowers, and is a regular haunt of the Atlantic seal, which breeds in the caverns on the east side of Navax Point, the last headland before Godrevy Point.

In the largely flat lands of the Somerset Levels, Glastonbury Tor is by far the most prominent landmark. It dominates most of the local landscapes, even when barely glimpsed from afar through a field gate or above a roadside hedge

The Heart of Avalon

Glastonbury Tor is one of the most magical spots in England, and legends are attracted to it like moths to a flame.

It is certain that the Tor was venerated as a holy place in very ancient times, and it may have been a centre for the worship of the prehistoric Earth Mother. Celtic folk believed it to be one of the entrances to the Otherworld – the land of the dead. The Tor and the higher land on which Glastonbury town stands was called Ynys Witrin, or the Isle of Glass, perhaps a reference to the mirror-like waters which once surrounded it, or perhaps linking it with the Castle of Glass frequently mentioned in Celtic myth. It later became Avalon, the land of apples, and of King Arthur.

The slopes of the Tor are circled by a series of ridges, and it has been suggested that these are the remains of a spiral maze laid out in prehistoric times as part of a religious ritual. It is said that there was once a temple on the summit, and that some of its stones are

Offshore is another island, Godrevy Island, on which stands Trinity Lighthouse, first erected in 1859. The coast here is so inhospitable that the light is now automatic and unmanned.

Parking west of Godrevy Farm and in lay-bys off B3301. On N side of B3301.

incorporated in the church tower that now crowns the Tor. The Tor's summit is also said to have been the setting of an invisible structure – the palace of the King of the Dead, who led the wild hunt of unearthly hounds in search of souls. Some say that the Tor is hollow, honeycombed with chambers and tunnels that echo a spiritual force which threads and weaves through the earth. Glastonbury and the Tor were sanctified by Christians at an early date, and it is claimed that Joseph of Arimathea brought to Glastonbury the chalice used by Christ at the last supper. This is the Holy Grail, sought for by the knights of King Arthur, and said by some to be hidden inside Chalice Hill, attached to the Tor, and reputedly linked to it by a tunnel.

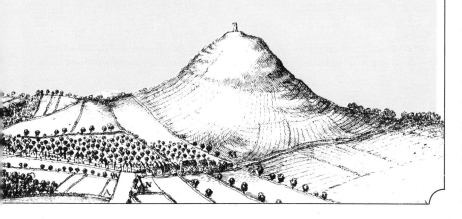

GOLDEN CAP ESTATE

Dorset   SY49

Spectacular cliffs and wide-sweeping views combine with a landscape of small, high-hedged fields and old stone farms in the Trust's Golden Cap Estate on Dorset's south coast. The estate takes its name from the band of bright orange sandstone which stands out above the grey rock of the cliffs along Lyme Bay, the highest of which is 619ft-high Golden Cap itself.

These 1,974 acres include about five miles of coast between Charmouth and Eypemouth, and are criss-crossed by about 15 miles of footpaths. The Dorset Naturalists' Trust manages reserves at Black Venn and Newlands Batch.

In the cliffs can be seen the fossils of ammonites and starfish. One of the great finds in the early days of palaeontology was made on the precipitous cliffs of Black Venn, when 12-year-old Mary Anning found the fossilised remains of an ichthyosaurus, now in the Natural History Museum in London. The sea can be reached by car at Charmouth, Seaton and Eypemouth, and a fine walk from Morcombelake leads to a beach at St Gabriel's and the remains of a 13th-century chapel.

4m E of Lyme Regis, 3m W of Bridport.

GOODAMEAVY

Devon   SX56

Here, the gorges of the rivers Plym and Meavy descend to join at the south-west corner of Dartmoor, before the river Plym continues through Bickleigh Vale to enter the sea at Plymouth. The waters of the two rivers tumble together beneath a canopy of oak at Shaugh Bridge. Before the rivers meet they are divided by the towering Dewerstone Rock, its sides made sheer by the wear of winter-swollen waters. On its cap are the remains of an Iron Age hill-fort, in which was found an unusual pottery cup of the middle Bronze Age, now kept in Plymouth City Museum.

6m NE of Plymouth, 2m S of Yelverton.

GREAT HANGMAN

Devon   SS64

The macabre name of this 1,043ft-high hill on Blackstone Point has a suitably gruesome tale attached to it. A sheep-stealer is said to have crossed the hill carrying the carcass of one of his victims by a rope over his shoulder. Overcome by weariness, he stopped to rest. He placed the sheep on top of a rock and fell asleep against it. While he slumbered, the sheep fell from the rock, and its weight pulled the rope taut around the thief's neck and strangled him.

Access by coastal footpath. Between Combe Martin and Heddon's Mouth.

THE GRIBBIN AND POLRIDMOUTH

Cornwall   *SX04, 15*

The 244ft summit of Gribbin Head encloses St Austell Bay to the east, and is marked by an 80ft tower painted red and white to help sailors distinguish it from its *doppelganger*, the Dodman, nine miles to the south-west. Wind-stunted sycamore, ilex, beech and rhododendrons cling to the slopes of the hill, and below are several sandy coves – difficult to reach but, because of this, delightfully secluded. Just east is a beautiful beach, Polridmouth Cove, sheltered by a backcloth of trees.

Cars should be left at car park outside entrance gate to Menabilly Barton. 2m W of Fowey.

HARDY'S COTTAGE

Dorset   *SY79*

This brick cottage under a thatch roof was built by Thomas Hardy's great-grandfather in 1800. It stands off Cuckoo Lane in Higher Bockhampton, at the top of the hill. Behind it stretches Hardy's 'Egdon Heath', now managed by the Forestry Commission. Here Hardy was born on 2 June 1840, and spent most of his first 30 years of life. His father was a master builder, and he paid his men through the barred window which opens on to the heath. Grandfather was known to smuggle brandy – a peep-hole in the porch is supposedly for watching for excise men.
   Under the Greenwood Tree (in which the cottage is described in detail) and *Far From the Madding Crowd* were written in the window seat in Hardy's bedroom. His letters and other memorials of his literary career are kept here.

Interior open by written appointment only. Garden open April to end Oct. Admission charged. Wheelchair access. Parking in woods nearby. 3m NE of Dorchester, ½m S of A35.

HEDDON VALLEY

Devon   *SS64*

The river Heddon has carved a great cleft through this seaward edge of Exmoor, and dug itself a vale 700ft deep where it enters Heddon's Mouth to spill into the sea. Inland, the valley is often the warmest and most sheltered spot on Exmoor. It can be explored along a footpath which hugs the east bank of the river from Hunter's Inn to Heddon's Mouth. Near Hunter's Inn the valley sides are overhung with oak, sycamore, poplar and fir. The stream bounces and bubbles along a boulder-strewn bed, the perfect habitat for the dipper, and often the haunt of the stately heron. At Heddon's Mouth the western cliff is a wall of grey scree, with only gorse and heather clinging precariously to the valley sides. The rocky cove itself is hemmed in by high cliffs, along the top of which runs a heady footpath, with exhilarating views of the coast and across the Bristol Channel to Wales.

4m W of Linton.

HELFORD RIVER

Cornwall   *SW72*

This long, wooded estuary, which finds its bridgehead five miles inland at Gweek, is a complete contrast to the Trust's cliffland properties. Several offshoots meander away from the main passage, and can only be properly

Every generation of the Acland family has added to the garden at Killerton, laid out after the Napoleonic wars. Near Killerton House is a terrace with dwarf shrubs and evergreen plants such as begonias, lavender and yucca. The sweeping lawns around the house are host to some fine specimen trees and shrubs

On the wooded slopes of Selworthy Combe, amid the glorious Dartmoor countryside of the Trust's Holnicote Estate, stand the white-washed thatched cottages of Selworthy, built in the early 19th century by the Acland family to house the aged and infirm. The idea was inspired by Blaise Hamlet at Henbury in Bristol, also a Trust property

Blacka Brook and Great Gnat's Head, present typical Dartmoor scenery – rounded, heather-clad hills punctuated by towering granite tors. Little life stirs on the hillsides, except perhaps for a few sheep and Dartmoor ponies and the occasional solitary bird. The property is above the headwaters of the river Plym which rises at the north-east tip of the Trust's land at Plym Head; it is accessible only on foot or horseback.

On SW flank of Dartmoor.

HOLNICOTE ESTATE

Somerset and Devon   *SS83, 84*

The National Trust's main property on Exmoor is the 12,443-acre Holnicote Estate, about half of which is unenclosed moor and hill, freely open to the public. The rest is largely agricultural land. Within this acreage is a good cross-section of all Exmoor's attractions and differing habitats.

The village of Selworthy lies at the heart of the estate, a charming 'model' village built in 1828 for estate pensioners. One of the cottages is a National Trust information centre. From the village there are footpaths to Selworthy Woods, north of the village, where oak, chestnut, Scots pine and silver fir grow, turning to evergreen oak towards the sea. The oak woods of Horner, to the south, are an important haven for wildlife and an example of a delicate and easily destroyed habitat. These woods were once valuable for the timber they produced for building and charcoal-making. From Horner the ground rises to the wide sweep of moorland which culminates at 1,705ft-high Dunkery Beacon – the wild, open countryside most people associate with the moor.

E and S of Porlock.

KILLERTON

Devon   *SX99*

This is a huge estate (over 6,000 acres in extent) which includes a country house, magnificent gardens, 1,000 acres of woodland and much of the Devon villages of Broadclyst and Budlake.

The house is a plain, low Georgian mansion, built in 1778–9. The interior was redesigned in the 1890s and again after a fire in 1924. The Aclands, whose family have lived in Devon since the 12th century and at Killerton since the period of the Civil War, gave the estate to the Trust in 1944. The dining room, drawing room and the upstairs of the house are used to display the Paulise de Bush collection of period costumes.

The 15-acre gardens are the work of nurseryman John Veitch, who was employed by the Aclands in the late 18th and early 19th centuries. The hillside site above the house is an arboretum of rhododendrons and conifers. Shrub borders, plant beds and large lawns surround the house, from where an avenue of

explored by boat. The Trust's properties here are scattered. A few acres are owned at Carne Vean, a small hamlet at the end of Gillan Creek; 40 acres are owned of secretive Penarvon Cove opposite Helford Passage, and also the narrow wooded east bank of Frenchman's Creek.

E of Helston, S of Falmouth.

HEMBURY

Devon   *SX76*

Here are lovely young oak woods and coppice on the west side of the river Dart, with woodland rides to the river and to open heathland.

High above the waters of the river Dart is Hembury Castle, an Iron Age hill-fort. The oval-shaped enclosure is surrounded by three ramparts, and is covered in bracken. This site may have been inhabited in the fourth century BC, but the ramparts were made in the third and last centuries BC. The remains of a Norman motte and bailey, Dane's Castle, lie within the fortifications.

Car park. 2m N of Buckfastleigh (A38), 1m S of A384.

HENTOR

Devon   *SX56, 66, 65*

Today it seems remarkable that these 3,333 desolate acres, like the rest of Dartmoor, were at one time well populated. Looking out over the cold granite cairns, standing stones and hut circles built by our prehistoric ancestors, and still to be seen scattered across the bleak, often inhospitable expanse of these rolling hills, it is hard to imagine why they settled here. The answer is in the climate. In prehistoric times Dartmoor was warmer, and lightly wooded. It had plenty of water, and stones for building, so it was a perfect place to settle.

The Trust's four miles of Dartmoor, between

ancient beeches (some planted 200 years ago by Veitch himself), sweeps up the hillside.

The gardens lie within a 300-acre park, at the eastern edge of which is the family chapel, designed in 1840. Inside, on either side of the west rose window, are carved swallows' nests. These commemorate 'Great' Sir Thomas Acland, who halted the building of the chapel so that a pair of swallows who had nested in the church could raise their young in peace.

Open April to end Oct. Admission charged. Free parking. Wheelchairs available. Restaurant. 7m NE of Exeter, W of B3181.

KNIGHTSHAYES COURT

Devon   SS91

William Burges, the creator of the fantastic Gothic towers of Cardiff Castle, is also responsible for this Gothic Victorian house. It was commissioned by John Heathcoat-Amory, the grandson of John Heathcoat, who in 1805 invented a lace-making machine that became the foundation of the family's fortune.

The foundation stone of Knightshayes was laid in 1869, and the house was largely completed by 1874 except for the finely-detailed interior decoration for which Burges is famous. An impatient Heathcoat-Amory fired his architect, and hired instead an artist-designer called Crace. He installed the painted ceilings and stencilled wall decorations popular at the time. The mock-Gothic architecture of the interior remains, but much of Crace's work was covered over in later decades. Some has been restored by the Trust, and recently a William Burges painted ceiling was uncovered.

However, it is the garden which is the main attraction. It is chiefly the work of the 1950s and 1960s, although Burges' formal south terraces remain. The Victorian garden has been simplified and extended to 25 acres. There is a mature woodland whose floor is planted with bulbs and shrubs, and a formal garden of paths and pools. A survivor of the older garden is a 50-year-old topiary depicting a fox and hounds.

Open April to end Oct. Admission charged. Free parking. Wheelchair available. Restaurant. 2m N of Tiverton, turn right off A396 at Bolham.

LANHYDROCK

Cornwall   SX06

Lanhydrock is set into a wooded hillside, a church standing behind it, in front of it a park stretching away down the Fowey Valley. A famous avenue of beeches and sycamores (some of the trees are over 300 years old) line the driveway to the house.

A merchant and banker from Truro, Robert Robartes, bought the Lanhydrock estate in 1620. He began building the present house in about 1624, the year in which he was created a baron by James I. Robartes died before it was

finished, but his son continued the work, adding the gatehouse which combines perfectly with house and church – a delightful composition best seen from the driveway.

Lanhydrock was originally built around a quadrangle, with the gatehouse as the entrance to a walled forecourt on the east side. In 1780 the east wing was demolished and the forecourt walls removed, leaving the quadrangle open with the charming gatehouse standing alone.

This grey-granite house, solid and respectable like its builder, was virtually destroyed by fire in 1881; only the gatehouse and the gallery in the north wing survive today. (In the magnificent 116ft-long gallery can be seen the fine original stucco ceiling made by local craftsmen in the 17th century.) The rest of the house was fortunately rebuilt to the same plan, even of the same stone, but with a Victorian interior. The rebuilders also added a servants' wing, which vividly illustrates the 'below stairs' life in a 19th-century country household.

Open April to end Oct. Admission charged. Free parking. Wheelchair available. Restaurant. 2½m SE of Bodmin, signposted from A38 or B3268.

LIZARD PENINSULA

Cornwall   SW71, 61

These southernmost acres of England, parts of which are owned by the Trust, are designated an Area of Outstanding Natural Beauty.

The most well-known property is Mullion Cove and Island; a picture-postcard Cornish fishing harbour nestling at the end of a small, steep valley. The cliffs on either side and the tall bulk of Mullion Island just outside the harbour

The largest freshwater lake in Cornwall, Loe Pool is a drowned valley separated from the sea by a bar composed mainly of flints. The waters of the river Cober trickle naturally through the bar, but in recent years an overflow channel has been created to control the depth of water and prevent damage from flooding

The entrance front of 17th-century Lanhydrock appears almost exactly as it did in 1780, despite a disastrous fire in 1881, which almost destroyed it except for the porch and north wing (the wing on the right of the picture). Fortunately, the owner, Lord Robartes, had the house rebuilt to exactly the same design using local materials, so retaining its delightful period appearance

give the stone quays and jetties of this delightful place a toy-like quality.

North lies Angrouse Cliff, where Guglielmo Marconi built the first radio station to transmit a message across the Atlantic. A granite monument on the cliff marks the site, and four bronze panels tell the story of this historic event.

At Predannack, south of Mullion Cove, the Trust owns 600 acres of typical Lizard scenery: heath, bog and rock, and a stream plummeting over the cliffs to the sea. Here the flora is a botanist's delight, and much of the land is leased to the Cornish Naturalists' Trust.

Further south, towards Lizard Point, the Trust owns beautiful Kynance Cove, where steep cliffs shelter a little bay of golden sands and serpentine rock can be found. This rock is streaked with red, white, yellow and black veins, and was very popular with Victorians – the moors above the cove are pock-marked with the excavations of amateur miners.

On the eastern side of Lizard Point, itself disappointing but for the views, is Bass Point, and beyond that, above Cadgwith Cove, is the extraordinary Devil's Frying Pan. Here the sea has eroded away a layer of soft rock to create an enormous cave. Its roof has fallen in to leave a rock arch over the entrance and a 200ft deep pit in which the water boils furiously.

LOE POOL AND BAR

Cornwall   SW62

Loe Bar, the Cornish will tell you, was created by Jan Tregeagle, a local folk hero, who was forced by the devil to clear nearby Berepper beach of sand. During his labours a teasing demon tripped the unwilling Tregeagle up,

causing him to spill his load across the mouth of the river Cober. However it got there, this 600ft wide dam of shingle has created Loe Pool, Cornwall's largest natural lake.

Where the river Cober flows into the pool is a marshy, reed-fringed area, a favourite haunt for wintering ducks such as teal, wigeon, shoveler and tufted duck. Water-lilies create a splash of colour in summer, and on the sand dunes grow sea campion and bird's foot trefoil.

This pool is also connected to the Arthurian legend – here, some say, Arthur's sword Excalibur was thrown into the water by Sir Bedevere, to to be caught by a ghostly hand.

Car parking. 2m S of Helston, 1m E of Porthleven.

LOUGHWOOD MEETING HOUSE

Devon   SY29

This is one of the earliest Baptist chapels in England, built in this remote spot by the Baptist congregation of Kilmington in 1650 to avoid harassment by the Puritans. It is a rectangular grey stone rubble building, with a thatched roof, with buttressed walls and round-headed clear glass windows. The inside is much as the 18th century left it. The walls are white, the floorboards and pews of scrubbed pine. A tall pulpit dominates one end, and beneath it is the baptismal tank, hidden by floorboards. Behind the pulpit are two retiring rooms, one for each sex, and each with a tiny fireplace.

Open all year. Admission free. 4m W of Axminster, turn right on Axminster-Honiton road (A35), 1m S of Dalwood, 1m NW of Kilmington.

LUNDY

Devon	*SS14*

A windswept granite island at the mouth of the Bristol Channel, Lundy has had a stormy history, not surprising in view of its strategic position as a rocky outpost at the mouth of the Bristol Channel. Its many owners at different times have included the powerful Knights Templar and the heroic Sir Richard Grenville, who in 1591 attacked 52 Spanish ships off the Azores with his ship the *Revenge*, beating off 15 and sinking two before succumbing to the superior force and to a fatal injury. Forty of Grenville's men, and 2,000 Spaniards, died during the action. The castle whose ruins can still be seen on the island was built by Henry III in 1243. As a Royalist stronghold during the Civil War, it was the last place in Britain to surrender to the Parliamentarians. The island frequently fell into the hands of pirates until the late 18th century, when it began to enjoy greater stability as the seas around our coasts fell under the overriding dominance of the Royal Navy.

There are several cottages on the island which, together with the old lighthouse, former schoolroom and old Admiralty lookout, are let as holiday cottages. Most visitors go to Lundy for its scenery, its peace and quiet, and its wildlife. The island's famous puffins are now scarce, but many other species of seabirds may be seen, as well as seals, Sika deer, wild goats and ponies.

Open all year (pedestrian access only; the island is traffic-free). Accessible all year by the island's own ship, the Polar Bear, *which runs from Ilfracombe, and from May to Oct also by helicopter in the summer from Hartland Point. Booking essential for both; apply to the Administrator, Lundy Island, Ilfracombe, Devon. Parking in Ilfracombe pier or harbour car parks. Occasionally, weather conditions make it impossible to land on Lundy. 11 miles N of Hartland Point.*

LYDFORD GORGE

Devon	*SX58*

Lydford Gorge lies on the western edge of Dartmoor and is one of the loveliest, and most exciting, places in the West Country. Nearly half a million years ago the river Lyd carved a deep gorge out of the rocks here. The narrowest part of the gorge is the most dramatic, a deep ravine filled with the excitement of rushing water, its steep rocky sides clothed in spray-dampened ferns and mosses. Its most awesome part, the Devil's Cauldron, through which the water fumes and boils, is a narrow cleft which can be approached along a path of wooden planks suspended just above the angry water.

Once past the ravine the river enters a gentler, wider valley, where oak trees cloak the sides. White Lady Waterfall, which when in full spate has a clear fall of a hundred feet, tumbles down the valley side to join the Lyd.

Open April to Oct (Nov to March open from

waterfall entrance as far as waterfall). Admission charge. Car parks at waterfall entrance and Bridge House. Refreshments. Near Lydford village, halfway between Okehampton and Tavistock.

LYNMOUTH

Devon	*SS74*

The most popular place in this extensive Trust property is undoubtedly Watersmeet, a well-known beauty spot at the meeting point of the East Lyn River and Hoaroak Water. The river here tumbles along a rocky bed fringed by luxuriant woodland. A charming 19th-century fishing lodge at Watersmeet is now a National Trust information centre and shop.

The sheer, red cliffs and wild moorland of Foreland Point and Countisbury Hill offer a complete contrast. The cliffs on the western side of the headland – the most northerly point in Devon – are, at 994ft, some of the highest in England. Around Wind Hill is an early Iron Age earthwork – possibly an invasion beach-head. The whole area is criss-crossed by footpaths.

E of Lynmouth, on both sides of A39. Refreshments at Watersmeet Cottage.

The sylvan ravine into which the waters of the White Lady Waterfall plunge from 100ft was created 450,000 years ago. That is when the river Lydd was diverted into the course of a much smaller stream and the suddenly increased volume of water gouged out dramatic Lydford Gorge

Built in the middle of the 15th century, the Great Hall at Lytes Cary is still lit by stained glass that was originally installed in the 16th century. Much of the furniture in the hall is made of oak and dates from the 17th century

LYTES CARY

Somerset   *ST52*

This pleasant, tucked-away Somerset manor house takes its name from the Lyte family, who lived here for 500 years from the 13th to the 15th centuries. The oldest part of the present house is the chapel, which was built around 1343. The Great Hall dates from the mid 15th century, while much of the rest of the house was built a century later, by John Lyte. His son, Henry, was a noted horticulturist. As well as transforming the garden at Lytes Cary, he also published in 1578 one of the foremost horticultural books of his day, the *Niewe Herball* – a translation from the original Flemish. Although his garden at Lytes Cary has not survived, the manor stands in an attractive and appropriately formal garden, parts of which are being re-stocked with plants that were commonly grown in Henry Lyte's day.

Limited opening March to end Oct. Admission charged. Wheelchair available. 1m N of Ilchester by-pass A303; signposted from A303/A37 roundabout nearby.

MAYON AND TREVESCAN

Cornwall   *SW32*

Land's End itself is one of the busiest and most crowded tourist 'honeypots' in England, but the magnificent cliffs on either side, although popular, are almost empty by comparison. The National Trust owns nearly 60 acres of cliffs to the north of Land's End, including the well-preserved Iron Age earthwork Maen Castle.

Between Land's End and Sennen.

MONTACUTE

Somerset   *ST41*

Built of the lovely stone from nearby Ham Hill, Montacute is a splendid Elizabethan mansion packed with fine furniture and superb paintings. The exterior of the house is strictly symmetrical, and the walls are pierced by the huge windows so beloved of the Elizabethans.

In 1787 the owner, Edward Phelips, rebuilt the west front of the house in keeping with the existing architecture. When the house came into the ownership of the National Trust in 1931 most of its furniture had been dispersed, but the Phelips family loaned their collection of family portraits, and furniture and ceramics were lent by the Society for the Protection of Ancient Buildings. Montacute was greatly enriched in 1960 when Sir Malcolm Stewart left a magnificent collection of paintings, furniture, ceramics and tapestries to the house. The Long Gallery was restored between 1973 and 1975 and now houses a collection of Elizabethan and Jacobean paintings on permanent loan from the National Portrait Gallery.

Open April to Oct. Admission charged. Free parking. Wheelchair available, access to garden only. Refreshment. 4m W of Yeovil.

MORWENSTOW

Cornwall   *SS21*

This 136-acre National Trust property is adjacent to the church of St Morwenna, noted for its fine Norman doorway richly decorated with zig-zag work. It also has associations with Sabine Baring-Gould's novel *The Vicar of Morwenstow*. The subject of the book was

Robert Stephen Hawker, a parson-poet who wrote many popular Cornish ballads while he was vicar of St Morwenna between 1824 and 1861. The church and Rectory Farm stand above some of the highest cliffs in Cornwall – once the haunt of gangs of wreckers, who signalled ships on to the rocks in order to plunder their cargoes.

Access by footpath from the gate beside the churchyard. 6m N of Bude near the Devon border.

NARE HEAD AND VERYAN BAY

Cornwall	SW93

The lonely, windswept promontory of Nare Head rises 330ft sheer from the sea. Its clifftops are covered in heather, gorse and rough grasses, while the inland acres are a patchwork of cornfields bounded by high hedgerows – the quintessence of Cornish coastal countryside. It forms the eastern boundary of Gerrans Bay (named after Geraint, one of the Knights of the Round Table), and from it are views of the Roseland Peninsula and the Lizard to the west, and of Dodman Point to the east.

Access to footpath. Car parks on S side of farm buildings and just inside headland gate. 4½m S of Tregony.

OLD BLUNDELL'S SCHOOL

Devon	SS91

Wealthy wool-merchant Peter Blundell built this old school as a gift to the people of Tiverton in 1604. Among its past pupils is R. D. Blackmore (1825–1900), the author of *Lorna Doone*. The sandstone, slate-roofed school is described in the novel as the setting for Jan Ridd's fight. Blundell's gift was used as a school for over 250 years, until 1882, when it was converted into houses. The building was given to the National Trust in 1954.

Access to forecourt only; open to pedestrians at all reasonable hours. Station Road (A373), on the eastern side of Tiverton.

OVERBECKS

Devon	SX73

The house and gardens here are named after Mr Otto Overbeck, who left them to the National Trust in 1937. Created early in the 20th century, the gardens, which extend to about six acres, contain one of the richest and most varied collections of trees, shrubs and flowering plants to be found in England. The climate is so mild here that palm trees seed themselves! It would be difficult to pick one plant species among so

many, but perhaps the magnificent blooms of magnolias in springtime call for special mention. Beside its plants the garden also has superb views across Salcombe Bay.

The house itself contains a museum that will be of particular interest to children. Among the exhibits are dolls, toys, natural history collections and a section devoted to shipbuilding, with models of ships and a display of shipwrights' tools.

Museum open April to Oct. Garden open all year. Admission charged. Small car park (admission charged). Picnicking permitted in garden. 1½m SW of Salcombe.

An unusual attraction in the Parke Estate is the Parke Rare Breeds Farm, where unusual and old-fashioned breeds of farm animals are kept to preserve them from extinction. The Longhorn cattle pictured above are probably direct descendants of the wild cattle domesticated by Stone Age man

PARKE

Devon	*SX87*

The park and mansion lie on the wooded floor of the river Bovey close to the Dartmoor National Park border. The house, a late Georgian mansion built in 1828, is not open, but the parkland is, and offers delightful walks beside the river or along the old railway track which ran between Newton Abbot and Moretonhampstead until 1959.

Within the park is the newly opened Rare Breeds Farm, a collection of rare, traditional breeds of livestock – cattle, sheep, pigs and poultry. Here it is hoped to continue breeds which otherwise may become extinct.

Park open all year. Rare Breeds Farm open from Spring 1983 to Oct. Admission to farm charged. Refreshments. Just W of Bovey Tracey on N side of B3344 to Manaton.

Standing high on a shelf above Splat Cove on the most southerly tip of Devon, Overbecks commands extensive coastal views. The garden was terraced and the retaining walls were built in 1901. Since then the garden has been planted with many tender and rare trees, shrubs and plants, which encourage the almost Mediterranean atmosphere of this surprisingly mild corner of England

PENCARROW HEAD

Cornwall	*SX15*

The coastline between Fowey and Polperro remains largely unspoilt and uncrowded. The National Trust owns some of the finest stretches – the cliffs above Lantic Bay, Pencarrow Head, and the cliffs on the east of Lantivet Bay. Lantic Bay and Pencarrow Head are best reached by the coastal path from Polruan, while Lantivet Bay can be reached by footpath from Lansallos.

Car parks at Lansallos and Frogmore, and lay-by above Lantic Bay.

PENTIRE HEAD

Cornwall	*SW98*

The east side of Padstow Bay, where Polzeath and New Polzeath lie, is an example of the damage that unrestrained development can do to the Cornish coastline.

However, just north of New Polzeath are some 700 Trust-owned acres which stretch around Pentire Point eastwards to Rumps Point and along the coast to Portquin, an unspoiled typically Cornish cove overlooked by an 18th-century folly, Doyden Castle.

Pentire Point and Y-shaped Rumps Point form the corners of a square-headed peninsula, from which there are impressive views of the north Cornish coast to the cliffs near Bude and beyond. In the opposite direction, across the mouth of the Camel estuary, can be seen Stepper Point and, in the distance, Trevose Head and its lighthouse. To the south, up the estuary, can be spied (from Pentire Head) the Doom Bar, a sandbank across the estuary mouth which has ended Padstow's role as a port. According to legend, the bar is the result of a curse cast by a mermaid who had been injured by a Padstow fisherman. Nearly 300 ships have foundered on the 150-year-old bar. On Rumps Head is an Iron Age hill-fort, where Celts are known to have lived 2,000 years ago.

6m NW of Wadebridge, on B3314.

PLYM BRIDGE WOODS

Devon	*SX55*

Only five miles from the centre of Plymouth the river Plym is a delightful stream running through a wooded valley. The National Trust owns about 124 acres of the valley to the north of Plym Bridge, including the remains of once-busy slate quarries. Also of interest to industrial archaeologists will be the massive brick-built viaduct which carries the old Great Western Railway Plymouth to Tavistock line across the river. Near to it are the massive stone piers of the original wooden viaduct, built by Isambard Brunel in 1858.

5m NE of Plymouth.

THE QUANTOCKS

Somerset   *ST14*

The gentle Quantocks stretch from the coast near Watchet inland to overlook the Vale of Taunton Deane. Much of the land is devoted to farming, but there are still areas of moorland in the northern and western parts and wooded valleys on the north-east slopes. Most of the woodlands are coniferous, but some of the original oak woodlands remain. The National Trust owns some of these at Shervage, just off the A39 between Holford and Nether Stowey. There is also an area of moorland at Shervage, and the Trust owns more Quantock moorland at Longstone Hill (which can be reached by footpath from Holford).

ROUGH TOR

Cornwall   *SX18*

Rough Tor can be reached from an unclassified road that leads from Camelford. Its moorland slopes are dotted with the remains of prehistoric fields and huts, and on its summit is a monument to men of the Wessex Division who died in World War II.

Car park at end of road 3m SE of Camelford.

ST ANTHONY-IN-ROSELAND

Cornwall   *SW83*

Roseland is a lovely peninsula tucked away south of Truro to the east of the river Fal. It is a landscape of small fields and farms glimpsed through hedges and farm gates.

The shore of the estuary opposite St Mawes belongs to the National Trust and can be reached by footpath from the little village of St Anthony. The Trust also owns a stretch of cliff scenery to the east of St Anthony, and this can be reached by footpath from Porth Farm.

Car park at St Anthony Head.

ST MICHAEL'S MOUNT

Cornwall   *SW52*

St Michael's Mount is a striking islet of granite that rises abruptly from the level sands or – at high tide – the waters of Mount's Bay. Beneath the sea around it, traces of ancient tree trunks have been discovered – a legacy from the days when the Mount was a knoll rising from an area of dense forest. However, the forest was submerged by the sea and even as early as the Iron Age, St Michael's Mount was an important

The saloon at Saltram is an exquisite example of a Robert Adam interior design. Every detail, including the position of the pictures and their subject matter, was included in the initial plans for the room. It was created in the 1770s, and was used for lavish entertainments such as concerts and county balls

Jack the Giant-Killer

Several high hills in Cornwall are linked with tales of giants, and St Michael's Mount lays claim to the best-known of them all. The story goes that the Mount was built by the giant Cormoran. He was feared and detested by the locals, for he made regular forays to the mainland to steal their cattle and sheep. One night, a local lad called Jack rowed out to the Mount and, while the giant slept, dug a deep pit in the hillside. At sunrise Jack blew his horn to wake the giant. Blinded by the brilliant sunlight, Cormoran careered down the side of the Mount and fell to his death in the pit. A well in the hillside is still shown to young visitors to the Mount as the pit dug by the heroic 'Jack the Giant-Killer'.

I WILL BROIL YOU FOR MY BREAKFAST.

port. Gold and copper from Ireland and tin from Cornwall were shipped from here to France and the Mediterranean.

In the 12th century the Abbot of Mont St Michel in Normandy – the Cornish islet's strikingly lookalike counterpart – established a Benedictine priory on the island. The first church was destroyed by an earthquake in 1275, and although some 70 years later the Black Death reduced the monastic community to three, the same century saw the building of the church that survives today.

The castle that crowns the 230ft Mount dates from various periods; parts of the masonry can be traced to the original priory buildings, while the entire south-east wing was built in the 1870s

by a cousin of the St Aubyns, the family which acquired the island in 1659 and kept it until 1954, when it was given to the National Trust. The most interesting parts of the castle to visit are the church, the Chevy Chase room – originally the monastery refectory – and the Blue Drawing Rooms, which occupy the former 15th-century chapel and display fine rococo plasterwork and Chippendale furniture.

Far below the castle lie the village and harbour, which grew to prosperity in the late 18th and 19th centuries – the heyday of the Cornish tin trade.

Open all year. Admission charged. Refreshments at Island Café (summer only). ½m S of A394 at Marazion. Access from Marazion at low tide by causeway or at high tide (summer only) by ferry.

SALCOMBE

Devon	SX73

Some of the finest cliff scenery in southern Devon lies on either side of Salcombe, and much of it belongs to the National Trust. The Trust owns the whole stretch from Bolt Tail round to Overbecks garden at Sharpitor. The walk along the cliffs here, a distance of about six miles, is one of the most exhilarating and lovely in England. On the other side of the entrance to Salcombe harbour the Trust owns a further three miles of coast, stretching from Mill Bay to Gammon Head, and also the headland of Prawle Point. The South Devon Coast Path, which follows the length of this outstanding scenery, can be joined at many points along the coast.

11m of coastline either side of Salcombe Harbour.

SALTRAM

Devon	SX55

Saltram is an almost perfect example of 18th-century architecture. However, behind its classical façade is a far older structure, a Tudor house that can still be glimpsed in an inner courtyard. The central part of the house, the west wing, was largely built at the very beginning of the 18th century, and the south and east wings date from about 1750.

It is the interior of the mansion which gives Saltram its special place among English houses, for Robert Adam did some of his finest work here. The saloon and dining room remain exactly as he planned them, right down to the design of the door handles. The house is also noted for its Chinese rooms and for its collection of paintings, a number of which are by Reynolds.

The kitchen at Saltram is one of the finest the Trust owns, a perfectly preserved example of the 'below stairs' world of the servants who ran the great country houses.

Open April to Oct. Admission charged. Wheelchairs available. Restaurant. 3m E of Plymouth centre.

SEDGEMOOR AND ATHELNEY

Somerset   ST43, 33

Throughout prehistory and well into medieval times, the part of Somerset which is known today as Sedgemoor was a wet and watery land.

Much of the area was drained by the monks of Glastonbury Abbey for agricultural purposes between the 10th and 14th centuries, and today Sedgemoor's rich alluvial soils, threaded by drainage ditches known as drains and rhines, nurture magnificent grazing crops and fine vegetables and fruits. The area is rich in wetland plant life.

The National Trust owns several small sites in this extraordinary landscape. Among these are; Cock Hill (off the A39 between Bridgwater and Glastonbury), which looks across the King's Sedgemoor Drain to the site of the Battle of Sedgemoor, fought in 1685 between forces led by the Duke of Monmouth and the army of King James I (the last battle to be fought on English soil); the twin ridges of Walton Hill and Ivythorn Hill, also along the A39; and a thatched 19th-century windmill (viewing by appointment only) just outside High Ham.

One of the most outstanding isolated hillocks in the Sedgemoor area is the Trust's Burrow Mump, which stands close to the A361 2½ miles south-west of Othery. Its summit has been occupied by a Norman castle, of which nothing remains, but it is now capped by the ruins of an unfinished 18th-century chapel.

SHUTE BARTON

Devon   SY29

This handsome manor house was begun in about 1380 and added to in the 15th and 16th centuries. Its exterior, including the impressive Tudor gatehouse, can be seen at all times, but those wishing to see the interior of the house – the spit in the kitchen is capable of roasting two oxen – must book in advance.

Open by appointment with the occupier April to Oct. 3m SW of Axminster.

SOUTHDOWN FARM

Dorset   SY78

The Dorset downs end abruptly at Weymouth Bay as a series of cliffs, owned by the Trust from Ringstead to White Nothe. Ringstead, on the edge of the cliffs, and Holworth, a mile inland, are both deserted villages. Only grass-covered banks and hollows betray where the streets and houses were. The villages failed in the 15th century, perhaps through the plague.

At the centre of Ringstead Bay is Burning Cliff, so named because the rock it is composed of – sulphurous oil shale – ignited spontaneously in 1826 and burned for four years. Here and towards White Nothe, landslip has created

inward facing cliffs, the ideal nesting sites for a variety of seabirds.

Access by foot, cars to crest of the Down only.

TEIGN VALLEY WOODS

Devon   SX78

Wooded valleys are very characteristic of the West Country, and the upper reaches of the Teign valley are cloaked in beautiful woodlands. The National Trust owns nearly 200 acres of these 'hanging' woods north-east of Moretonhampstead. Such woodlands were usually carefully managed, often by workers in the tanning industry, who used the bark to tan leather. Many of the oak trees in the Teign valley were coppiced regularly until fairly recent times. A nature trail leads through the woodland on the north bank of the river.

Near Steps Bridge, on both sides of the B3212 NE of Moretonhampstead.

The manor house of Shute Barton marks a distinct turning point in English medieval history; it was built virtually without defences. The law and order imposed by Edward I encouraged the nobility to build more comfortable houses, and abandon the utilitarian castles of their forebears

TINTAGEL

Cornwall   *SX08*

The National Trust owns the cliffs overlooking the glorious sands of Trebarwith Strand, and Glebe Cliff, which lies between Tintagel Church and the sea. To the north of Tintagel the Trust owns Barras Nose and the headland called Willapark. The Old Post Office in Tintagel village also belongs to the Trust, and this lovely 14th-century stone house, originally built as a manor, has been restored by the Trust.

Old Post Office open April to Oct. Admission charged. Wheelchair access. In centre of village.

TINTINHULL HOUSE

Somerset   *ST51*

This small mansion, built as a farmhouse in the 17th century and given its elegant west front in about 1700, is set off to perfection by its lovely gardens. Careful planning of the gardens, which were laid out in the early part of the 20th century, ensures that as visitors move from one part to another they are constantly delighted by new sights and new vistas.

Open April to Sept. Admission charged. Wheelchair available, access to garden only. 5m NW of Yeovil, ½m south of A303.

TREEN CASTLE

Cornwall   *SW32*

A footpath leads across open fields from the car park in Treen village to the breathtaking tumble of rocks that makes up the promontory of Treryn Dinas. This natural defensive site was fortified at different periods of the early Iron Age. The earthwork nearest the tip of the headland is the most remarkable, and probably the last to be built. It is approached over a causeway across a deep ditch and consists of a bank faced with huge masonry blocks.
    Immediately beyond this defensive structure is the famous Logan Rock, a rocking stone left isolated by the forces of nature.

Car park in village at Treen. 4m SE of Land's End, 7m SW of Penzance.

The Logan Rock at Treen is a huge boulder left balanced by the forces of nature so that its massive bulk can be relatively easily rocked. However, in 1824, a naval lieutenant overturned it, a feat recalled by the sign of the local inn (inset). Local outrage was so great he was made to replace it at his own expense, but it now takes some effort to move it

LOGAN ROCK

TRELISSICK

Cornwall   *SW83*

Cornwall's mild climate lends itself to gardens
which contain exotic and delicate plants, and
the garden at Trelissick has an exceptional
collection from all over the world. Among the
plants which can be seen are tree ferns from
New Zealand, evergreen ferns from Chile, and
many beautiful varieties of rhododendron.
There are superb views of the Fal Estuary and
Falmouth harbour from the immaculate lawns.

Open April to end Oct. Admission charged.
Wheelchairs available. Refreshments. 4m S of
Truro.

TRENGWAINTON

Cornwall   *SW43*

Facing due south, overlooking Mount's Bay, this
98-acre garden and park enjoys a wonderfully
mild climate, which fosters many plants that
will not normally grow outdoors in Britain.

The garden at Trengwainton is almost
entirely a 20th-century creation though there
has been a house here at least since the 16th
century (present house not open). Many of the
plants have been grown here from seed collected
on expeditions to the Far East and the Southern
Hemisphere. Trengwainton's speciality is
rhododendrons, which are ideally suited to the
acid soil here. Magnolias also grow in profusion.

Open March to end Oct. Admission charged.
Wheelchair access. 2m NW of Penzance, ½m W of
Hea Moor on B3312.

TRERICE

Cornwall   *SW85*

Set in a quiet valley and reached by typical
Cornish lanes, Trerice is a charming small
Elizabethan manor house standing in 14 acres of
grounds. It was built in 1573 for Sir John
Arundell, whose military career included a spell
in the Low Countries – which may account for
the curved and scrolled Dutch-style gables that
are such a striking feature of Trerice's handsome

THE BUILDER OF TRERICE
Richard Carew, the 16th-century
Cornish historian, wrote of Sir
John Arundell, the builder of
Trerice:
   '. . . all who knew him shall
testify with me; that of his enemies
he would take no wrong nor on
them any revenge, and being once
reconciled, embraced them
without scruple or remnant of gall.
Over his kindred he held a wary
and chary care, which bountifully
was expressed when occasion so
required, reputing himself not only
principal of the family but a
general father to them all.'
   Carew, who lived at Anthony
House (also a Trust property), was
Sir John's son-in-law.

E-shaped main façade. The interior of the house is notable especially for its 16th-century plaster-work ceilings. One of the best is that of the hall, an imposing room lit by a huge window which contains 576 separate panes of glass – most of them original. The drawing-room is also a lovely sunny room, with a great south-facing bay window. This room, too, is rich in fine plasterwork, including its elaborate ceiling and richly sculpted overmantel. The furniture includes a set of Chippendale armchairs and other 18th-century pieces.

Open April to end Oct. Admission charged. Wheelchairs available. Refreshments. 3m SE of Newquay via A392 and A3058 (turn right at Kestle Mill).

WEMBURY BAY AND YEALM ESTUARY

Devon	*SX54*

The National Trust owns two stretches of coast at the mouth of the Yealm: a 1½-mile stretch on the north side of the estuary from Warren Point to Wembury, and a two-mile stretch on the south side from Mouthstone Point to Blackstone Point. On Wembury Beach is a medieval watermill which houses a café and shop.

Open all year (shop April to end Oct only). Refreshments in Mill Café. 5-6m E of Plymouth.

WESTWARD HO! KIPLING TORS

Devon	*SS42*

The National Trust owns a stretch of land near Westward Ho!, the resort that was named after Charles Kingsley's novel. Literary connections are continued by its name, Kipling Tors. Consisting of 18 acres of gorse-clad land to the west of the resort, it was given to the National Trust by the Rudyard Kipling Memorial Fund, for it is the setting of much of his well-known novel *Stalky & Co.*

W of Westward Ho! off B3236.

WHEAL BETSY

Devon	*SX58*

In a dramatic setting on the western edge of Dartmoor, Wheal Betsy is the roofless, ruined engine house of a former mine. The ore it produced was lead but this was worked on account of the silver it contained. The mine itself functioned from the early 19th century, but Wheal Betsy was not built until 1868, to house the beam engine that, with the advent of steam power, replaced the two huge waterwheels. The mine was worked until 1877. Wheal Betsy fell in to disrepair, but conservationists protested at an attempt to blow it up as a military exercise and it was eventually acquired by the National Trust in 1967.

5m N of Tavistock, just E of A386.

WHITESAND BAY

Cornwall	*SW35*

The National Trust owns two sections of the coast between Portwrinkle and Freathy. The westerly one is 69 acres at Trethill Cliffs. The easterly one extends to 284 acres around Higher Tregantle and Sharrow Point. At the foot of the cliffs is a cave which has a curious history . Measuring 15ft deep and 7ft high, Sharrow Grot, as it is known, was cut at the time of the American War of Independence by a naval

Smoke issued from the tall chimney stack of Wheal Betsy for the last time in 1877, when the giant beam engine it housed ground to a halt. In nine years of service 4,000–5,000 ounces of silver had been extracted from the mine beneath it

Trelissick's exceptional gardens are complemented by 376 acres of immaculately kept parkland, where walks lead through broad lawns beneath towering beech trees and ancient oaks. The views across the Carrick Roads, a most beautiful tree-lined stretch of water four miles long by one mile wide, are superb

lieutenant called Lugger, who not only excavated the chamber but also carved verses on its rock walls. All this hard work was undertaken to cure his gout – apparently it worked! The Grot has recently been sealed off because it is now unsafe.

5m W of Torpoint, 3m NW of Rame Head. In between the two NT properties lies a series of firing ranges, which are out of bounds.

WOODY BAY

Devon	SS64

Steep, tree-clad slopes, rugged cliffs, waterfalls and wild moorland combine to make this one of the Trust's most attractive properties in Devon. It stretches from Wringapeak Point to the old pier at Woody Bay. There is a lime kiln near the pier – a reminder of the days when limestone from south Wales was landed here and made into agricultural lime. The conditions are ideal for many species of wildlife; guillemots and razorbills are among the seabirds that rest on the rocky ledges of the cliffs.

3m W of Lynton.

ZENNOR

Cornwall	SW43

The cliff scenery to the north of Zennor is some of the most spectacular in Cornwall, and Zennor Head, which belongs to the National Trust, is a bright jewel in a string of majestic headlands. It can be reached by a footpath from Zennor village and its granite rocks are home to many seabirds and a remarkably rich flora. On a bench-end in Zennor church there is a unique carving of a mermaid. This is said to depict the Mermaid of Zennor, who lured a young man to her home in the waters below Pendour Cove.

N of Zennor village, off the B3306 between St Ives and St Just.

The coastline at Zennor Head. From here can sometimes be seen the 'green flash', a phenomenon which can occasionally be seen on a summer's evening, when a green light will suddenly flood the sunset just before the sun sinks below the sea

OTHER PROPERTIES

AVON

Bath
Bushey Norwood. *ST76*
Farmland with prehistoric sites. Between Claverton Manor and golf course. Footpath access.

Rainbow Wood Farm. *ST76*
Farmland with Iron Age fort. On Claverton Down. Footpath access.

Bristol
Blaise Hamlet. *ST57*
Group of ten thatched cottages built in Picturesque style by John Nash in 1809. 4m N of Central Bristol, N of B4057. Not open.

Frenchay Moor. *ST64*
Common land. 5m NE of Central Bristol.

Leigh Woods. *ST57*
Woodland, with Iron Age fort, by Clifton Suspension Bridge on left bank of Avon.

Shirehampton Park. *ST57*
Partly golf course; overlooking Avon 4m W of Central Bristol.

Westbury College. *ST57*
15th-century gate-house. In College Road, Westbury-on-Trym. Key with vicar, 44 Eastfield Road.

Failand. *ST57*
Farm and woodland. 4m W of Central Bristol, overlooking Severn.

Horton Court. *ST78*
Cotswold manor house with a 12th-century Norman hall and farmland. 3m NE of Chipping Sodbury. Limited opening April to end Oct.

Little Solsbury Hill. *ST76*
Flat hilltop with Iron Age fort. Views. Between Swainswick and Batheaston.

Middle Hope (Woodspring). *ST36*
Two miles of coastline; views across Bristol Channel and Somerset Marshes. 5m N of Weston-super-Mare. Access from Sand Bay to most of property.

Monk's Steps, Kewstoke. *ST36*
The Monk's (or St Kew's) Steps, and 2½ acres. Views. On N edge of Weston-super-Mare.

Redcliffe Bay. *ST47*
Coastal belt, 200yds long; crossed by mariners' footpath from Clevedon to Portishead.

Sand Point, Kewstoke. *ST36*
Coastal headland adjoining Middle Hope (qv). 5m N of Weston-super-Mare.

CORNWALL

Bedruthan. *SW86*
Clifftop land overlooking Bedruthan Beach and Steps (not NT). 6m SW of Padstow.

Bodigga Cliff. *SX25*
Cliffland and foreshore. 1m E of Looe.

Camel Estuary. *SW97*
Fishing Cove Field. Cliff field at Trebetherick.

Cudden Point. *SW52*
Headland, 3m SE of Marazion. Coastal footpath; access also from lane leading south from Rosudgeon.

The Dizzard. *SX19*
Wild headland, cliffland and pasture. 2m NE of Crackington Haven. Coastal footpath.

Duckpool to Sandymouth. *SS21*
Cliffs and beaches. 5m N of Bude. Access at Duckpool and Sandymouth, coastal path traverses whole length of the property.

Erth Barton and Erth Island. *SW35*
Saltings and foreshore at confluence of rivers Tiddy and Lynher. 1½m SE of St Germans.

Fal Estuary. *SW84*
Ardevora and Trelonk. Foreshore on E bank of the Fal.

Gunwalloe Fishing Cove. *SW62*
Farmland between coast road and beach, including Mullion Golf Course. 4m S of Helston.

Hor Point and Hellesveor Cliff. *SW54*
Rocky coast with views. 1½m W of St Ives. Access by coastal footpath.

Lanyon Quoit. *SW43*
Granite capstone; part of long barrow. 4m NW of Penzance.

Lawrence House, Launceston. *SX38*
18th-century town house. In Castle Street. Open April to end Sept.

Lerryn Creek. *SX15*
Ethy House (not open) and wooded park. On E bank of Fowey estuary. Access by waterside walk.

Lesceave Cliff. *SW52*
Cliffland 5m W of Helston. Access by coastal footpath.

Maer Cliff, Bude. *SS20*
Clifftop pastures running north to Northcott Mouth; also foreshore.

Newton Cliff, St Mawes. *SW83*
Meadows at water's edge, the steep escarpment behind, and foreshore. On E side of Falmouth Harbour.

Northcott Mouth. *SS20*
Grassland and foreshore. 1m N of Bude. Access via narrow lane from Poughill, or by coastal footpath.

Park Head, St Eval *SW87*
Wild headland and sea. Round barrows. 6m SW of Padstow.

Pendower Beach. *SW93*
247 acres overlooking large sandy beach. 1m SW of Veryan.

Polperro
Chapel Cliff. *SX25*
Farm and cliffland on W side of harbour; terraced walks.

The Warren. *SX25*
Cliffland on E side of harbour.

Port Gaverne. *SX08*
Beach, foreshore and fish cellars on W side of stream, ¼m E of Port Isaac.

Porthcothan. *SW87*
The north side of the inlet. 5m SW of Padstow.

Porthminster Point. *SW53*
Cliffs and small fields between railway and sea on S edge of St Ives. Views.

Rinsey Cliff. *SW52*
Heather-clad cliff and ruin of Wheal Prosper Mine Engine House. 1m SW Ashton between Helston and Marazion. Car park on cliff.

Rosemergy and Trevean Cliffs. *SW43*
Wild cliff with viewpoint. 1m E of Morvah Church.

Rosemullion Head. *SW72*
Headland with views over Falmouth Bay, N of Helford river mouth. Access by coastal footpath or on foot by road to Mawnan Church.

St Just-in-Roseland. *SW38*
Farmland on E side of Falmouth Harbour. Access by coastal footpath or by track from road to Churchtown.

St Levan Cliffs. *SX08*
Headland of Pedn-Men-An-Mere, and part of Rospletha Cliff. Between Land's End and Porthcurno.

Tregardock Beach. *SX08*
Cliffland and beach 3m S of Tintagel. Access on foot from public highway, or via coastal footpath.

Tregassick and Trewince. *SW83*
Farmland and hamlet of Porthcuel with 1½ miles of St Mawes estuary shore (E bank). Waterside footpath.

Trencrom Hill. *SW53*
Gorse-covered hillside with Iron Age fort and the Bowl Rock. 3m S of St Ives.

DEVON

Beesands Cliff. *SX84*
Cliffland with disused slate quarry at north end of Beesands Beach, ½m S of Torcross.

Burrough Farm, Northam. *SS42*
Farmland running from edge of Northam Down to low wooded cliffs on left bank of Torridge estuary. Access by cliff and field paths; also to a small cove.

Clematon Hill, Bigbury-on-Sea. *SX64*
Hillside with views to Bolt Tail and Burgh Island. On S side of B3392.

Clovelly
Beckland Cliffs. *SS22*
Cliff and farmland. 2½m NW of Clovelly.

The Brownshams. *SS22*
Farm and woodland with two ancient farmhouses. Access by footpaths to cliffs and Mouth Mill Beach. Part is a nature reserve.

Fatacott Cliff. *SS22*
Cliff and farmland 4m W of Clovelly. Access by coastal footpath.

Gawlish. *SS22*
Cliffland. Access by coastal footpath.

Mount Pleasant. *SS32*
An acre just above Clovelly; view over Bideford Bay.

Combe Wood, Combe Raleigh. *ST10*
Woodland 1m N of Honiton.

Dunsland. *SS40*
Woodland and the site of a house which was completely destroyed by fire in 1967. 4½m E of Holsworthy.

East Titchberry Farm. *SS22*
Farmland and a mile of cliff with an old farmhouse and farm buildings. Access to cliff only; not to farmland; motorists please use car park at farm entrance.

Golden Cove, Berrynarbor. *SS54*
Wooded cliff W of Combe Martin.

Holdstone Down. *SS64*
Moorland and cliff halfway between Combe Martin and Heddon's Mouth.

Holne Woods. *SX77*
2½m of woodland on S and W banks of river Dart. 10m W of Newton Abbot. Paths give fine views.

Ilfracombe. *SS44*
Coastal land from outskirts of town to W of Lee village, including farmland and woods.

Lee to Croyde. *SS44*
Five miles of some of Devon's finest coast, continuous from Lee to Woolacombe, and then some gaps to Croyde. Access by footpath.

Little Haldon. *SX97*
Heathland; views over Exe estuary and Dartmoor. 3m E of Teignmouth.

Lympstone. *SX98*
Land on E side of the Exe 7m SE of Exeter overlooking the estuary.

Orcombe and Prattshayes. *SY07*
A mile of high red sandstone cliff, cliff fields and foreshore 2½m SE of Exmouth. Access by footpath to cliff and by Orcombe Point Steps and Rodney Steps to foreshore.

Rockbeare Hill *SY09*
(Prickly Pearblossoms Park). Hill and woodland 3m W of Ottery St Mary.

Southdown Cliffs, Brixham. *SX95*
Cliff and farmland between Sharkham Point and Man Sands, ½m E of Brixham.

Peak Hill Field, Pond Meadow and Sid Meadows, Sidmouth. *SY18*
Meadow and pasture land.

Thurlestone. *SX64*
Part of Thurlestone Sands known as South Milton Sands 4m W of Kingsbridge.

Welcombe and Marsland Mouths. *SS21*
An acre above Welcombe Mouth on Devon/Cornwall border.

Withleigh. *SS91*
Coppice, water meadow, hanging woodland and steep pasture fields in the valley of the Little Dart, 3m W of Tiverton.

DORSET

Belle Vue Farm. *SZ07*
Rough grazing above cliffs on Isle of Purbeck, 2m SW of Swanage. Public footpaths.

Burton Cliff, Burton Bradstock. *SY48*
High cliff running west to Freshwater Bay and sloping inland to river Bride. Riverside and cliff walks.

Crook Hill, Beaminster. *ST40*
Viewpoint near Winyard's Gap (qv).

Eggardon Hill. *SY59*
Downland; views over Marshwood Vale and the sea.

Hardy Monument. *ST68*
Erected 1846 to Vice Admiral Thomas Masterman Hardy, flag captain of *Victory* at Trafalgar.

Lambert's Castle Hill. *SY36*
Hilltop and surrounding land with woodland. 4½m E of Axminster. Iron Age fort. Views.

Lewesdon Hill. *ST40*
Part of wooded summit; views over Devon, Dorset and Somerset. 3m W of Beaminster.

Lime Kiln Hill and Labour-in-Vain farm, Puncknowle, West Bexington. *SY58*
Former stone workings, rough grazing and farmland overlooking Chesil Bank.

Martyrs' Memorial, Tolpuddle. *SY79*
A commemorative seat to the martyrs. 7m NE of Dorchester.

Pilsdon Pen. *ST40*
Landmark with Iron Age hill-fort. Rough grazing. Access by footpath from B3164.

Whitecliff Farm and Ballard Down. *SZ08*
Downland, steep slopes and undercliff on Isle of Purbeck. Public footpaths and bridleways; also coastal footpath along cliff edge.

Winyard's Gap. *ST40*
Woodland above Chedington, 4m SE of Crewkerne.

SOMERSET

Brean Down. *ST25*
Headland with Iron Age promontory fort. 2m W of Weston-super-Mare.

Brent Knoll. *ST35*
Part of hill in Somerset Levels with Iron Age hill-fort. 3m E of Burnham on Sea. Access by footpath to summit.

Cheddar Cliffs. *ST45*
North side of famous gorge. 318 acres, part of which is a nature reserve with limited access. 8m NW of Wells.

Fyne Court. *ST23*
Former pleasure grounds of now demolished house. Headquarters of Somerset Trust for Nature Conservation and visitor centre for Quantocks. 6m N of Taunton at Broomfield.

Grabbist Hill, Dunster. *SS94*
Wooded oak hillside; views over Dunster Castle, the Quantocks and Exmoor. Public footpaths and bridleways.

Priest's House, Muchelney. *ST42*
Late medieval house 1½m S of Langport. Access by appointment.

Tor Hill, Wells. *ST54*
Hill just E of city; views of cathedral and surrounding country.

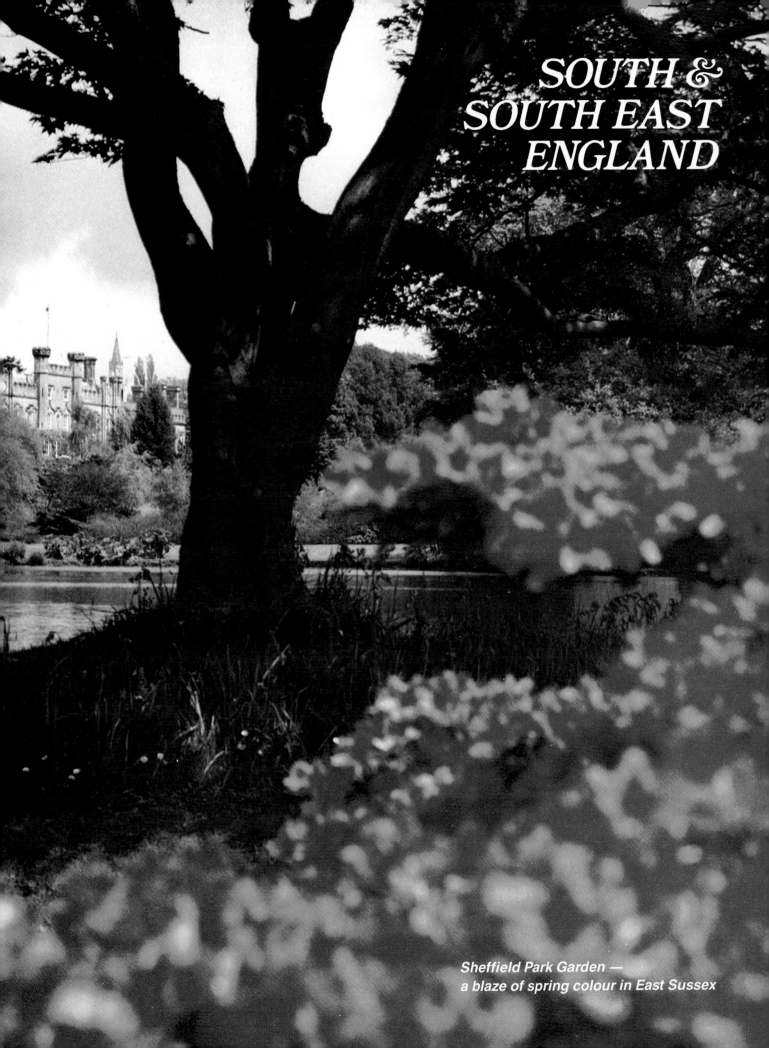

SOUTH &
SOUTH EAST
ENGLAND

*Sheffield Park Garden —
a blaze of spring colour in East Sussex*

SO

SP

BANBURY

MILTON KEYNES

M50

M5

M5

Hidcote
Manor Gdn.

Dover's Hill

The Coneygree
Market Hall

Snowshill
Manor

Hailes Abbey

Chantry
Chapel

Boarstall
Duck
Decoy

Claydon House

Stow-on-the-Wold

A34

Waddesdon
Manor

AYLESBURY

GLOUCESTER

A40

Ashleworth
Tithe Barn

May Hill

A40

Westbury Court

Blackstable
Wood

Crickley Hill

Chedworth
Roman
Villa

Long
Crendon

King's
Head

Princes
Risborough
Manor

Whiteleaf

Haresfield Beacon

Stockend &
Maitland Woods

A429

Arlington Row

OXFORD

M40

Aston Wood

Coombe

Bradenham

Hugh

Rodborough Common
St Chloe's Green

Besbury Common
Hyde Common

Cirencester

Ruskin
Reserve

West Wycombe
Park

Frocester Hill

Watledge Hill

Minchinhampton
Commons

Buscot
Park

A420

A34

Watlington Hill

Greenlands
Estate

Clive

Westridge Woods

Coleshill

A419

Great Coxwell
Barn

Uffington
White Horse

Priory Cottages

A423

M4

Ashdown House

Lardon Chase

Lough Down

Greys Court

Basildon Park

A4

M4

Pangbourne
Meadow

READING

Chippenham

Cherhill Down

A4

Avebury

A4

NEWBURY

A4

Finchamps
Ridges

A30

Great
Chalfield
Manor

Lacock

A361

Marlborough

A338

Falkland Memorial

Sandham
Memorial
Chapel

Ambarrow Hill

M4

A350

The Courts

The Chase

M34

The Vyne

Westwood
House

BASINGSTOKE

M3

ST

Warminster

Cley Hill

Andover

FARNHAM

Wey & G
Navi

SU

Eashing Brid
Wit
Con

A303

Stonehenge
Down

A36

A338

A30

M3

A31

Frensham
Common

Fre
Mer

Liphoo

Stourhead

A303

Dinton Park

Figsbury Ring

SALISBURY

Mompesson

A30

A338

A354

Win Green Hill

Hale Purlieu

Mottisfont
Abbey

Pepperbox Hill

Winchester
City Mill

WINCHESTER

Ludshott

Selborne Hill

Durford Heath

Marle

Petersfield

Woolbe

Uppark

Dro
S
E

M27

SOUTHAMPTON

Hamble River

A27

Ringwood

Hightown Common

A31

M27

Quay Meadow

CHI

PORTSMOUTH

East Head

Cowes

RYDE

Horestone Point

Newtown

Newport

St Helen's Common

SZ

Freshwater

St Helen's Duver

Bembridge
Windmill

Borthwood
Copse

Sandown

Bembridge and
Culver Downs

West
Wight

Knowles
Farm

Ventnor

The Clappers

A6

A428

BEDFORD

A1

A505

TL

Puckeridge

A5

Dunstable Downs

ott

A1M

A6

Shaw's Corner

Pitstone Windmill

Ashridge Estate

Hatfield Forest

Braintree

A604

A1034

Colchester

A604

Harwich

TM

Bourne Mill

Ray Island

CLACTON ON-SEA

Northey Island

A414

CHELMSFORD

A12

Danbury and Lingwood

EPPING

M25

A110

BRENTWOOD

M11

M25

A128

Rayleigh Mount

A12

den nor

WATFORD

SOUTHEND ON-SEA

A13

Hogback Wood

Dorneywood House

Fenton House

LONDON

Eastbury House

DENHEAD

Gray's Monument

M4

Osterley Park

Carlyle's House

Blewcoat School

East Sheen Common

Rainham Hall

George Inn

DARTFORD

Goswells

STAINES

nymede

Ham House

Wandle Park

St John's Jerusalem

Sheerness

MARGATE

Morden Hall

Hawkwood

Owletts

A299

Claremont Landscape Garden

Happy Valley

CROYDON

Petts Wood

Tudor Yeoman's House

Faversham

Golden Hill

Sandwich Bay

Watermeads

M20

Coldrum Long Burrow

CANTERBURY

Sandwich

Cedar House

Selsdon Wood

M26

Wrotham Water

M2

A2

A258

Bookham Commons

LEATHERHEAD

Quebec

SEVENOAKS

MAIDSTONE

Stoneacre

A22

Chartwell

Emmetts

Knole

A20

TR

St Margaret's Bay

Polesden Lacey

Box Hill

Headley Heath

South Hawke

Gdn

Old Soar Manor

DFORD

Hatchlands

Ranmore Cmn

Gatton

Limpsfield Common

Toys Hill

One Tree Hill

Wool House

ASHFORD

DOVER

ord Mill

Netley Park

North Downs

Grange Farm

I de Hill

Mariner's Hill

TQ

M20

Great Farthingloe

A20

almington ions

Abinger Roughs

Hackhurst Down

Harewoods

Chiddingstone

A259

FOLKESTONE

Blackheath

Holmwood Common

Leith Hill

Sprivers Garden

Royal Military Canal

Winkworth Arboretum

M23

Wakehurst Place Garden

Standen

Scotney Castle Garden

Sissinghurst Castle

Smallhythe Place

Hydon's Ball

East Grinstead

Nap Wood

A21

Bodiam Castle

HORSHAM

The Warren

Black Down

Nyman's Garden

Bateman's

Lamb House

Petworth House

A24

Sheffield Park Garden

A22

Wickham Manor Farm

Rye

A29

Lavington Common

Ditchling Beacon

Lake Meadow

Sullington Warren

A23

Fairlight

Estate

Warren Hill

on

Bramber Castle

Newtimber Hill

A27

Monks House

Alfriston Clergy House

HASTINGS

Arundel

Cissbury Ring

A27

Highdown Hill

Shoreham Gap

BRIGHTON

A2 59

Exceat Saltings

Crowlink

EASTBOURNE

TV

M1

M3

M25

A3

0   10   20   30 Mls.

0   10   20   30   40   50 Kms.

ALFRISTON CLERGY HOUSE

East Sussex   TQ50

The National Trust bought this small medieval building in 1896 – for £10. A modest acquisition it might have been, but it was the first house to be owned by the Trust, which makes it more than a little special.

It is a timber-framed, thatched house in which the Roman Catholic parish priests of the area lived. Great events, such as the defeat of the French at Crécy in 1346, the advent of the Black Death, and the routing of the French at Poitiers are contemporary with its building.

The main body of the house is the hall, open to the timber roof. At each end is a two-storeyed section. The east end has its own entrance, and here the housekeeper lived; at the other end stores were kept on the ground floor, with the priests' rooms above. The floor of the hall is made of rammed chalk sealed with milk, as it would have been originally. When the Trust renovated the building in 1977, 30 gallons of sour milk were used on a new floor. The smell, apparently, was unbearable for several days.

Open April to end Oct. Admission charged. Parking in village car park. 4m NE of Seaford in Alfriston, adjoining church.

ARLINGTON ROW

Gloucestershire   SP10

Bibury is an enchantingly pretty Cotswold village. Here, framed against a backdrop of trees, are the much-photographed stone cottages of Arlington Row, which strike a chord in every visitor's heart. Arlington Row was a sheep-house in the 14th century, but when Arlington Mill began in the 17th century to full (cleanse and thicken) cloth as well as grind corn, it was converted into a row of cottages to house the weavers.

The nearby meadow, called Rack Isle, is also owned by the Trust. Here wool washed in the Row was hung to dry on racks which gave this spot its name. The river Coln, well-stocked with trout, bounds one side, while a stream runs along two other sides. The meadow is now a nature reserve.

Arlington Row interiors not open. In Bibury village, on S side of A433.

ASCOTT

Buckinghamshire   SP82

People come to Ascott in hordes, not so much to see the house, but for the gardens and the magnificent Ascott collection of art.

Somewhere in the midst of this large, rambling 19th-century house, half-timbered and whitewashed, is a small farmhouse of 1606, which disappeared within the fabric of the

present house first in 1874, and was buried even deeper in 1937. The only plainly visible relic of the original house is a beam over the present front door, dated 1606.

Ascott, or Eastcote, was bought by Baron Mayer de Rothschild in 1873. In 1937 the house was inherited by Antony de Rothschild who, with the help of his wife, created the existing interior and exterior; and most importantly, consolidated the family's remarkable collection of *objets d'art*.

To gain entry to the house, visitors often have to wait some time in the garden. This is no hardship. These 30 acres were designed by Leopold de Rothschild with the advice of horticulturist Sir Harry Veitch, and are an exceptional example of 19th-century gardening. The garden is a blend of formal and natural. Rare shrubs and trees planted singly or in groups give a richness to the site, especially in autumn, when the varied species glow with colours. The garden overlooks the Vale of Aylesbury, beyond which rise the Chilterns, a

The medieval Clergy House in Alfriston, on the edge of the South Downs

NATIONAL TRUST INFORMATION

For details of opening times and further information about properties in South and South-East England, contact the Regional Information Officer at the following addresses:

Essex: Blickling, Norwich NR11 6NF Tel. Aylsham 3471

Kent, East Sussex and South-East London: The Estate Office, Scotney Castle, Lamberhurst, Tunbridge Wells, Kent TN3 8JN Tel. Lamberhurst 890651

Gloucestershire: 34–36 Church Street, Tewkesbury, Glos GL20 5SN

Ascott – a house filled with world-famous art treasures

Tel. Tewkesbury 292427 and 292919

Hampshire, Surrey, West Sussex and South-West London:
Polesden Lacey, Dorking, Surrey RH5 6BD
Tel. Bookham 53401

Bedfordshire, Berkshire, Buckinghamshire, Hertfordshire, Oxfordshire and North London:
Hughenden Manor, High Wycombe, Bucks HP14 4LA
Tel. High Wycombe 28051

Wiltshire: Stourton, Warminster, Wiltshire BA12 6QD
Tel. Bourton, Dorset 840224

view best seen from the series of formal grass terraces below the house. One terrace leads to an unusual sundial, the roman figures carved out of box, a yew casting the shadow. West of the terraces lies a perfect sunken Victorian garden, while to the north a lily pond is resplendent with flowers in summer.

Open April to end Sept. Admission charged. Free parking. Wheelchair access. 2m SW of Leighton Buzzard, on the A418.

ASHDOWN HOUSE

Oxfordshire   *SU28*

Looking for all the world like a doll's house, Ashdown is a pretty, tall, square house with a steep, hipped roof topped by two massive chimneys and an octagonal cupola. It sits almost isolated, with only two unattached pavilions for company, high up on the Berkshire Downs.

Here it was built in about 1665 by the First Earl of Craven as a gift to the greatest passion of his life, Elizabeth Queen of Bohemia, the sister of Charles I.

The rooms retain few original features. Only the hall, stairs and cupola are open to the public, along with the grounds and formal garden, designed by the Trust, who took possession in 1956. The staircase climbs the full height of the house to the cupola, from where splendid views can be enjoyed. In the hall and stairway are hung portraits from the Craven collection, a fascinating record of the family and friends of the Queen of Bohemia.

Limited opening April to end Sept. Admission charged. Free parking. Wheelchair access to grounds only. 2½m S of Ashbury, 3½m N of Lambourn, on W side of B4000.

ASHLEWORTH TITHE BARN

Gloucestershire   *SO82*

Tithe barns are among the most atmospheric of medieval survivals, impressive by their size and structure, and among the few domestic buildings of that age left to us. Ashleworth is no exception. Measuring 125ft long by 25ft wide, the 15th-century barn is built of limestone faced with jointed blocks of stone, and is roofed with stone slates borne by massive roof timbers. The interior is dimly lit and church-like, with high walls reaching up to the open timbered roof, and is entered through one of two giant gabled porches with carved wooden lintels.

Open all year. Admission charged. 6m N of Gloucester, 1¼m E of Hartpury (A417), on W bank of Severn, SE of Ashleworth.

ASHRIDGE ESTATE

Hertfordshire   *SP91*

Here the Trust owns a 4,000-acre slice of the Chilterns, divided into two distinct parts – the chalkland of Ivinghoe Beacon and Steps Hill, and the clay-with-flint plateau below.

The chalk downland harbours a treasure-trove of wild flowers; cowslips, vetches, violets, exotic orchids such as the bee, frog and fragrant orchids, and the extraordinarily named squinancywort.

The plateau woodlands of oak, beech, wild cherry, ash, hornbeam and ancient sweet chestnut are rich in wildlife. Among the animals the most dramatic are perhaps the fallow and muntjak deer, the most unusual the edible dormice. These are twice the size of our own common dormice, and are found only in parts of the Chilterns. Lord Rothschild introduced them into the country in 1902; they were considered a delicacy on the Continent.

3m N of Berkhamsted, between A41 and B489, astride B4506.

AVEBURY

Wiltshire   *SU17*

The small downland village of Avebury has a large claim to fame. It is half built within a Bronze Age temple, perhaps the most important in Europe, and actually larger than Stonehenge 18 miles away. A great ditch runs in a circle enclosing an area 360yds across; on its inner lip stand the remains of a huge ring of sarsen stones, smaller than those at Stonehenge, but still impressive. Within the enclosure stand two more rings, side by side. The ditch is broken by gateways to the north, south, east and west.

Where a stone is missing, a modern concrete post marks its site, and it is mostly a line of these which outline an avenue, 50ft wide, leading to Overton Hill, 1½ miles away. The remaining stones in the avenue show that the way was marked by 100 pairs of ancient sarsens, each pair comprising a tall, thin stone opposite a squat, roughly diamond-shaped rock; perhaps these represented male and female figures in some forgotten fertility rite. Overton Hill, it seems, was the site of religious buildings, probably built of wood; here too a small ring of stones stood.

A barn in Avebury village, actually within the henge, houses an excellent display of Wiltshire rural life. The Alexander Keiller Museum houses exhibits of pottery and other finds from Avebury itself.

Stone circle open every day. Great Barn open April to end Sept. Alexander Keiller Museum open mid March to mid Oct, limited winter opening mid Oct to mid March. Admission charged to museum and Great Barn. Wheelchair access to Great Barn and museum. Refreshments in Barn, and in pub in village (within henge). 1m N of the Bath road (A4) at junction of A361 and B4003.

An ancient mystery

It is one of the most famous, and certainly the largest prehistoric monument in Britain. Thousands of people visit it every year, and countless books, pamphlets and theses have been written about it. Yet Avebury remains a mystery; little is known about the people who built and used it and next to nothing is known about the reasons for its construction.

Henge monuments like Avebury seem to have been developed independently in Britain, but further impetus and sophistication was lent by immigrants arriving from the Low Countries and the mouth of the Rhine in about 2,000 BC. These people are known as Beaker Folk because of their distinctive and refined pottery. The Beaker Folk may have worked with the existing Neolithic population, although it is more likely that they became overlords. But it is possible these dynamic people spurred on the building of Avebury, and are responsible for it becoming the most important structure in the country before its eventual eclipse by Stonehenge.

It is generally accepted that Avebury is a sacred, or at the very least a ceremonial structure, and the theories developed by Professor Alexander Thom are given credence by many archaeologists. He has argued that the henge monuments are astronomical calendars, constructed so that a priestly or kingly class could predict eclipses and calculate the movements of heavenly bodies. He also suggests that in a society reliant on the successful growing of crops it would be essential to have precise knowledge of when to sow and when to harvest.

It is probable, however, that the entire truth about Avebury will never be known. And that, of course, is one of its fascinations. Many visitors return time and time again, mystified by its purpose, and entranced by the beauty of the setting and by the sculptural beauty of the huge stones.

BASILDON PARK

Berkshire   *SU67*

A Yorkshireman, Sir Francis Sykes, employed a Yorkshire architect, John Carr, to build this gracious Palladian mansion. Work began in 1776. The house, built of Bath stone, overlooks the Thames valley. The state rooms are on the first floor, reached by climbing the magnificent staircase which is lit by semi-circular windows high up in the roof. The finest room is the Octagon Room. This was finished in the 1840s, rather later than the rest of the house's interior, which still keeps in the main to the original designs of the 1770s. Richly coloured walls and a heavily decorated ceiling create a nest of luxury from which to view the Thames valley and the beech hangers of the opposing slopes.

Paintings and furniture of the 18th century fill the house, some of them very fine, especially the beds in the Crimson Bedroom and Bamboo Room. The Anglo-Indian Room is particularly interesting (Sykes made his money in India), and so too is the decorative shell room. The doors and fireplaces came from Panton Hall in Lincolnshire, another house by Carr, now sadly demolished.

Open April to end Oct. Admission charged. Free parking. Refreshments. Between Pangbourne and Streatley 7m NW of Reading, on W side of A329.

Kipling describes how he and his wife first set eyes on Bateman's from their very early motor car in 1902.

'It was the heart-breaking Locomobile that brought us to the house called 'Bateman's'. We had seen an advertisement of her, and we reached her down an enlarged rabbit-hole of a lane. At very first sight the Committee of Ways and Means (Mrs Kipling and himself) said: 'That's her! The Only She! Make an honest woman of her – quick!' We entered and felt her Spirit – her Feng Shui – to be good. We went through every room and found no shadow of regrets, stifled miseries, nor any menace though the 'new' end of her was three hundred years old.'

Bateman's garden was designed by Rudyard Kipling to suit the house and to blend harmoniously with the surrounding Sussex countryside

One of the largest ceremonial monuments in Europe, Avebury's stone circle is bathed in an atmosphere of tranquillity not found at over-popular Stonehenge. Some of the stones were destroyed during the 14th and 18th centuries

BATEMAN'S

East Sussex   *TQ62*

The 17th century saw the Wealden iron industry at its height, and Bateman's is a house built for a successful ironmaster – large, solid and comfortable. Charcoal made from the Sussex woods was soon superseded as a fuel for iron-smelting by the newly discovered coal of the Midlands, which led to a decline in the Sussex industry. In consequence many fine houses such as Bateman's fell into use as farmhouses. Bateman's was not rescued until the 1890s by Mr Macmeikan, who bought it with 100 acres and restored it. In 1902 it was sold, with a further 200 acres, to novelist Rudyard Kipling.

This almost perfect example of Jacobean architecture retains many original interior features, such as the stone doorways, oak wainscoting and oak staircase. Most of the furnishings are 17th-century: English and Continental pieces of solid oak, Mortlake and Brussels tapestries and the fine painted Spanish leather from Cordova, bought by the Kiplings, which lines the dining room. The Kiplings also left many mementoes of their love-affair with India – an Indian silk-embroidered fire-screen in the dining room, Indian brasses in the hall, and in the author's study, the heart of the house, Indian rugs made to Kipling's order. Here, at the large ink-stained desk, he wrote many of his novels, including *Puck of Pook's Hill*; the hill is visible from the window.

The garden, through which the Dudwell Stream flows, was partly designed by Kipling. A member of the family once said of it; 'The house stands like a beautiful cup on a saucer to match'. Here, house, garden and countryside blend together admirably. There are lawns and yew hedges, a pool and a rose garden; Kipling's designs for the last two hang in his study. Park Mill, in which Kipling installed a turbine to provide the house with electricity, lies over the Dudwell Stream, and has been restored to working order.

Open March to Oct. Admission charged. Free parking. Refreshments. ½m S of Burwash on A265.

BLACK DOWN

West Sussex   *SU93*

The silhouette of Black Down juts out like a headland into the calm ocean of the Weald. 'The dark sentinel of the Western Weald' as it has been described, is one of the wildest tracts of land in an otherwise domesticated southern England, and offers walkers and riders the matchless pleasures of open countryside and far-reaching views.

Heather, gorse and bracken cover much of the 600 acres of hill, but as the practice of sheep grazing has declined, Scots pine, birch and even rhododendrons have moved in.

From the Temple of the Four Winds, a stone seat half an hour's walk from the upper car park (also a nature trail – leaflet available from Haslemere Museum), the views are among the finest in the south-east. East and south lies the Weald, westwards magnificent views over Hampshire.

2m S of Wellington (A38), ½m E of the Wellington-Hemyoch road.

BOARSTALL DUCK DECOY

Buckinghamshire   SP62

Charles II was responsible for introducing the duck decoy into England in the 18th century. Its purpose is to catch waterfowl in large numbers. To do this the birds are attracted, by the use of a 'decoy' or dummy duck, on to a small patch of water. Parts of this are partitioned into funnels using nets. The birds are herded into these netted over 'pipes' by a decoyman and his dog, rather as a shepherd herds sheep. Once trapped the birds can be caught at leisure.

The duck decoy at Boarstall, set in 13 acres of woodland, is still in use. However, the birds are no longer killed for food, instead they are caught and ringed for ornithological study. A collection of European wildfowl is kept on the lake, and in the woods is a nature trail. There is an exhibition hall on the site, and notes are supplied to those interested in natural history.

Limited opening April to Aug. Admission charged. Nature trail suitable for disabled. Midway between Bicester and Thame, 2m W of Brill.

BODIAM CASTLE

East Sussex   TQ72

At the mid-point of the Hundred Years War, England lost control of the Channel for fifteen years. During this time the French wreaked havoc along the south coast, attacking and burning English ports. At that time the river Rother was navigable as far as Bodiam Bridge. The owner of the Bodiam estate was Sir Edward Dalyngrigge, whose manor house overlooked the Rother valley, making it a natural site for defence against a possible invasion. In October 1385 Richard II directed Sir Edward 'to strengthen and crenellate his manor house . . . for resistance against our enemies'. However, Sir Edward decided to build a new castle instead.

England regained the Channel before the castle was finished, so its defences were never put to the test. It was inhabited until the 16th century when, during the Civil War, the undefended castle was taken and the interior wrecked by Commonwealth troops. It remained deserted until early this century when Lord Curzon bought it and restored the towers and walls. He also landscaped the surrounding countryside, making his 'most fairy of English castles' as he called it, even more the quintessential relic of the legendary, chivalrous days of medieval England.

Open all year. Admission charged. Parking charged (except NT members). Wheelchair access. Refreshments at car park and Castle Inn (NT) nearby. 3m S of Hawkhurst, 1m E of A229.

BOOKHAM COMMONS

Surrey   TQ15

Peasants turned their pigs out to forage on these commons in the 11th century; in the 16th century oak from the commons' woods was used in the building of Henry VIII's Nonesuch Palace; during the 17th century it is recorded that here villagers still had the right to graze their horses, oxen, cows and sheep, and gather wood. In 1941 the commons were used for military exercises. Today the grasslands are partially overgrown with scrub; the practice of grazing ceased some 60 years ago after perhaps 1,000 years of such use. Together with the

The defences of Bodiam Castle were formidable. The Postern Gate, seen here across the moat, is the 'backdoor' of the castle. If this was taken by an attacker, the main gatehouse could still be isolated, and the inner walls defended, virtually creating a castle within a castle

Bourne Mill, in Colchester, is thought to have started life as an Elizabethan fishing lodge. There has been a mill on this site since the 12th century, but the present building was probably constructed with materials taken from St John's Abbey after the Dissolution of the Monasteries. In its turn a woollen mill and then a flour mill, the building still houses a 26ft waterwheel and three pairs of millstones. It has been restored since the National Trust acquired it in 1936

mature oak woodlands, the grasslands are now preserved for the flowering plants (500 species recorded) and rich birdlife.

2¼ W of Leatherhead, just N of Bookham Station, between A245 and A246.

BOURNE MILL

Essex   TM02

Sir Thomas Lucas built Bourne Mill in 1591. It was possibly originally a fishing lodge – the little building's stepped Dutch gables and finials, chimneys with octagonal shafts, mullioned windows and the Lucas arms over the door seem unusually finicky features for a mere mill.

The building was used by Dutch refugees for processing cloth in the 17th century, but this trade declined and in 1825 the mill was converted to grind flour. The old machinery was finally halted just before the outbreak of World War II, but is now again restored and working.

Open April to end Sept. Admission charged. 1m S of centre of Colchester in Bourne Road, off the Mersea Road (B1025).

BOX HILL

Surrey   TQ15

This hill, one of the highest (and most popular) along the North Downs, rises as a 400ft cliff above the river Mole, shrubs barely covering the bare white chalk where the water has carved one of the few gaps which breach the line of these hills. The property includes 800 acres of chalk downland and woods, part of it designated a country park including nature walks. The area is one of the richest in the south for its wildlife and flowers.

The hill was named after the box trees cultivated on its slopes, which provided shade for walkers, and wood for the makers of mathematical instruments, and for cabinet makers, who used it extensively as a veneer.

The summit is bare and carpeted with springy turf, and from here are glorious views across the Weald, to the South Downs.

Open all year. Information Room and Exhibition open April to end Oct, limited opening March and Nov to mid Dec. Wheelchair access to summit area only. Refreshments. 2½m S of Leatherhead, 1m N of Dorking, E of A24, close to Burford Bridge.

BRADENHAM

Buckinghamshire   SU89

The National Trust owns virtually all of this delightful village, including Bradenham Manor. The fine red brick manor was for a time the home of Benjamin Disraeli, the 19th-century Prime Minister, who lived here with his father Isaac, a writer. Queen Elizabeth was entertained here in about 1670, during one of her frequent tours of the countryside.

Manor house not open. 4m NW of High Wycombe, 4½m S of Princes Risborough, on E side of A4010.

BRAMBER CASTLE

West Sussex   TQ11

Set on the river Adur, Bramber was once an important port, and the large natural mound here on which the remains of Bramber Castle stand was a natural site for fortification by the Normans. It was an administrative centre in the early days of Norman rule, but when the river silted up the port died, and by 1833 Bramber was recorded as a 'mean village' – although it still returned two MPs to Parliament.

Little remains of the great Norman castle, except the deep fosse, or defensive ditch, remnants of wall and one dramatic and romantic survival – a 76ft-high fragment of the keep. The Trust keeps the site undisturbed, overgrown and wild, with sheep-cropped grassy banks and self-sown trees, to preserve the age-old spirit of the place and its romantic appeal.

SE of Steyning, in Bramber, just N of A283.

BUCKINGHAM CHANTRY CHAPEL

Buckinghamshire SP63

Chantry chapels were built by respected citizens in order that Mass could be sung for their souls in perpetuity – a sort of insurance policy securing a place in heaven. This one is particularly attractive, and is also the oldest building in Buckingham. It was first built in 1260, but the only survivor from the original Norman building is the recessed doorway with zig-zag moulding around the arch. The Chantry Chapel of St John, as it is known, was rebuilt in 1475, and in the reign of Henry VIII it became the Royal Latin School. It remained a school until 1907. It was restored by Gilbert Scott in 1875, and passed to the Trust in 1912.

Open all year, apply to Mr Aris, 4 West Street, for admission. On Market Hill, Buckingham.

BUSCOT PARK

Oxfordshire SU29

One Walter Loveden bought the manor of Buscot in 1557; the house which stands today and houses the fabulous Faringdon Collection of art did not appear until Edward Loveden Townsend, a great nephew of the last Loveden descendant, inherited the estate in 1749. It was he who designed this classical house in 1780.

The period which stands out in Buscot's history was that of its ownership by Robert Campbell, a wealthy Australian. He bought the estate in 1859 as 4,000 acres of almost derelict land on either bank of the Thames. Campbell instituted a daring agricultural scheme way ahead of its time. At the centre of the plan was the production of sugar-beet and its by-products. He built a distillery on an island in the Thames (still called Brandy Island), a narrow-gauge railway round the estate, an extensive irrigation network, a gas works, and concrete farm buildings – 30 years before anyone else. He was also an enlightened land-owner, introducing a nine-hour day and other benefits for his workers. Unfortunately his grandiose schemes bankrupted him – the enormous capital cost could not be recouped quickly enough.

Sir Alexander Henderson, the First Lord Faringdon, bought the estate in 1889, and began the art collection which is the house's outstanding attraction. Exceptional are the paintings in the saloon, a series by Edward Burne-Jones depicting *The Legend of the Briar Rose*, bought from the artist in 1890. The Second Lord Faringdon, one of the 'Bright Young Things' of the 1920s, added to the collection, but in 1948 sold the house to Ernest Cook on a lease-back basis and the collection was put in trust to ensure its survival. The house itself passed to the National Trust in 1962.

Open April to end Sept. Admission charged. Free parking. Refreshments. Between Lechlade and Faringdon, off A417.

CARLYLE'S HOUSE

London TQ27

There is nothing extraordinary about the early 18th-century houses in Cheyne Row, Chelsea, except that in No. 5 (now No. 24) Thomas Carlyle lived for 47 years, from 1834 until his death in 1881.

Carlyle, son of a poor Scottish stonemason, became perhaps Victorian England's most eminent and respected writer, historian and philosopher. His works, the most famous being *Frederick the Great*, are little read today, but during his lifetime he attracted to this then unfashionable part of London many of the great men of his age: Dickens, Tennyson and Gladstone numbered among his visitors.

The house is three storeys high, with a basement, and in the attic is a study built specially for Carlyle. The building is full of the Carlyles' possessions – mementoes, presents, correspondence and all the bric-à-brac of day-to-day life.

Open April to end Oct. Admission charged. No. 24 Cheyne Row, Chelsea SW3, off Cheyne Walk, between Battersea and Albert Bridges on Chelsea Embankment.

THE CHELSEA HOUSE
Shortly after moving to Cheyne Row, Jane, Carlyle's wife, wrote:
'. . .We have got an excellent lodgement, of most antique physiognomy, quite to our humour; all wainscoted, carved and queer-looking, roomy, substantial, commodious, with closets to satisfy any Bluebeard . . . Two weeks ago there was a row of ancient trees in front, but some crazy-headed Cockneys have uprooted them. Behind we have a garden (so called in the language of flattery) in the worst order, but boasting two vines. . . and a walnut tree, from which I gathered almost sixpence worth of Walnuts.'

Buscot owes its present dignified appearance to a 1930s restoration, which swept away Victorian additions that were out of character with the original 18th-century classical lines

CHARTWELL

Kent   TQ45

Churchill's studio at Chartwell, where the statesman retired to paint and to escape the pressures of his political life. On the walls of this little building, hidden away in a corner of the garden, hang a number of canvases in various stages of completion

Sir Winston Churchill bought Chartwell in 1922, when he was 47 years old and, for the first time since 1900, out of Parliament and out of office.

The Victorian ex-farmhouse (only 25 miles from Westminster) had little to commend it architecturally, but its setting and fine views over the Weald were what swayed Churchill to buy. Philip Tilden, a popular architect of the time, was employed to remodel the house. Nineteenth-century trimmings were swept away and a new wing added, Victorian gloom banished and a light, airy interior created. Although not an architectural success, the house was, and still is, practicable and comfortable – a house in which to work and raise a family. The garden, too, was taken in hand. The keynote here is simplicity; wide lawns, a lake, rose gardens and ornamental pools, all plainly but effectively planted. The wall around the kitchen garden (now grassed over) was built largely by Winston himself.

The interior of the house is dedicated to Churchill's memory. The library, the study, and the drawing and dining rooms are kept as the great statesman left them when he died in 1964. The upstairs rooms form a museum of his life, displaying his medals, uniforms and the many gifts he received from heads of state and the famous throughout his career. The study reflects Churchill at work; it is where he did much of his writing as an historian, and much of his thinking and planning as a politician. The studio in the garden, however, reflects Churchill at leisure. The walls are hung with his paintings, and on an easel is an unfinished canvas.

Open March to end Nov. Admission charged. Free parking. Wheelchair available. Restaurant. 2m S of Westerham, fork left off B2026 after 1½m.

Churchill at Chartwell

If there is one word that could never apply to Winston Churchill it is the word 'average'. And yet careful notes have been kept of an average day for the great man at Chartwell. He was awoken at 8.00 am and ate a hearty English breakfast. He remained in bed for the rest of the morning, first reading the papers and then either dictating to one of his secretaries or writing memos. He dresssed for lunch, and after eating walked in the garden where he fed the fish or went to look at the wildfowl on the lake. One of these, a Canada goose, became a close friend of Churchill's, emerging from the water when he appeared and then following him round the garden. Churchill had an affinity with animals, having at various times a pet badger, a fox, a tame robin, several dogs and cats and even a pet sheep.

After returning from his walk Churchill slept for an hour or two, a habit learned many years before, which stood him in good stead when great stamina and staying power were needed. On waking he worked again till dinner time. He retired to his study at about midnight and often worked through till four in the morning – a schedule that would appal most people.

Of course, Churchill did much that is not described in his 'average' day. For instance he built the famous wall at Chartwell, but what is not so well known is that he also built the little summer-house in the south-east corner of the kitchen garden. He spent much time painting, a hobby of which he said: 'If it weren't for painting, I couldn't live'.

CHEDWORTH ROMAN VILLA

Gloucestershire　　　　　　　　　　　*SP01*

A gamekeeper digging for a lost ferret discovered Chedworth in 1864. Subsequent excavations revealed a villa which must have belonged to a very wealthy Roman landowner. The building – 32 rooms have so far been excavated – dates from AD 180-350. By the fourth century the inhabitants were Christians, perhaps Romano-British. The finest and best excavated villa in the country, Chedworth shows a sophisticated household with sauna baths and turkish baths, a dining suite, a court garden and verandah, which must have been an oasis of civilisation and luxury in an otherwise untamed countryside.

A small museum, erected soon after the first excavation, contains many fascinating objects found on the site.

Open March to end Oct, limited winter opening Nov to mid Dec and Feb. Admission charged. Wheelchair available. 3m NW of Fossebridge.

CHIDDINGSTONE

Kent　　　　　　　　　　　　　　*TQ54*

Across the street from the churchyard the Trust owns a row of superb 16th- to 17th-century houses, among the best in this outstanding village in a county famous for its vernacular architecture. The houses are half-timbered, infilled with plaster or brick. Perhaps the finest is the house in the middle of the row; with its steep-pitched roof and three overhanging gables, the middle gable is supported by oak posts to form a porch. The Trust also owns the Castle Inn. In the grounds of Chiddingstone Castle is the 'chiding' stone, a large sandstone block, from which this delightful village supposedly takes its name. What the chiding stone was used for remains a mystery, but it could have been where nagging wives were taken to be scolded.

Houses not open. 4m E of Edenbridge off B2027, 1½m NW of Penshurst.

CISSBURY RING

West Sussex　　　　　　　　　　　*TQ10*

On the highest point of a southern spur of the Downs is one of the largest and most impressive Iron-Age hill-forts in the country. Cissbury is an oval of 60 acres enclosed by a single bank and ditch, constructed in about 260 BC. The tribe that built it had to move 60,000 tons of chalk to fortify the site.

Also on this hill, and underneath the fort, are about 200 Stone Age flint mines hidden away among the gorse and bracken. Some are over 40ft deep with several galleries interlinking underground. In these two skeletons were found, one of a young woman who perhaps fell down the shaft and was accidentally killed, the other of a young man, probably a miner. The mines were already more than 2,000 years old when the fort was built over them.

1½m E of Findon on A24, 3m N of Worthing.

CISSBURY MINES RE-DISCOVERED

The flint mines of Cissbury Ring were first excavated by General Pitt-Rivers, a charismatic and eccentric Victorian who is generally regarded as the founder of scientific archaeological field work. When excavating the flint mines some 100 years ago (he was then confusingly known as Colonel Lane-Fox), he recorded one particularly ghoulish experience which happened while he was exploring one of the galleries: 'Presently a well-formed and perfect human jaw fell down from above, and on looking up we could perceive the remainder of the skull fixed with the base downwards, and the face towards the west, between two pieces of chalk rubble.' It was the head of a young woman. More common finds were the antler picks and shovels made from the shoulder blades of ox, deer, and pig, with which the mines were dug in about 3,500 BC.

Chedworth Roman Villa contains some interesting mosaics. This figure, carrying what looks like a rabbit in one hand and a branch in the other, represents winter

Chiddingstone's superb half-timbered houses date from the 16th to 17th centuries. The old row across the street from the churchyard is preserved by the Trust

CLANDON PARK

Surrey   TQ05

A large, square red-brick block, Clandon does not look particularly prepossessing. The formal gardens, canals and courtyards which were designed with the house and may have softened its impact were swept away by the landscape gardener 'Capability' Brown. But it has a saving grace; inside is an outstanding collection of rooms beautifully decorated in exuberant baroque style.

This is superbly illustrated by the Marble Hall, the first room entered. Two storeys high, it has two magnificent fireplaces in marble, marbled columns and a profusion of the best plasterwork the 18th century can offer, exquisitely modelled. It is painted in two tones of white, designed to cool the strong, warm colours of the state rooms beyond.

Complementing these splendid rooms are the paintings, 18th-century furniture, and a collection of rare ceramics bequeathed to the Trust by Mrs David Gubbay. Another gift allowed the Trust to redecorate and recreate the colourful interiors originally intended by Giacomo Leoni, the architect. A Venetian, he was employed in the 1730s by Thomas, the Second Lord Onslow, to replace the family's old Elizabethan mansion. His house, apart from the addition of a 19th-century porch, survives largely as he envisaged it.

Open April to mid Oct. Admission charged. Free parking. Wheelchair available. Restaurant. At West Clandon on A247, 3m E of Guildford.

CLAREMONT LANDSCAPE GARDEN

Surrey   TQ16

The architect John Vanbrugh bought this plot of land on the outskirts of Esher as a country retreat in about 1710. The house was small, but so were Vanbrugh's finances, and on the death of his mother in 1711, he sold it to Pelham-Holles, created Earl of Clare in 1714 – hence the name Claremont. Vanbrugh, ironically, became the Earl's architect, and Charles Bridgeman was employed to create the landscaped garden, one of the first to spring up in reaction to the strict formality of 17th-century gardens. He created the great grassy amphitheatre and the pond below it, and planted splendid avenues of trees. Vanbrugh made some contributions, building the belvedere (small look-out-tower) and devising the winding, wooded walks around it. Vanbrugh's death in 1726 temporarily halted work, but in the 1730s, William Kent, the new arbiter of taste, was asked to draw up further plans. He enlarged Bridgeman's pool, did away with formality, and built the island pavilion.

Finally, 'Capability' Brown, perhaps the most famous of the 18th-century landscape gardeners, took a hand in the garden in the 1770s. He was hired by Clive of India, who had bought the property in 1769, and who built the present house. Brown's main contribution was the realignment of the Portsmouth road away from the lake, and the obliteration of any remaining formality except for Vanbrugh's kitchen garden and Bridgeman's amphitheatre Claremont is, therefore, a living illustration of the evolution of the landscape garden as developed by some of its finest exponents.

Open all year (house not open). Admission charged. Wheelchair access. Refreshments. On S edge of Esher, on E side of A307.

CLAYDON HOUSE

Buckinghamshire　　　　　　　　　　*SP72*

The Second Earl of Verney was extravagant, politically ambitious and fanatical about art and music. He succeeded to his family home in 1752, and proceeded to rebuild it, primarily, it appears, in an attempt to outshine the house of his greatest political opponent, Earl Temple of Stowe. He began by adding four large rooms and an impressive staircase to the front of the old brick mansion, and then on to this recklessly built an enormous ballroom and a vast rotunda. But most extraordinary is the suite of rococo rooms decorated with the carvings of Luke Lightfoot. Everywhere – ceilings, cornices, walls and overmantels – is fancifully adorned with delicately carved birds, beasts, fruits, flowers and all manner of other things – a complete contrast to the rather sober exterior of the house. The fantastic Chinese room is perhaps unique – here Lightfoot achieved heights in the art of *chinoiserie* (the European interpretation of Chinese art) only dreamt of by his contemporaries.

Not surprisingly, all this flamboyance bankrupted the Earl by 1783. He sold up and fled to France. The rotunda and ballroom were found unsafe and were demolished in 1792. Years later a stable lad found the old Earl wandering inside the closed house, and cared for the broken old man in secret there for several weeks. The Earl's successor demolished two-thirds of his house in order to pay for the upkeep of the remainder. What he left was given to the Trust in 1956.

One of the bedrooms was kept solely for the use of Florence Nightingale, a regular visitor to Claydon (Parthenope Verney was her sister). Relics of her Crimean adventure are shown in an adjacent room.

Open April to end Oct. Admission charged. Free parking. Wheelchair available. Refreshments. In Middle Claydon 13m NW of Aylesbury, 3½m SW of Winslow.

CLIVEDEN

Buckinghamshire　　　　　　　　　　*SU98*

The driveway to Cliveden winds through a valley of rhododendrons, is checked by a huge marble fountain, and then continues in stately manner along an avenue of lime trees to the house, a vast 19th-century Italianate giant. Before it lie lawns and a forecourt hedged by yews. Beyond, from the terrace on the other side of the house, a sweeping expanse of lawn overlaid with a design of box hedges introduces one of the finest views from any country house – the gloriously wooded stretch of the river Thames known as Cliveden Reach.

Cliveden, built by Charles Barry in 1851 for the Duke of Sutherland, passed in 1893 to the American millionaire, William Waldorf Astor. During the reign of the Second Viscount Astor between the two World Wars, Cliveden became a social and political centre: the hostess, Lady Astor, was the first woman to become a Member of Parliament. The Second Viscount gave Cliveden to the National Trust in 1942, and today it is used by Stanford University of California as its British base. Because of this only two rooms are shown. These are furnished by the Astors with fittings from France, such as the splendid 16th-century fireplace in the hall, Louis XV panelling and Brussels tapestries.

The delightful park, however, is open. It stretches from Cliveden on its hillside perch down wooded slopes to Thameside walks. There is an Italian garden, a water garden, topiary, box and yews and an unusual rose garden. Scattered about the formal gardens are Roman carvings and Italian Renaissance statuary collected by William Astor. High above the Thames stands Canning's Oak, where Lord Canning, the 19th-century prime minister, is reputed to have sat for hours admiring the spectacular view.

House opening limited April to end Oct. Gardens open March to end Dec. Admission charged. Free parking. Wheelchair access. Refreshments. 2m N Taplow on B476.

Cliveden mansion from the parterre, or formal garden. This was originally a simple flat lawn. In the mid 19th century this was replaced by the present flawless sward and geometrical, box-lined beds, much to the sorrow of the young Lord Ronald Gower, who later recorded his grief at the loss of a 'huge field of grass and wild flowers'

Luke Lightfoot, the creative genius responsible for the extraordinary decorations at Claydon House, was said by a contemporary to have had 'no small trace of madness in his composition'. It is in the breathtaking Chinese Room that Lightfoot's 'madness' can be seen at its height. Here wooden carvings of remarkable delicacy surround doors and overmantels and, most outstandingly, form a complete alcove

COLDRUM LONG BARROW

Kent TQ66

The closely-clustered standing stones of Coldrum enclose a rectangular tomb, once chambered and capped by a roofing stone. All around them large fallen sarsen stones lie, marking an area some 60ft by 45ft. This would have been the size of the earthen mound or barrow which covered the tomb, for these stones once formed walls which held the earth in place.

When the tomb was opened in 1910, inside were found 22 skeletons, a flint saw and some pottery. The skeletons ranged from those of infants to old men and women, and dated from about 3,000BC. These people belonged to a small, long-headed people of the New Stone Age, and were perhaps members of the same family. A few of the bones are kept in the porch of nearby Trottiscliffe Church; the rest were destroyed in London in a bombing raid of 1942.

Between the Pilgrim's Way and the A20, 1m E of Trottiscliffe.

COLESHILL

Oxfordshire SU29

Like the Trust's neighbouring Buscot property, the 3,620 acres of farm and woodland comprising the Coleshill estate also include a village. However, the great house, one of the finest 17th-century examples in England, burnt down in the 1950s; only the gate piers remain. Cotswold stone and tile, cottage gardens enclosed by box hedges and dry-stone walls make Coleshill an attractive place. The surrounding farmlands and woods do not have unrestricted access, but there are many public footpaths. Above the village is Badbury Hill,

cloaked in beech wood. Here there is an Iron Age hill-fort, from which there are far-reaching views over the upper Thames Valley.

Adjoining and S of Buscot, astride B4019, and bounded on the SE by A420.

CROWLINK

East Sussex TV59

Quite fittingly, the National Trust owns over 600 acres of these green, rolling downs, which suddenly and dramatically finish in cliffs of gleaming white chalk, enduring symbols of unconquered Britain in the last world war. The cliff walk along their tops is not for the timid, but the rewards – wide skies, rolling hills, the ocean views and wheeling gulls below – amount to a delicious sense of freedom.

The Trust also owns over 60 acres at Birling Gap (one of the few chinks in the great chalk wall which runs between the Seven Sisters and Beachy Head), some to the west adjoining Crowlink, some to the east approaching Beachy Head. In these particular cliffs an 18th-century clergyman, Parson Darby of East Dean, hollowed out a cave in which he hung lamps to warn passing ships of their proximity.

5m W of Eastbourne, just S of Friston on A259.

DANBURY COMMON

Essex TL70

Danbury Common was used by smugglers during the Napoleonic Wars, being not far from the Crouch or Blackwater estuaries on the Essex coast. Lingwood Common (also NT), rather more remote from the village, is visited less and is wilder, rougher, prettier – it has now reverted to mature woodland. Danbury Common, on the other hand, is still a mixture of heath and birchwood which perhaps the medieval tenants of Danbury might still recognise.

Parking provided on the Camp Ground by village. 5m E of Chelmsford. N and E of A414.

EMMETTS GARDEN

Kent	*TQ45*

The garden is chiefly an arboretum, a fine collection of trees and shrubs within a four-acre garden on a hilltop site. It was begun by Frederick Lubbock between 1893 and 1895. The Shrub Garden was planted in 1900–8. There is no particular plan or design to the garden, each tree and shrub is grown for its individual interest, but in spring, when the woodland floor is flooded with bluebells, or in autumn when the foliage of the many strange bedfellows mingle their various hues, it is an enchanting spot.

Limited opening April to end Oct. Admission charged. Wheelchair access to parts of garden. 1½m S of A25 on Sundridge to Ide Hill road, 1½m N of Ide Hill off B2042.

FENTON HOUSE

London	*TQ28*

Hampstead was still a village, still a rural ride from London, when Fenton House was built at the end of the 17th century in the reign of William and Mary. Of dark-coloured brick, it is a simple but pleasant house, standing in a large, walled garden, and approached through impressive wrought-iron gates.

It is the two collections housed here which make this such a popular (and over-crowded) property. First is the collection of 18th-century furniture and porcelain, given to the Trust in 1936 by Lady Binning. The second is the collection of equally exquisite keyboard instruments – harpsichords, spinets, clavichords and early pianos.

Open April to end Oct, limited winter opening Nov, Feb and March. Admission charged. Windmill Hill, Hampstead, on W side of Hampstead Grove.

FINCHAMPSTEAD RIDGES

Berkshire	*SU86*

The Trust owns 60 acres of wood and heathland along the ridge, from where there are fine views over Berkshire, Hampshire and Surrey. A topograph at the south end maps out the obvious landmarks visible on a good day. The Devil's Highway, an old Roman road, leads to Heath Pool and Simons Wood, two further Trust properties just to the north-east. Simons Wood harbours a particularly wide range of tree species, and one of the approaches is along a magnificent avenue of giant Wellingtonias, a species of sequoia which has produced some of the tallest trees in the world.

¾m W of Crowthorne station, 4m S of Wokingham, on S side of B3348.

Fenton House contains both Major Benton Fletcher's collection of keyboard instruments and Lady Binning's 18th-century porcelain, of which Meissen's Harlequin (c 1738) is a prime example

The George Inn is London's last galleried inn. The original pub on this site was built in 1554, but burnt down in 1676. The new George Inn was rebuilt to exactly the same plan. Inside it retains its original floorboards, old fireplace and blackened beams

FRENSHAM COMMON

Surrey SU84

This is a popular beauty spot of over one square mile of open heathland, wood and water. The great attractions are the two ponds; Great Pond, which covers more than 100 acres, the mecca of all local fishermen and dinghy sailors; and Little Pond, resplendent with flowering water lilies in late spring and summer.

The presence of water, and the scrub cover provided by the gorse and heather, attract a wide variety of bird life – the Common is a favourite haunt of bird-watchers. Over 200 species have been spotted here.

Astride the Hindhead-Farnham road, the A287.

GEORGE INN

London TQ37

Close to London Bridge, this old inn is the last galleried inn to survive in the city of London. It stands on the site of a previous George Inn known to have burnt down in the Southwark fire of 1676. Shakespeare is said to have acted in the courtyard of that inn. His plays are still sometimes staged in the present courtyard.

The galleries (balconies which range the length of the building) provide the only passage from room to room on the first and second floors. Unfortunately a large part of the galleried inn was demolished in 1899. Charles Dickens almost certainly knew this place when it was a busy and popular coaching inn, and he

mentions it in *Little Dorrit*. It is still a public house, and still popular; the Coffee Room retains its Victorian box pews, the bar its welcoming open fire, but it no longer offers accommodation.

On E side of Borough High Street, close to London Bridge Station.

GREAT CHALFIELD MANOR

Wiltshire   ST86

The Corsham stone of Great Chalfield's north front exudes antiquity. The stone-mullioned windows and jumbled, gabled roofline of the great hall – flanked by two gabled wings, the pinnacles of each bearing a carved soldier in armour – suggest that this must have been the family home of a medieval knight. But this rare survivor of the 15th century was built by Thomas Tropnell, a businessman and one of a new class of people – the middle class – which arose after the collapse of feudalism following the Wars of the Roses. He built the house in about 1480 on the site of an old fortified manor. No fortifications remain, apart from the moat.

Inside there is a finely-timbered great hall divided from the pantry and kitchen passage by a copy of the original screen. At the other end a spiral staircase leads to the solar or living room. Spy-holes from this room, designed as stone

masks with their eyes cut out, allowed the ladies to watch the proceedings in the great hall below. The splendid condition of Chalfield is largely due to Harold Brakspear, who restored the building in the early years of this century to its appearance as shown in some drawings made in 1837, when it was still in its original state.

Limited opening April to Oct. Admission charged. Free parking. 3m NE of Bradford-on-Avon, via B3109.

GREAT COXWELL TITHE BARN

Oxfordshire   SU29

This massive medieval barn was where tenants of the surrounding lands, which belonged to Beaulieu Abbey in Hampshire, came to pay their tithes – usually a portion of their crops – and had them stored. The lands were granted to the Cistercian monks of Beaulieu by King John in 1204, and the barn was built around the middle of that century. The Church's role as a powerful landowner is often shown in the size of its barns; this one, built of stone, with a roof of Cotswold stone tiles, is 152ft long and 48ft high. All is original, except the doorways at either end; these are 18th-century additions.

Open all year. Wheelchair access. 2m S of Faringdon between A420 and B4019.

Hailes Abbey, although now a peaceful ruin of mellow stone in a green meadow, was at the time of the Dissolution in 1539 the twelfth richest Cistercian abbey in the country, a position reached after more than 250 years of varying financial fortune and hard struggle

Great Coxwell Tithe Barn, seen here amid its tranquil riverside setting, has a suitably church-like appearance for a place once owned and run by the Cistercian monks of Beaulieu. Mountains of crops given in payment of taxes were stored within the Tithe Barn's huge walls

GREYS COURT

Oxfordshire   *SU78*

The de Grey family were the first builders here, and they were licensed to fortify their manor house in 1347. This original house is gone, but the Great Tower, some walling and three smaller towers of the defences survive. These remains seem now to belong more to the garden than to the present house of Greys Court. This stands across a small stretch of lawn from the old tower. The 16th-century house of brick and stone was built by the Knollys family, who secured the estate during the reign of Henry VIII. It is a charming house, much altered and added to over the centuries (a 17th-century oriel window and an 18th-century wing are among the additions), with little to boast of except some good plasterwork (especially in the drawing room) of 1760 and fine furniture of the late 17th and 18th centuries. But it has a well-lived in air, and a sense of timelessness accentuated by the delightfully informal gardens in and around de Grey's ruins. A network of ancient walls creates little pockets of sheltered calm, each differently planted.

Adjacent to the house is a small group of Tudor outhouses, among them a well-house with a donkey wheel and 200ft-deep well.

Open April to end Sept. House limited opening. Admission charged. Free parking. Wheelchair available. Refreshments. 2½m W of Henley-on-Thames adjoining the village of Rotherfield Greys.

HAILES ABBEY

Gloucestershire   *SP03*

Richard, Earl of Cornwall and younger brother of Henry III, founded this abbey in fulfilment of a vow he made on escaping shipwreck in the Isles of Scilly in 1242. By 1251 the abbey church had been consecrated. The pride of the abbey was a phial of the Holy Blood, guaranteed by Pope Urban IV and brought to Hailes in 1272 by Richard's son, Edmund. A shrine was specially built to house the holy relic, and this became a famous centre of pilgrimage: Chaucer refers to it in *The Pardoner's Tale*: 'By the blode of Crist that is in Hayles'. Like many abbeys, Hailes succumbed to Henry VIII's Dissolution of 1539. After its fall, the stones of the abbey were being used by the 18th century for building elsewhere, but extensive ruins – crumbling walls and rows of beautifully proportioned arches – have survived in this still remote spot.

Open mid March to mid Oct, limited opening rest of year. Admission charged. Wheelchair access. 2m NE of Winchcombe, 1m E of Broadway road (A46).

HAM HOUSE

London   *TQ17*

This superb riverside mansion was built by Sir Thomas Vavasour, a courtier of James I, but its golden age, during which its name became a by-word for luxury, did not arrive until it came into the possession of the Duke of Lauderdale. He married Elizabeth, the heiress to Ham, in 1672. She was, apparently, 'restless in her ambition, profuse in her expense and of a most ravenous covetousness; she was a violent friend and a much more violent enemy'. The Duke, by all accounts, was equally unpleasant. But they had good taste, and lavished an extraordinary amount of money on the house.

Ham began as an H-shaped brick Jacobean house. The Lauderdales filled in one half of the H to provide a new suite of rooms, and commissioned artists and craftsmen from Germany, Holland and Italy to decorate it.

The Lauderdales flaunted their wealth. It can be seen in the silver fireplace furnishings – thought ostentatious by the couple's contemporaries – in the sumptuous damasks, velvets and silks which hang on the walls, in the elaborate moulded plasterwork and carved and gilded wood, and in the most expensive furniture and *objets d'art* of the age. These 17th-century rooms are the finest example in England of the wealth and confidence of the Restoration.

As the house is such a perfectly preserved slice of the 17th century, the gardens have been remodelled to their original plan, but the planting is still far from mature.

Open all year. Admission charged. Free parking. Wheelchair available. Refreshments. On S bank of the Thames, 1m SW of Richmond off the A307.

HATCHLANDS

Surrey   TQ05

'Old Dreadnought' as Admiral Boscawen was known, bought Hatchlands in 1749, and lived there for seven years before pulling down the old house and building the red-brick one that the Trust now owns. He paid for it with money won from the French during his much-acclaimed naval encounters.

Hatchlands is largely decorated and furnished in Victorian style, but in the library and drawing room the ceilings and sculptured marble fireplaces (and probably the ceiling in the hall) are by Robert Adam. These are the earliest examples of his work, made when he was 31 years old, and they signal the beginning of his distinguished career as an interior designer.

Limited opening April to mid Oct. Admission charged. Free parking. Wheelchair access. Refreshments. Just E of East Clandon, on N side of the Leatherhead-Guildford road (A246).

HATFIELD FOREST

Essex   TL52

Much of southern England once resembled this 1,000-acre forest. It has survived where other great forests have declined because for centuries, since before the Norman kings, it was a royal hunting preserve protected by special laws. These majestic woodlands, with their magnificent pollarded hornbeams and centuries-old oaks, are criss-crossed by broad rides or 'chases', open stretches of grassland dotted with clumps of hawthorn.

The forest is designated a country park, and at its centre is a lake which offers boating and fishing. Nearby is a marsh kept as a nature reserve, where several species of orchid flower. The Shell House, on the shores of the lake, is open at weekends as an information centre, and is the starting point for a 1½-mile nature trail.

3m E of Bishop's Stortford, on S side of A120.

HIDCOTE MANOR GARDEN

Gloucestershire   SP14

When Major Lawrence Johnstone bought Hidcote Manor in 1905, the garden comprised little more than two fields and a clump of beeches. Over forty years his expertise created a small but beautiful garden which has played an important part in the development of British garden design.

Covering 10 acres of the Cotswold escarpment, Hidcote is divided by walls and hedges into a series of separate, intimate gardens each of different character, planted in a seemingly haphazard manner yet bound together by an overall design which ensures all is in harmony. The gardens, of varying size, offer a boundless variety of plants and colour – and by careful planning show attractive flower and foliage at any time of the year. In complete relief are the two unexpected vistas which open out on to glorious countryside, and a wide spacious lawn. The combination of cottage-style gardening and formal design give Hidcote its special character, and is both a source of inspiration to any amateur gardener and a magnificent showpiece of 20th-century gardening.

Open April to end Oct. Admission charged. Wheelchair available. Refreshments. 4m NE of Chipping Campden, 1m E of A46 on B4081.

HIGHDOWN HILL

West Sussex   TQ00

Crowning Highdown Hill is the ditch and rampart of an Iron Age hill-fort, built between 550 and 300 BC. Beneath this archaeologists have found traces of a Late Bronze Age settlement, probably lived in by a tribe originally from northern France, a pastoral people who used a primitive plough to till the land. Romano-British people re-occupied Highdown, no doubt looking for safety in a world no longer held together by the might of the Roman rule. Pottery they left behind dates them to the third century. After their departure

The eleven-acre grounds of Hidcote Manor have been imaginatively divided up into a series of different formal gardens. Many rare trees and shrubs are to be found here, and a variety of skilfully arranged hedges helps protect the more delicate plants from the weather in this exposed site on the Cotswold edge

A statue of Benjamin Disraeli in the outer hall at Hughenden Manor, the Buckinghamshire country house in which he lived for 33 years. A more atypical country squire could not be imagined. He wore rings on his fingers, brightly striped socks and flowery waistcoats. He did not hunt or shoot. He was a Jew, and lacked the stable of aristocratic ancestors possessed by his hunting, shooting, Church of England peers. But within 14 years of entering Parliament (after four unsuccessful attempts) he became the Conservative Party leader

(perhaps enforced), the war-like Saxons used the enclosure as a cemetery. When excavated in 1892–4, this yielded rich finds which are kept in the Worthing museum. Among these are knives of iron, spearheads, and from the Late Roman era, four glass drinking horns.

1m N of Ferring, 3m NW of Worthing, 1m S of A27, between South Downs and the sea.

HINDHEAD COMMONS

Surrey   *SU83*

Footpaths criss-cross these 14,000 acres of mainly sandy heathland punctuated by deep combes. The most fascinating of these to explore is the Devil's Punch Bowl. The Bowl's steep slopes are covered in gorse, birch and pine, and along its floor the Smallbrook flows through a wooded valley which harbours four species of deer, and badgers who live in setts perhaps first dug centuries ago.

A 2½-mile nature trail explores the Bowl, beginning at its southern rim, while another, slightly shorter trail begins a little to the south from a car park on the A3 on Gibbet Hill. Upon this 894ft-high summit, from where there are magnificent views, three ruffians were hanged in 1786 for the murder of a sailor. A memorial tablet marks the spot.

12m SW of Guildford, on both sides of A3.

HUGHENDEN MANOR

Buckinghamshire   *SU89*

This house is known first and foremost as the country home of Benjamin Disraeli. The future Prime Minister and leader of the Conservative Party acquired the Hughenden estate in 1847 when the manor house was still a typical country house of the early 19th century. It was Mrs Disraeli who directed the remodelling of the simple stuccoed building and produced the curious red-brick Victorian Tudor façade it wears today. The interior was at the same time revamped in Gothic style. There have been few changes since Disraeli's day, and a tour of the house gives a good idea of Victorian taste and of Disraeli's character, especially in the particularly evocative study. There are pictures of his contemporaries and gifts from his admirers (among them Queen Victoria), and other bits and pieces which together form a museum of his life and career.

Disraeli's self-confessed passions were trees and books. His library stands intact, and the sweeping parkland which surrounds the house boasts many fine specimens of lime, beech, whitebeam and many more which thrive on the chalky hill on which the house stands.

Open April to Oct, limited opening March and Nov. Admission charged. Free parking. Wheelchair available. Refreshments. 1½m N of High Wycombe, on W side of Great Missenden road (A4128).

Disraeli at Hughenden

Disraeli was never rich. He had no inheritance, nor did he marry a rich heiress. He was certainly not the hunting, shooting peer of the realm that a country house owner and a Tory leader was expected to be. Hughenden was bought for him by his supporters to give him respectability, for political reasons. But he loved his house, and devoted to it as much time and money as he could.

For such a colourful character – a favourite of Queen Victoria – Hughenden is remarkably subdued, homely and unpretentious. The Disraelis came here to relax every year during the long Parliamentary recess, which at that time lasted from the end of August until after Christmas. Disraeli would spend his time wandering about his park, or watching 'the sunbeams on the bindings of the books' in his library. Here he wrote novels (the only prime minister ever to do so), and here, as each new Parliament approached, he would plan his political strategy. Mary Anne, his wife, ran the household, embroidered and, it is said, talked a good deal. The Disraelis enjoyed the company of friends, who came to stay in great numbers – though finances were said to be tight enough to cause Mary Anne to return a joint to the butcher with a request for a refund after some friends had failed to turn up for lunch one day. They were an odd couple, eccentric in some respects, but very ordinary in their love for their home, which still shines through at Hughenden.

ISLE OF WIGHT

BEMBRIDGE AND CULVER DOWNS

Isle of Wight   SZ68

The Isle of Wight has a great backbone of chalk highland, which in the east takes the form of these 343ft high downs, ending abruptly as spectacular high and white cliffs. The downs are typical chalkland – green, rolling hills open to the elements, acres of windswept turf offering a sense of freedom few other landscapes can give. Sheep, now a rarity on the island, crop the grass; at Culver cliffs, where the land drops sheer to the sea, seabirds nest on precarious ledges.

BEMBRIDGE WINDMILL

Isle of Wight   SZ68

The last remaining windmill on the island, this four-storey tower-mill has been a familiar landmark to sailors for over 250 years. Flour, meal and latterly bran and cattle feed were ground here from about 1700 until the last harvest before World War I. During World War II it was used as a look-out post.

The mill is built of local stone, with a wooden cap and four 60ft-long wooden sails which can be turned to face the wind. Bembridge windmill has now been fully restored, and visitors can see all the machinery and follow the flour-milling process from start to finish.

Open Good Fri to end Sept. Admission charged. ½m S of Bembridge.

KNOWLES FARM

Isle of Wight   SZ47

On the southerly tip of the Isle of Wight the Trust owns some particularly beautiful land at Knowles Farm, which includes cliffs and foreshore around St Catherine's Lighthouse. Between the cliffs and the sea, this land is composed of a gault clay called Blue Slipper. This clay is prone to land slippage, and over the centuries has produced a peculiar landscape of hills and valleys. It is let for farming but there is access by public footpaths. As a result of a landslide in 1928, the western parts are particularly rough, with hillocks and sheltered hollows abundant with wild flowers, forming the perfect cover for birds. St Catherine's Point itself is where thousands of migrating birds gather in spring and autumn.

Above the Point, St Catherine's Hill has superb views over West Wight. At the southern end stands St Catherine's Oratory, an early lighthouse built in the 14th century (now in the

Bembridge Windmill – a familiar landmark to local yachtsmen

care of the DoE). This 38ft 'pepperpot' was supposedly built by the locals, who felt guilty about the booty they salvaged from shipwrecks.

Access by public footpath to Knowles Farm, unrestricted access by footpath to St Catherine's Hill and Down. Car park for St Catherine's Hill near Blackgang.

NEWTOWN

Isle of Wight   SZ49

Records of this place reach back to the ninth century, but Newtown as a borough took form at least as early as 1256, when Aymer de Valance, Bishop Elect of Winchester, gave the borough a charter. At this time it was known as Franchville. By the 14th century Newtown was a busy and important port, and had a prosperous salt industry and famous oyster beds. However, the town's fortunes changed after a particularly disastrous attack by the French in 1377. It never recovered from the blow, and quickly declined.

In 1636 Newtown had only 12 inhabited houses, yet in 1700 the town hall was built, a simple brick and stone building where elections were held and the burghers met. Copies of ancient documents and a facsimile of the mace are kept here. As well as the town hall, the Trust also owns much of the rest of the town – where hedges mark former house plots and grassy lanes

FERGUSON'S GANG

During the 1930s there appeared an extraordinary secret society dedicated to raising funds for the National Trust. It was named Ferguson's Gang, and its members were known only by such pseudonyms as Sister Agatha, the Nark, Red Biddy, and the Artichoke. Money they collected was delivered to the Trust, in used coins and notes, by masked messenger. But money was not the only gift. Newtown Town Hall was one of several properties donated by the gang. The Artichoke, known to be an eminent architect, restored the building before it was given in 1933.

Membership 'is terminable only by death; but this is not so difficult as may be supposed' states the gang's constitution. However, it celebrated its 40th anniversary in 1967, and although little has been heard of it in recent years, surviving members still retain their anonymity.

the roads of the past. The quay, the entire Newtown estuary and five miles of Solent foreshore are also Trust-owned. Much of this land is now a nature reserve, where up to 4,000 waders and 2,000 wildfowl have been seen at one time, and 170 species recorded.

Town Hall open June to Aug, limited opening Easter to end May. Admission charged. Midway between Newport and Yarmouth, 1m N of A3054.

VENTNOR

Isle of Wight — SZ57

Around the popular resort of Ventnor, the Trust owns three major tracts of downland, each giving wide views of the coast and the island, and offering exhilarating walks. From Littleton and Luccombe Downs to the east of Ventnor there are views over the channel and north across the island to the Solent and Hampshire, and eastwards to the Sussex Downs. The downland and meadow of Luccombe Farm between Ventnor and Shanklin adjoins Luccombe and Bonchurch Downs, and leads to beaches and cliff. Above and behind Ventnor St Boniface Down, rising to 764ft, is the highest point on the island.

Littleton and Luccombe Downs accessible by car from Ventnor, Luccombe Farm by public and coastal footpath, St Boniface Down by footpaths from old Ventnor Station, Nansen Hill and Mitchell Avenue.

WEST WIGHT

Isle of Wight — SZ38

In the west of the island the Trust owns several properties of high chalk downland, cliff and coast between Chilton Chine and Freshwater Bay. Among these are Compton Beaches, where there is safe bathing and the best surfing on the island; Brook Chine, again with access to the sea; and Afton, Compton, Brook and Mottistone Downs. The Mottistone Estate also includes the charming village of the same name which shelters in a wooded valley inland and below the downland. Just south-west of Freshwater is Tennyson Down, named after the Poet Laureate, Lord Alfred Tennyson, who took his daily walk here when he lived at Farringford.

In the westernmost corner of the island, the Trust owns the Needles Headland. Here the downs rise to nearly 500ft with magnificent views over sea and island. The whole area is a bird sanctuary. Built near the cliff edge, 250ft above the sea, stands an old battery, constructed under Lord Palmerston's government in the last century. An extraordinary feature is a 200ft tunnel from the fort to the cliff face, from where there are unique views of the towering chalk stacks of the Needles. A museum in the former Powder Magazine tells the history of the headland from the time of the battery's construction to the present day.

Needles Old Battery open Easter to end Oct. Admission charged.

Cliff scenery at Tennyson Head

TENNYSON DOWN
The Poet Laureate Lord Tennyson lived at Farringford on the Isle of Wight between 1853 and 1868. Tennyson was enormously fond of the outdoors, and his favourite walk was across the downs now named after him. *The Sea-Fairies* was written on the Isle of Wight, and the following extract is a delightful evocation of the magic of downland, coast and sea:

Mariner, mariner, furl your sails,
For here are the blissful downs and
*   dales,*
And merrily merrily carol the gales,
And the spangle dances in bight and
*   bay,*
And the rainbow forms and flies on
*   the land*
Over the islands free;
And the rainbow lives in the curve of
*   the sand;*
Hither, come hither and see;
And the rainbow hangs on the poising
*   wave,*
And sweet is the colour of cove and
*   cave,*
And sweet shall your welcome be:

KING'S HEAD

Buckinghamshire   *SP81*

The old market square in Aylesbury was ringed by inns in medieval times. The only one to remain in any way intact is the King's Head. The large, timber-framed building, approached through a medieval gateway, has been an inn since the 15th century. Before that, it was the guesthouse of a monastery.

In the bar, near the old refectory, is the inn's chief glory, a great Tudor window of 20 lights, dating from about 1450. The ancient heraldic glass shows the arms of both Prince Edward, killed at Tewkesbury, and Henry VI and his Queen Margaret of Anjou, among other ancient heraldic emblems.

Open normal opening hours. At NW corner of Market Square, Aylesbury.

KNOLE

Kent   *TQ55*

What began as a simple medieval manor house grew to be both the palace of an Archbishop and a King, and one of the largest of England's country houses. Thomas Bourchier, Archbishop of Canterbury, bought Knole for £266.13s.4d in 1456, and set about transforming it into his palace. His successor, Cardinal Morton, was succeeded by Cardinal Cranmer, who was persuaded to give Knole to Henry VIII in 1538. The King spent little time there, but spent a fortune extending beyond Bourchier's

additions. In 1556 Elizabeth I gave the house to her cousin Thomas Sackville, whose family kept the freehold for ten subsequent generations. Sackville is responsible for a great deal of the interior furnishing; he employed an army of workmen to plaster, upholster, glaze and build, including 300 specially imported Italians. Most Elizabethan houses had one long gallery, a huge room in which to walk during inclement weather – Sackville built three. When he had finished, the house looked much as it does today. There are said to be 365 rooms, there are seven courtyards, and the whole covers four acres of ground. The jumble of rooflines, chimneys and turrets and towers makes the place look, from outside the great encircling wall, like a fortified town rather than a single home.

The state rooms, furnished with pieces from the 17th and early 18th centuries, are a rich architectural feast; on the elaborately plastered walls hang valuable paintings – Reynolds and Gainsborough are among the artists exhibited.

From these sumptuous rooms, views of the 26-acre garden can be enjoyed through the Tudor mullions or Georgian sash windows. Formal walks, flower beds, roses, shrubs, fruit trees and lawns are a welcome relief to the richness within. Beyond the encircling wall is a 1,000 acres of deer park, a landscape of undulating pasture dotted with old and stately trees, copses of oak and beech, vales, and knolls and bracken-clad rides that Elizabethan huntsmen might well recognise.

Open April to end Sept, limited winter opening Oct and Nov. Admission charged. Wheelchair access to park. Parking charged for non-members of NT. At S end of Sevenoaks town; just E of A225.

Half-timbered houses near the churchyard in Lacock, one of the most beautiful villages in England. It is wholly owned by the National Trust, which keeps it as a living, working village for local people – houses are not let to 'outsiders'. Measures such as employing one television aerial on a nearby hillside for the entire village help prevent too many 20th-century intrusions on a scene that has remained little changed for centuries

of Sherrington's descendants, in the family name of Talbot, until its transfer to the Trust in 1944. Beyond the Abbey gates, which allow access to the park, is an old barn converted into a museum about Henry Fox Talbot, a member of the family who was known as a pioneering photographer. In 1835 he made the world's first photographic negative.

Open April to end Oct, Museum March to end Oct. Admission charged. Free parking. Wheelchair available at house and museum. Refreshments in village. 3m S of Chippenham, just E off A350.

LAMB HOUSE

East Sussex   TQ92

James Lamb, vintner and 13 times mayor of Rye, gave his name to this house. He built it in about 1721, a fine two-storeyed Georgian house of red brick. Worthy James Lamb came to the rescue, in 1726, of George I, who was shipwrecked on nearby Camber Sands. The King slept for four nights at Lamb House, where he was snowed in. The first night Mrs Lamb gave birth to a son, to whom George I acted as godfather at the baptism two days later.

For almost 150 years the Lamb family lived at Lamb House, until in 1864 it was sold to a local banker. At his death in 1897 it was leased to its most famous inhabitant, the novelist and critic, Henry James. He made some minor alterations, chief among them the addition of French windows in the two rooms shown, which open onto an immaculate garden. In these rooms are portraits of James from childhood to old age, a few of his possessions and his furniture.

Limited opening April to end Oct. Admission charged. West Street, Rye; facing W end of church.

LEITH HILL

Surrey   TQ14

Just within 40 miles of London, the Trust owns several sites of considerable beauty around Leith Hill. The summit of the hill itself, 967ft high, is one of them. It is topped by a stone tower built in 1766 by Richard Hull, a local man who wished that he and his friends might better enjoy the remarkable views of 13 counties visible from this spot. So enamoured was he of this place that he now lies buried beneath his tower.

Fine old oak and beech woods can be explored near Leith Hill Place (house not open) at the foot of the hill. They are especially beautiful in spring when there is a profusion of bluebells. To the east lies Mosses Wood, which stretches almost from the Wealden floor to the summit of the ridge. On the north slope of the hill the Trust also owns Duke's Warren, 193 acres of heathland originally kept aside as a preserve for rabbits, which provided both sport and food.

3m W of junction of A29 and A26, W of B2126.

Fallow deer browse in front of Knole's impressive façade. This huge mansion, reputed to have as many rooms as there are days in the year, has remained substantially unchanged for four centuries. It has been the home of the Sackvilles since 1556, when Elizabeth I gave it to her cousin, Thomas Sackville, who spared no expense in extending and embellishing the house to give it its present dimensions and richness

LACOCK

Wiltshire   ST96

Lacock Abbey and the greater part of Lacock village are owned by the Trust, and form a complete community of great house and attendant village, which have grown up together over some 700 years.

The buildings of the village date from the 14th to 18th centuries, a delightful array of timeless half-timbered and stone-built houses, built on the proceeds of the wool trade, which flourished here prior to the Industrial Revolution.

The Abbey was founded in 1232 by Ela, Countess of Salisbury, who became its first abbess. At the Dissolution the nuns were found to be 'of virtuous living' and were all given pensions, but the abbey – the last to be dissolved in England – was sold off. The buyer was William Sherrington, a Tudor profiteer who destroyed the church, and converted the domestic buildings into his home. He made some alterations, using a craftsman familiar with the new style of the Italian Renaissance. In 1754 John Ivory Talbot asked Sanderson Miller to design a new entrance hall – which turned out to be a superb example of the new Gothic Revival, and a great success.

The house and village remained in the hands

LONG CRENDON COURTHOUSE

Buckinghamshire	*SP60*

In a village of 60 or so cottages of the 16th and 17th centuries, the Courthouse still stands out as something a little out of the ordinary. It is a long, two-storeyed timber-framed building probably built at the beginning of the 15th century. Although the windows and doors have been altered, and the great chimney stack was added in Tudor times, the magnificent open timber roof is original.

The building was probably designed as a wool store, but it was also used as a manorial court house from the time of Henry V, early in the 1400s, until the late 19th century. The Trust acquired the Courthouse in 1900 as one of its first possessions.

Limited opening (upper floor only) April to end Sept. Admission charged. 2m N of Thame, via B4011, close to church.

LUDSHOTT

Hampshire and Surrey	*SU83*

During the 16th and 17th centuries the southern counties were at the centre of England's industrial production. The heartland of this industrial ferment was the Weald, but ironworks were scattered across neighbouring areas. One of these was Waggoners' Wells, west of Hindhead. The string of three lakes here were hammer-ponds for an iron foundry in the 16th century. Hammer-ponds were formed by damming to supply water for turning the mill wheels which operated the huge trip-hammers that tempered the iron ore. Today the lakes are surrounded by magnificent beech woods.

Above the lakes is Ludshott Common, 370 acres of typical Surrey heathland.

1½m W of Hindhead.

MOMPESSON HOUSE

Wiltshire	*SU12*

The Cathedral Close in Salisbury is reckoned the most beautiful in England. Overlooking a part of it known as Choristers' Green is Mompesson House, a perfect Queen Anne house of 1701. It was begun by Thomas Mompesson, a staunch Royalist who suddenly found himself in favour and fortune at the Restoration under Charles II. His son, a lawyer, completed the work after his death.

The beautifully proportioned front, beneath a hipped roof, is stone-faced and very impressive behind its high wrought-iron railings. The interior is notable for its fine stucco ceilings of about 1740 and its finely carved oak staircase. Recent wall paintings brighten the hall, and good period furniture fills the rooms. But perhaps more impressive is the splendid collection of 18th-century English glasses kept here, and the several paintings which originally hung at Stourhead.

Open April to end Oct. Admission charged. Parking in Cathedral Close. On N side of Choristers' Green, near High Street Gate.

MONK'S HOUSE

East Sussex	*TQ40*

In 1919 Leonard and Virginia Woolf, leading lights of the literary Bloomsbury group, bought this small weather-boarded farmhouse in the main street of Rodmell village. The view across the river Ouse to hills beyond and the large garden outweighed the disadvantages – oil lamps for lights and a well as the only source of water. Many literary lions of the day visited this humble country retreat, including T. S. Eliot. The Woolfs divided their time between Monk's House and their London home until 1940, when the latter was bombed. In 1941 Virginia drowned herself in the Ouse, and her ashes are buried in the garden of Monk's House. Leonard remained here until his death in 1969.

Limited opening April to end Oct. Admission charged. 2½m S of Lewes, on unclassified road to Newhaven, in Rodmell village near the church.

The shell of the gutted house at Nymans forms the nucleus of the garden. It burnt down shortly after World War II, but with time and careful planting it has been absorbed into the garden. The lawn which surrounds it is fringed by Himalayan rhododendrons, hydrangeas and camellias. The lime-free soil and mild climate here encourage the growth of many rare and beautiful shrubs – and the propagation of new hybrids, as the beautiful Nymans forsythia and eucryphia, and the Camellia 'Leonard Messel' and Magnolia 'Leonard Messel' testify

Architectural historians recognise the elegance of the plasterwork ceilings and overmantels at Mompesson House in Salisbury

MOTTISFONT ABBEY

Hampshire   *SU32*

In 1536, at the Dissolution, the 13th-century Priory of Holy Trinity at Mottisfont went to William, Lord Sandys, who, improvidently some might say, gave the King the villages of Paddington and Chelsea in exchange for it.

Lord Sandys and his immediate descendants converted the nave and tower of the priory into the principal apartments of a large Tudor mansion. In 1684, when the last of Lord Sandys' descendants died, the house passed to the Mill family. Sir Richard Mill transformed the Tudor house into a Georgian house in the 1740s, reducing the Tudor influence but keeping the monastic remains – the former Tudor south front is now plainly red-brick Georgian, whereas in the north front the old medieval church can clearly be seen.

The remains of the abbey are open to the public, including the almost complete vaulted cellarium, the monk's storeroom. Only three rooms of the house are shown. One of them is the outstanding Rex Whistler Room painted with false columns, pelmets and plasterwork.

A great deal of Mottisfont's charm is bound up in its setting. It is surrounded by large lawns shaded by mature trees on the west bank of the river Test, which runs through a particularly gentle and beautiful valley. Complementing the old house is a garden of old fashioned roses, planted just a few years ago but already a popular feature. Nearby, the spring which gave the place its name fills a crystal-clear pool in the chalk hillside.

April to end Sept (limited opening for house). Admission charged. Free parking. Wheelchair available. Refreshments. 4½m NW of Romsey, ¾m W of A3057.

NYMANS GARDEN

West Sussex   *TQ22*

The oldest part of the garden, the Wall Garden, was originally an orchard. Here are some fine specimen trees (now dwarfing the old fruit trees), borders and flowering shrubs, first laid out by the 19th-century creator of the garden, Ludwig Messel, and his son Leonard. A Victorian laurel walk leads from a wood, renowned in spring for its floor of daffodils, to a sunken garden, where bedding plants grow surrounded by camellias. Near here is a heather garden. Each of these gardens spells variety, each overflows with a multitude of species, some of them rare and unusual.

From the road lawns sweep upwards from a pergola to the ruins of the house – now the shelter of choice climbers and tender plants. Other features include a wild garden, glasshouses, and an enormous collection of rhododendrons.

Open April to end Oct. Admission charged. Free parking. Wheelchair available. Refreshments. At Handcross, 4½m S of Crawley, just off London-Brighton M23/A23.

OLD SOAR MANOR

Kent   *TQ65*

This is a precious survival, because the remote knight's manor of Old Soar was built of stone when most of its 13th-century contemporaries were made of less durable wood. Even so, only the solar block remains; the great hall was knocked down and the present adjoining Georgian farmhouse built in its place. The solar, on the first floor, was the private bed-sitting room of the lord and lady. Two small rooms lead off the solar. At one end is the chapel, also used as a study, and at the other, the garderobe or privy. The ground floor was used as storage space for winter food.

Open April to end Oct. Admission charged. 2m S of Borough Green (A25); approached via A227 and Plaxtol.

OSTERLEY PARK

London   *TQ17*

Sir Thomas Gresham, founder of the London Royal Exchange, built at Osterley an Elizabethan mansion 'faire and stately'. Much of his house still stands, but little can be seen, for it has been enshrined within an 18th-century masterpiece by architect Robert Adam. His employers were first Francis Child and then Francis' successor and younger brother Robert. These were the grandsons of Francis Child, a man dubbed 'the father of banking'.

Adam kept the Elizabethan arrangement of a courtyard built round on three sides with towers at each corner. The fourth side he closed in with a massive Ionic portico, encasing the rest within a Palladian façade. But it is the interior which makes Osterley so special. Adam designed every feature; even the firegrates and door handles were designed as a part of the whole effect. The drawing room was, according to Horace Walpole, a leading 18th-century commentator, 'worthy of Eve before the fall'.

The park is large but not particularly striking, although there is a chain of lakes.

Open all year, afternoons only. Admission charged. Parking charged. Wheelchair available. Refreshments. Just N of Osterley station (Piccadilly line); access from Syon Lane, N side of Great West Road, or from Thornbury Road (¼m E of station).

OWLETTS

Kent	*TQ66*

Bonham and Elizabeth Hayes, farmers of cherries, hops and corn, built this fine red-brick house in the reign of Charles II. The interior was finished in 1684, the date marked on the superb plaster ceiling over the staircase.

The house passed to the Baker family in 1794; Thomas Henry Baker had ten children, so he added the north wing. He also turned the farmyard into a garden and built new stables.

Sir Herbert Baker, architect of the Bank of England and partner of architect Sir Edward Lutyens in the building of New Delhi, was born here, and he stayed here throughout the war until his death in 1946. Much of the furniture

was collected or commissioned by him, including the unusual clock in the living room which tells the time simultaneously in all parts of the British Empire.

Limited opening April to end Sept. Admission charged. Wheelchair access. 1m S of A2 at W end of Cobham village, at junction of roads from Dartford and Sole Street.

PETWORTH HOUSE AND PARK

West Sussex	*SU92*

Charles Seymour, Sixth Duke of Somerset, rebuilt Petworth on his marriage to the heiress of the estate. She was a member of the Percy family, who had owned the house in an unbroken line from the 12th century. All that remains of the original Percy house is the chapel and parts of the basement. The rest disappeared between 1688 and 1696 as the present house was built – it has changed little through the intervening centuries.

It is the contents of the house that make Petworth especially famous. On its walls is hung one of the finest collections of paintings in England outside an art gallery. Most outstanding among these are the works by Turner.

The landscaped park which surrounds Petworth is well recorded by Turner. The sweep of hills, clumps of trees and tranquil lake look sublimely natural, which simply reinforces the genius of the man who created these views – for

Turner at Petworth

Turner first came to the attention of Lord Egremont, the owner of Petworth, in about 1802, when Lord Egremont began to buy the painter's work. It marked the beginning of a relationship that was to blossom, especially in the years 1827–31, when Turner spent considerable periods at Petworth, working and enjoying the convivial company there. While at Petworth Turner had his own studio, the old library above the chapel, and was given virtually free run of the place. The sketches he made at that time reveal him to be interested in everything visual – there are drawings of flowers, groups of people, furniture, and of course, landscapes.

A good many of the paintings remain at Petworth. They include four which were designed to hang in the Grinling Gibbons room. They depict two views of Petworth Park, and studies of the Chichester Canal and the Old Chain Pier at Brighton. The last two seemingly haphazard choices were in fact ventures with which Lord Egremont was associated. Also at Petworth is *Jessica*, a painting loosely based on a Shakespearian character. A critic said of it: 'If it resembles anything conceivable, and that is scarcely so, it is a lady jumping out of a mustard pot'.

Such remarks never deterred Turner, who produced some of the most astonishing and original works ever to come from the hand of an English artist.

In 1970 Pitstone Windmill again ground corn after 68 years of standing idle. The mill was declared open once more by Viscountess Davidson, and the grinding of corn has continued here ever since. Pitstone's immense sails have a span of 51 ft from tip to tip

Petworth Park is the masterpiece of 'Capability' Brown. Work began on this tremendous re-shaping of the landscape in about 1754, and today it is still maintained as a perfect example of the landscaper's art.

House open April to end Oct. Park open all year. Admission charged. Wheelchair available. Shop and refreshments. 5½m E of Midhurst.

PITSTONE WINDMILL

Buckinghamshire   SP91

How old this mill is can only be guessed at. A date of 1627 found carved on one of the beams is genuine, and old records show that at about that time carpenters were employed to repair the mill. In any case, it is one of the oldest mills in England still standing; built without drawings or plans, every piece handmade from raw materials by local craftsmen. This mill is a post mill; it revolves about a huge central post in order to face the wind.

A freak storm of 1902 caught the mill with its sails facing the wrong way – and damaged it so extensively that it had to be closed. In 1937 it was offered to the Trust, but it was not until the 1960s that funds were available to repair it properly. In 1970 the mill again ground corn.

Limited opening May to end Sept. Admission charged. ½m S of Ivinghoe, 3m NE of Tring.

POLESDEN LACEY

Surrey   TQ15

Set in the rolling chalklands on the edge of the North Downs, Polesden Lacey is an unassuming country mansion dating mostly from the 1820s. Various alterations have been made to it since that time, but it still retains its air of restrained Regency elegance. A good many other houses have stood on this site, but little is known about them. One of these belonged to the 18th-century playwright Richard Brinsley Sheridan.

Much of the appearance of the interior of the house and most of the contents are owed to the Honourable Mrs Greville, who inherited the house in 1908. She was a well-known society hostess, and an enthusiastic and knowledgeable collector of paintings, porcelain and fine furniture. Nearly all of her collections are preserved intact, as was her wish when she bequeathed the house to the Trust in 1942.

Adjoining the 1,000 acres of parkland and farmland attached to the house are the 500 acres of Ranmore Common.

House open April to Oct, limited opening March and Nov. Garden open all year. Admission charged. Wheelchair available. Shop and refreshments. 3m NW of Dorking.

The elegant south front of Polesden Lacey was built to the designs of Thomas Cubitt, who completed the house in 1823 for Joseph Bonsorat at a cost of £7,600. The total cost of house and park was estimated by Bonsorat to be in excess of £47,000

QUEBEC HOUSE

Kent   TQ45

Formerly known as Spiers, this handsome 17th-century house was renamed to commemorate James Wolfe, the hero of the battle which took place on the heights above Quebec in 1759. Wolfe was entrusted to capture Quebec during the struggle to expel the French from Canada. He succeeded against great odds, but died in the hour of his victory. His family had come to live here in Kent in 1726, and it was Wolfe's home until he was 11. He would no doubt recognise it today, for very little has changed, and alterations made in the 19th century have been swept away. Many of Wolfe's personal possessions, including his dressing gown and travelling canteen, have been carefully gathered together and are now on show in the house.

Open April to end Oct, limited opening in March. Admission charged. At junction of Edenbridge and Sevenoaks roads (A25 and B2026) at E end of Westerham.

RUNNYMEDE

Surrey   TQ07

This famous spot, close to the Thames near London, has become a symbol of freedom and of the sacrifices that men will make for freedom. Here, on 15 June 1215, King John signed the Magna Carta, a document which is held to be the cornerstone of democratic governments in Britain, the USA and the Commonwealth.

Three monuments mark the site. The first, and most impressive, is built on Cooper's Hill and stands in tribute to 20,456 men and women of the Air Forces of the British Commonwealth and Empire who died in World War II and who have no grave. The names of all the dead are inscribed on the walls of a great cloister block attached to a tower overlooking seven counties.

The second monument is a simple circular pavilion, within which stands a cylinder of English granite inscribed 'To commemorate Magna Carta, Symbol of Freedom under Law'. It was a gift of the American Bar Association. Nearer the Thames is the third of the monuments. It is a block of Portland stone dedicated to the memory of John F. Kennedy. It, with an acre of English ground, was presented to the American people in memory of a much-loved president of the United States.

Off A308 between Windsor and Staines.

SANDHAM MEMORIAL CHAPEL

Hampshire   SU46

From the outside, this brick-built chapel looks pleasant but unremarkable. Once the door is opened, however, visitors are transported from the quiet countryside of rural Hampshire to the landscapes of Macedonia and World War I. The walls are entirely covered in a series of paintings, executed between 1927 and 1932, which depict the world in upheaval as seen through the eyes of painter Stanley Spencer.

The chapel was specially built so that Stanley Spencer could paint these pictures, and it is named after Lieutenant H. W. Sandham, who died in 1919 from an illness contracted while on service in Macedonia.

Open all year. Admission charged. Wheelchair access. 4m S of Newbury.

Parts of Scotney Old Castle were specially demolished in 1837 to leave the romantic ruin that stands today beside the wide moat, whose waters are home to black swans

Sandham Memorial Chapel boasts beautiful murals crafted by artist Stanley Spencer. They are the outcome of Spencer's experiences in the Great War of 1914–1918

Gilbert White at Selborne

Gilbert White was born in the vicarage at Selborne on the 18th July 1720. He died in the house (now called The Wakes) which lies just across the village green on the 26 June 1793. Throughout his life he rarely spent long periods away from home, and he always returned as quickly as he could. It is fair to say that everything that White became he owed to Selborne.

He explored the hills, heaths and water meadows that lie within walking distance of the village, and he made careful studies of creatures like crickets and swallows which were to be found literally outside his back door, and faithfully recorded all he saw in his famous *National History of Selborne*. He never travelled further than Derbyshire, and described the Sussex downs as 'that vast range of mountains', so alien did they seem to him.

White was never vicar of Selborne, as is often supposed, but for many years he was curate of Farringdon, a village only two miles away, and from 1784 until his death he was curate of Selborne. There is still much of White's work to be seen in the village; there is the garden he created at The Wakes, the famous Zig-zag leading up to the Hanger, and numerous trees which he planted himself. But his real contribution to Selborne was to make its hills, trees, wild flowers, birds and animals the cornerstone of modern natural history, a subject he made accessible to everyone in a tradition now perhaps most graphically practised by the natural history film maker.

SANDWICH BAY

Kent   TR36

The river Stour negotiates a tortuously curving course, and an astonishing about-turn in direction, before it enters the sea at Pegwell Bay. The land between the river and the sea is made up of freshwater marshes, sand dunes, mud flats and sand bars. This variety of habitats attracts an excellent cross-section of Britain's birdlife, and the area is also frequently visited by migrant waders and a good many rare species of other kinds. The Trust owns nearly 200 acres here which are managed as a nature reserve.

Access by footpaths from Royal St George Golf Links clubhouse, or along the beach from Deal. 2m NE of Sandwich.

SCOTNEY CASTLE GARDEN

Kent   TQ63

This is a candidate for the original fairytale castle. Although genuine, it was carefully 'knocked about a bit' in the early part of the 19th century to make it look more picturesque.

First detailed records refer to a fortified manor house built by Roger Ashburnham in about 1378. It is the south tower of this building which looks so romantic today. Attached to it is a house dating from the end of the 16th century which incorporates parts of the original castle structure. In 1774 the Darrells, to whom Scotney had belonged since 1411, sold the house at auction to Thomas Hussey. His great grandson, Edward, commissioned a young architect called Anthony Salvin to build a new house on the hill overlooking the castle and its lovely lily-filled moat. The stone from which the house was built came from the quarry which now forms an integral part of the gardens.

The marvellous gardens were begun in the 1840s. They are superb examples of 'natural landscaping', and were created before the informal landscaping ideas of gardeners such as Gertrude Jekyll came into vogue.

Open April to end Oct. Admission charged. Wheelchair available. 1½m S of Lamberhurst.

SELBORNE HILL

Hampshire   SU73

Gilbert White is one of the most famous naturalists of all time, and it was Selborne that inspired him.

The great chalk shoulder behind the village is where White spent much of his time. It is covered for the most part in woodland, the commonest tree being beech. Although chalk is the principal soil type, there is also a band of clay beneath the hill and outcrops of 'malm' (a rich black soil) at various points. These have created a diverse soil structure which is a naturalist's paradise. The hill is still approached via the Zig-zag, a steep, winding path constructed under White's supervision. From the summit of the hill there are far-reaching views over the Hampshire countryside.

4m S of Alton, W of B3006.

SHALFORD MILL

Surrey   *TQ04*

This lovely old water-mill on the river Tillingbourne dates from the 18th century, but it was still grinding corn at the outbreak of World War I, two centuries after its great waterwheel first turned. The ground floor is built of brick, but the two upper floors have a massive timber frame which is filled with brick-nogging faced with tiles and timber cladding. Much of the mill's machinery remains intact.

The mill was presented to the National Trust in 1932 by a mysterious fraternity called 'Ferguson's Gang', which is still active today. This anonymous group has done much to help the Trust since its formation in 1930 by raising funds and presenting gifts of property and money to it regularly over the years. The original 'Ferguson's Gang' used to hold meetings in the mill.

Part open during daylight hours; apply to 45 The Street, Shalford.

SHAW'S CORNER

Hertfordshire   *TL11*

This ordinary country house was the home, for 44 years, of a most extraordinary man. It has remained unaltered since 1950, and stands as an intimate reminder of George Bernard Shaw, undoubtedly the finest playwright of his day and one of the giants of English literature.

He came here in 1906, when he was 50 years old, apparently because he had heard that people in Ayot St Lawrence lived a long time. It was certainly true for Shaw, who lived an astonishing 94 years.

The house is packed with mementoes of him. Here will be found Shaw's collection of hats (including one that he wore for 60 years), his piano, his study in which can be seen all the paraphernalia of a writer's life and the dining room in which he ate his vegetarian meals while reading. In the study Shaw's desk remains as he left it, with pictures of close friends hanging beside it, and adjacent a small reading desk displaying the record of the award of the Nobel Prize Shaw received in 1925. At the bottom of the garden is a little revolving summerhouse to which Shaw retreated for peace and quiet. The playwright's ashes were scattered in the garden after his death in 1950.

Open April to end Oct, limited opening March and Nov. Admission charged. At SW end of Ayot St Lawrence village.

The living room at Shaw's Corner has remained unchanged since the playwright's death in 1950

SHAW AT HOME

No biography of Shaw can impart a greater sense of intimacy than a visit to his home. Personal relics, left in their long accustomed places, fire the imagination. Here is the dining room where the playwright ate his vegetarian meals, and here, in his old age, he sat by the fire reading or listening to the wireless late into the night. On the walls are pictues of Dublin, where he spent his early years, and photographs of those who influenced him – Gandhi, Lenin, Stalin and Ibsen among them. Kept here are Shaw's fountain pen and steel-rimmed spectacles, his favourite pocket watch, his admission ticket to the British Museum Reading Room for 1880, and his membership card for the Cyclists' Touring Club dated 1950. These and numerous other mementoes help to colour the picture history has painted of one of our finest dramatists.

began to transform it into one of the most
beautiful gardens in Europe.

Originally Sissinghurst had been a great,
square Elizabethan house surrounded by a moat,
but most of it was demolished in the 19th
century, leaving odd little buildings scattered
about the site. It was on this plan that the garden
was laid out. Each part of the garden is
conceived to be self-contained, but each is
linked to the other parts by walks and vistas.
Perhaps the finest gardens are the White
Garden where lovely old roses are massed with
other white and silvery flowers, the Cottage
Garden with its assortments of red, orange and
yellow flowers, and the lime walk in spring when
it is carpeted with flowers.

Open April to mid Oct. Admission charged.
Wheelchair available. Refreshments. 2m NE of
Cranbrook, 1m E of Sissinghurst village.

SLINDON ESTATE

West Sussex   *SU90*

Lovely old cottages, a church, a manor house
and quiet fields make up the village of Slindon,
tucked away on the slopes of the South Downs.

This delightful, unspoilt village so typical of
Sussex is only 200ft above sea level, but it has
breathtaking views across the coastal plain all
the way to the sea. On the downs above the
village there are several prehistoric monuments,
an Iron Age hill-fort and part of Stane Street, a
Roman road which ran from Chichester to
London. More recent is Nore Folly. It is set on a
hill a little to the north of the village and
consists of an arch that is all that remains of a
hunting lodge.

One of the most extraordinary things on the
Slindon Estate is an inland beach. It is a relic of
Paleolithic times, when the sea reached much
further inland than it does today. By some
geological freak the beach, of shingle and
pebbles, was not covered by later deposits of
chalk and remains high and dry to this day.

6m N of Bognor Regis. Accessible via public
footpaths and bridleways.

SMALLHYTHE PLACE

Kent   *TQ83*

Part of a tiny hamlet with only a handful of
houses scattered near an ancient church,
Smallhythe Place is a beautiful and remarkably
well-preserved example of early 16th-century
architecture. It is timber-framed, and has an
overhanging upper storey. For nearly 30 years
Smallhythe Place was the country retreat of the
actress Ellen Terry. The house is kept as a
memorial to her, and as a tribute to other great
actors and actresses of her age.

Open March to end Oct. Admission charged. 2m S
of Tenterden.

SISSINGHURST

A tired swimmer in the waves of time
  I throw my hands up: let the surface
close:
Sink down through centuries to
another clime,
And buried find the castle and the
rose.
  Buried in time and sleep,
  So drowsy, overgrown,
That here the moss is green upon the
stone
  And lichen stains the keep.
I've sunk into an image, water-
drowned,
Where stirs no wind and penetrates no
sound,
Illusive, fragile to a touch, remote,
Foundered within the well of years as
deep
As in the waters of a stagnant moat.

These lines are taken from
'Sissinghurst' by Victoria
Sackville-West, written in 1931.

Shalford Mill is a restored, three-
storey mill in a beautiful setting on the
river Tillingbourne. Its brick ground
floor and timber-framed upper floors
contain a 12ft by 8ft iron wheel

SHEFFIELD PARK GARDEN

East Sussex   *TQ42*

All those who love trees will delight in this
beautiful garden, which covers over 100 acres
and includes five lakes. It is perhaps best visited
in the autumn, when the leaves turn to a myriad
golds, yellows and browns.

The garden was originally landscaped by
Capability Brown in about 1775, and it was he
who created two of the lakes. Much of the work
which resulted in the garden's present beauty
was done in the years following 1909, when the
then owner, A. G. Soames, extended and
transformed Capability Brown's original
conception.

As well as its thousands of superb trees, the
garden is enhanced by numerous shrubs and a
splendid array of flowers.

Open April to mid Nov. House not open.
Admission charged. Wheelchair available.
Refreshments nearby (not NT). 5m NW of
Uckfield.

SISSINGHURST CASTLE GARDENS

Kent   *TQ83*

Victoria Sackville-West and Harold Nicolson
created this garden. She was a poet and novelist
and he wrote biographies, histories and diaries.

SNOWSHILL MANOR

Gloucestershire   SP03

'Ne quid Pereat' means 'let nothing perish', and it is as well to have that phrase in mind when visiting Snowshill. It was the motto of Charles Wade who, between 1919 and 1951, packed into an outwardly normal Cotswold manor house an immense collection of objects of almost every conceivable sort.

But all that comes towards the end of the story of Snowshill, for its written history stretches back to AD821, when the estate belonged to Winchcombe Abbey. For 700 years the manor helped to fund the abbey, but at the Dissolution of the Monasteries the manor became Crown property. It passed through many hands during the ensuing centuries, usually being occupied by tenants, until Charles Wade purchased the house and about 200 acres of land. He was affected by the taste for all things Tudor that was prevalent in the early 20th century, and arranged his house and his life around the lifestyle of centuries past. He refused to have electric light fitted, slept in an ancient cupboard bed and worked in a reconstructed forge using period tools. To give a taste of the astonishing contents of the house – there are model boats, bicycles, Chinese and Japanese armour, cloth-makers' tools, horse brasses, policemen's truncheons and several leather fire buckets.

Open May to end Sept, limited opening April and Oct. Admission charged. Wheelchair access. 3m S of Broadway.

STANDEN

West Sussex   TQ33

One of the most original architects of late Victorian times was Philip Webb. His architectural output was not large, partly because he usually insisted on being responsible for every part of his buildings, which took time, and partly because he was reluctant to work for clients who he felt would not be sympathetic to his ideas. Little of his work now survives intact, and Standen, built near the end of his career as a country retreat for a solicitor, is one of his finest houses. It remained in the same family until it was bequeathed to the National Trust in 1972, and as well as being little changed, still contains most of its original furnishings and fittings. These include wallpaper, carpets and textiles designed by Morris, furniture designed by Webb and other craftsmen, and a number of paintings by members of the Beale family, who owned the house. Webb was concerned that his buildings should reflect traditional building styles and incorporate traditional materials, so Standen has weatherboarded gables, tilehanging, bricks of different colours, pebble-dash, and Georgian-style windows as well as stone that was quarried in the garden.

Limited opening April to Oct. Admission charged. Wheelchair available. 1½m S of East Grinstead.

STONEHENGE DOWN

Wiltshire   SU14

In prehistoric times Salisbury Plain was the home of a sophisticated and extensive culture which was centred on Stonehenge, the great stone temple which still attracts speculation and baffled admiration.

Clustered thickly round Stonehenge are hundreds of burial mounds, most of them carefully aligned in distinct cemeteries. Many of these tombs have been excavated, and it is the objects found in them which have supplied much of the knowledge we have of the people who lived on these rolling chalk downlands between 2,000 and 5,000 years ago. At the crossroads of the A303 and the A360 is a long barrow, the largest monument in the so-called Winterbourne Stoke cemetery. All the kinds of Neolithic barrow – bowl, bell, disc, pond and saucer barrows – are represented here. To the north of the A344 is Fargo Plantation, which partly encroaches on another cemetery made up of barrows of different sorts. Also partly within the plantation is the Cursus, one of the most mysterious earthworks in an area that is packed with enigmas. It comprises a parallel pair of banks and ditches, which meet to form rounded ends and enclose an area 1¾ miles long. It is thought that the Cursus was some kind of processional way, and was probably associated with Woodhenge and Durrington Walls, the precursors of Stonehenge.

3m W of Amesbury.

A 17th-century German suit of armour in Snowshill Manor, the home of an eccentric collection of objects from around the world

EARLY SETTLERS

The earthen long barrows and the Cursus on Stonehenge Down were built by early farming colonists known as the Windmill Hill people.

These New Stone Age tribesmen arrived from the Continent in about 3,000 BC, crossing the Channel in wooden-framed skin boats loaded with seed grain of wheat, barley and oats, and cattle, sheep and goats. They also brought pet dogs with them. They were a peaceful people, who herded cattle, grew crops and hunted small game with bows and flint-tipped arrows. Their tools and weapons were made from flint, wood, bone and antler. They clothed themselves in leather and made bag-shaped pottery, a trademark by which archaeolgists recognise their settlements. From 2,000 BC onwards this peaceful society began to change as it became amalgamated with the dominant Beaker people, who inspired the great building period of Stonehenge.

The view south-east from Toys Hill, a popular spot for walkers. A century ago the beech woods were cut to provide charcoal for drying hops in the local oast houses

WELLS AT UPPARK

In this short extract from H. G. Wells's *Experiment in Autobiography*, the author offers an example of the kind of discoveries a young boy might make in a huge, rambling country house like Uppark, where his mother was housekeeper.

'And there was a box, at first quite mysterious, full of brass objects that clearly might be screwed together. I screwed them together, by the method of trial and error, and presently found a Gregorian telescope on a tripod in my hands. I carried off the wonder to my bedroom. By daylight it showed everything upside down, I found, but that did not matter – except for the difficulty of locating objects – when I turned it to the sky. I was discovered by my mother in the small hours, my bedroom window wide open, inspecting the craters of the moon. She said I should catch my death of cold. But at the time that seemed a minor consideration.'

STOURHEAD

Wiltshire	*ST73*

Without a doubt Stourhead is one of the finest landscaped gardens in the world. That its sweeping views, great banks of trees and enticing walks and avenues look so natural is due largely to the imaginative genius of Henry Hoare, who came to live here in 1741. He inherited the estate from his father, who had purchased the estate in the early years of the 18th century. Subsequent generations of Hoares added further touches and embellishments, but none obscure the original brilliant design.

Some of the vistas are as famous and cherished as great works of art. The view from near Stourton village green of the lovely medieval Market Cross (rescued from a builder's yard in 1765) across the lake towards the Pantheon is breathtaking at all times of year. The Pantheon is one of several ornamental temples which enrich the landscape at Stourhead, somehow they contrive to make the garden seem even more natural, and each is placed to make particular vistas as nearly perfect as possible. The mansion at Stourhead was begun in 1721 and enlarged in 1800. Although it was partly burnt down in 1902 it is still a fitting foil to the gardens and a fine repository for furniture by Chippendale.

House open May to Sept, limited opening April and Oct. Garden open all year. Admission charged. Wheelchair available. Refreshments at Spread Eagle Inn (new entrance). 3m NW of Mere.

TOYS HILL

Kent	*TQ45*

This lovely spot, comprising 90 acres of wooded slopes with distant views, was well known to Octavia Hill, one of the founders of the National Trust. Her sister lived nearby, and Octavia sank a well near the cottages on the south side of the hill for the benefit of local people. The Trust has recently acquired a further 180 acres of woodland adjoining the original property, with a fine range of listed farm buildings and oast houses at Outridge Farm which can be reached by public footpath from the car park at Toys Hill.

2½m S of Brasted, 1m W of Ide Hill.

UPPARK

West Sussex	*SU71*

Uppark stands high on the chalk downs of Sussex, commanding extensive views southwards towards the sea. That a late 17th-century mansion should stand in such a position is in itself remarkable. Such places were inevitably built in valleys, because of the difficulty of supplying hilltop houses with water. This was solved with the invention by Sir Edward Ford, owner of the Uppark Estate, of an efficient water pump which made the building of the house possible. But it was Ford's grandson, Lord Grey, who fashioned the house we see today.

In 1747 the estate was purchased by Sir Matthew Featherstonhaugh. He and his wife Sarah had great taste and greatly improved the house and its contents. Sir Matthew died in 1774 and the estate passed to his son Harry. He was only 20 at the time, wild and extravagant, and a close friend of the Prince Regent. He also had great taste, and an admiration for beautiful women. He brought 15-year-old Emma Hart to Uppark, to entertain his guests. She stayed a year, but left pregnant. She later became Nelson's Lady Hamilton.

Later in life Harry employed Humphry Repton to improve the house and park. He remodelled the dining-room, added the north portico, and redesigned the entrance passage. At the age of 70 Sir Harry married his dairymaid, aged 20. He paid for her education, adopted her sister, and left the entire estate to her when he died, aged 92. His wife died in 1874, to be succeeded by her sister, who assumed the name Featherstonhaugh. Uppark remained unchanged throughout the 19th century, due to the care Mrs Featherstonhaugh and her sister lavished on the house. H. G. Wells moved to Uppark when he was 13 years old, when his mother became housekeeper in 1880. In later years he used the house as the model for 'Bladesover' in his novel *Tono-Bungay*.

Open April to end Sept. Admission charged. Free parking. Wheelchair available. Refreshments. 5m SE of Petersfield on B2146, 1½m S of South Harting.

THE VYNE

Hampshire	*SU65*

It is possible that a house has stood on this site since Roman times. It may have been called *Vindomis*, or the house of wine, which would explain the present name. Whatever the facts of that story, it is known that the mansion that stands here today was built by William Sandys, confidant of Henry VIII, during the first decade of the 16th century. Sandys was a fortunate man, for in a reign when most of the powerful seemed to lose their heads, he went from strength to strength. He was created Lord Sandys in 1523, and entertained his monarch at the Vyne on three occasions. Subsequent Sandys inherited the house after the first Lord died in 1540, and all attained high office.

The Sandys family were impoverished as a result of the Civil War, and were obliged to sell the Vyne to Chaloner Chute, a successful barrister. The house remained in the Chute family until it was bequeathed to the National Trust in 1956.

From the outside the house retains much of its early 16th-century character, but there have been several major changes through the centuries. The most outstanding additional feature is the 17th-century portico on the north side. This is especially important because it was the first classical portico to become part of an English country house. Inside, the house has been altered and re-arranged several times. There are two exceptional rooms – the chapel, not much changed since the 16th century and complete with its lovely original stained glass, and the Oak Gallery. It too is largely of the 16th century and is famous for its linenfold panelling. This is unsurpassed in England. Other treasures include the 18th-century tomb chamber and the staircase – both features designed by John Chute, who inherited the house in 1754.

Open April to end Oct. Admission charged. Free parking. Wheelchairs available. Refreshments. 4m N of Basingstoke, between Bramley and Sherborne St John.

WADDESDON MANOR

Buckinghamshire	*SP71*

Set on a wooded hilltop overlooking very English scenery is the very French-looking château of Waddesdon Manor. The house, and the landscaped grounds in which it stands, were created in the late 19th century for Baron Ferdinand de Rothschild, the great grandson of the founder of the famous banking family. Most of the astonishing collections of furniture, paintings, china and other works of art which he amassed are still in the house, as are many other works added by members of the family who inherited the estate.

Waddesdon is most famous for its collections of French 18th-century art, which include furniture, paintings, hangings, panelling, carpets and ornaments, but there are equally exciting collections of English paintings (notably by Gainsborough and Reynolds) and works by Dutch and Flemish Masters.

The grounds cover 160 acres and include wooded parkland, lawned areas and a large aviary stocked with birds.

Open late March to Oct. Admission charged (no children under 12). Free parking. Wheelchair available. Refreshments. 6m NW of Aylesbury.

The Vyne remained in the Chute family from 1653 until its acquisition by the Trust in 1956. When Anthony Chute died in 1754, the house passed to his brother, John, an amateur draughtsman. His skills are revealed in more than 70 drawings he made for the new Staircase Hall, pictured here. The task he set himself was an ambitious one – to transform the functional Tudor 'stone hall and staircase', as it is described in the records, into the grandest possible staircase hall. The space he had to work with was a mere 18ft by 44ft, but his elegant classical stairway became one of the most imposing features of the house

Waddesdon Manor is a huge château in French 16th-century style with tall roofs, spires, towers and chimneys. Not surprisingly, it was designed by a Frenchman, Hippolyte Destailleur, employed in 1874 to create a grand house for the owner, Baron Ferdinand de Rothschild – a name synonymous with wealth

WAKEHURST PLACE

West Sussex   TQ33

Bequeathed to the National Trust in 1963, the house and grounds of Wakehurst Place were leased to the Ministry of Agriculture, Fisheries and Food in 1965 to become an addition to the Royal Botanic Gardens at Kew. It was a move of advantage to the nation and would no doubt have been approved by previous owners of Wakehurst, since the work already done here could be extended and the immeasurably valuable work done at Kew could be continued in a more hospitable environment.

Many paths lead through the gardens, but visitors will be able to see the most beautiful parts by making a circular tour beginning and ending at the car park. Quite close to the mansion are the Rhododendron Walk, Heath Garden and Rock Outcrop, where specimen plants grow among sandstone outcrops close to the waters of Mansion Pond. On the north-west side of the house are two walled gardens, one laid out in muted, subtle colours in memory of Sir Henry Price (who left the gardens to the Trust). South-west of Mansion Pond is the little valley known as the Slips, and the Water Garden, with its wetland plants from Britain

and across the world. The Westwood Valley, with its rhododendrons, can be followed to Westwood Lake, around which there are many superb trees. To the east are the collections of coniferous trees in the pinetum.

Beyond Westwood Lake are Horsebridge Woods, mainly of native oak, and carpeted with acres of bluebells in the spring. Rock Walk, to the east of Horsebridge Woods, is a magical place where the exposed roots of yew, oak and beech can be seen growing over great natural outcrops of sandstone. Rock Walk leads to Bloomer's Valley, with specimen trees from all over the world, and Bethlehem Woods, from where a track leads back to the car park.

Open all year. Admission charged. Free parking. Wheelchair available. Refreshments. Near Haywards Heath, 1½m NW of Ardingly.

WESTBURY COURT GARDEN

Gloucestershire   SO71

Westbury Court is an example of a kind of water garden very popular in the late 17th or early 18th century. Such gardens were very much influenced by Dutch designs, and Westbury retains many of its original formal aspects and architectural features. In gardens like these the emphasis was on intimate spaces rather than large vistas, and on the horticultural content of the garden. Such gardens were very expensive and time-consuming to maintain, since the small areas, hundreds of yards of hedges, expanses of gravel, and thousands of plants, shrubs and trees had to be constantly cared for and replanted. When the new theories of 'natural' landscaping and gardening swept through the country in the 18th century, landowners were quick to replace the knot gardens, parterres and rows of pleached trees with huge parkland vistas and areas of shrubs. Not only was it fashionable, in the long run it was cheaper too!

But Westbury, created by two generations of the Colchester family at the very beginning of the 18th century, was not destroyed. It simply fell into quiet decay. By 1960 the long canals were choked with weeds and half full of silt, the formal hedges had either died or become trees and the gardens themselves were lost under brambles, thistles and nettles. In 1960 a speculator purchased the site, intending to build houses on it, but before the damage done became irreparable, the Gloucestershire County Council bought the site and offered the garden to the National Trust.

Today the canals, the lovely summerhouse, and the formal gardens have been restored and replanted. Hayfields which were once lawns were ploughed and resown, and the original planting records followed; Westbury is once more a beautiful garden.

Open May to Sept, limited opening April and Oct. Admission charged. Wheelchair available. Car park. 9m SW of Gloucester.

WESTWOOD MANOR

Wiltshire ST85

This is a lovely example of a Wiltshire manor. Its interest is increased by the variety of styles and periods which can be traced in the house. The earliest parts of the building date from about 1400, and there was further work done in about 1480, 1530 and the early 17th century. Features of the house include the great hall and the King's Room, which has painted panels depicting 22 English sovereigns up to the reign of Charles I. Much of the fine plasterwork and panelling dates from the house's remodelling in the 17th century at the hands of its owner, John Farewell. The formal gardens include excellent topiary work, including a tree cottage which has a doorway to walk through.

Limited opening April to Sept. Admission charged. 1½m SW of Bradford-on-Avon.

WEST WYCOMBE PARK

Buckinghamshire SU89

Sir Francis Dashwood, politician, traveller and man of letters created the mansion, temples, nearby church and landscaped grounds at West Wycombe with a fortune that he inherited at the age of 16. He was born in 1708, and spent many of his formative years on a series of Grand Tours that had a vital influence on the way in which he shaped West Wycombe and its surroundings. The mansion had originally been a substantial Queen Anne house, but between 1735 and 1771 Sir Francis remodelled it, with the aid of various architects, designers and friends, so that today it has a Palladian north front, an Ionic west portico, a portico of Doric columns on the east, and a superb double colonnade on the south front. These dramatic set pieces act as superb frames to the interior of the house with its sumptuously decorated rooms and the works of art they contain.

The landscaped grounds contain a number of temples and architectural conceits, which also fulfilled roles as backdrops to the lavish masques with which Sir Francis often entertained his friends. Virtually the whole of West Wycombe village, with an array of handsome old buildings, also belongs to the National Trust.

Open June to Aug. Admission charged. Free parking. Off A40, 2m W of High Wycombe.

WEY NAVIGATION

Surrey SU94

The National Trust owns the 15½-mile stretch of the Wey Navigation that runs between Weybridge and Guildford. Begun in 1635, the canal was the brainchild of Sir Richard Weston, one of Britain's greatest pioneering agriculturalists, who also introduced the principle of the canal-lock. The work involved

the canalisation of the river Wey along several stretches and the construction of new channels along others, as well as the building of 12 locks. In 1760 an Act of Parliament enabled the navigation to extend a further four miles to Godalming. In its heyday the canal carried corn, timber and other agricultural produce, but it was superseded by the railway from London to Guildford which was built in the 1840s. Today the canal is a popular leisure amenity and is busy with pleasure craft. Despite the fact that it flows through one of the most urbanised areas of England, the immediate vicinity of the canal, especially between Byfleet and Guildford, is remarkably rural and retains an air of quiet pastoral beauty.

Between Guildford and Weybridge.

West Wycombe Park is very prettily laid out around the house built by Sir Francis Dashwood. It embraces a lake and a collective of interesting 18th-century garden buildings

At one time used only for the passage of timber, corn and other agricultural produce, the Wey Navigational Canal is now host mainly to pleasure craft and gaily painted houseboats

A Figure in the Chalk

Horse or dragon? For something like 2,000 years an elegant creature has been galloping across the chalk downs, and no one is able to say with certainty what it is or what its function was. The White Horse of Uffington is one of the many enigmas which are scattered across the British landscape, and like all strange things it has attracted its fair share of legends.

Just below the figure is an oddly shaped hillock which is said to have been the spot where St George slew the famous dragon. The dragon's blood fell on the top of the hill, killing the grass that grew there, and ever since the spot has been bare. Those who wanted their wishes granted would stand in the figure's eye to bring the luck along.

Great ceremonies attended the regular scouring of the figure, which was done every few years to keep it clear of grass. The best known activity was cheese-rolling. Whole cheeses were rolled from the side of the hill into the coomb known as the Horse's Manger. All the local young men chased after them, those catching the cheese not only gaining the cheese itself, but good luck as well.

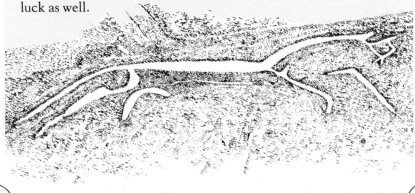

WHITE HORSE HILL

Oxfordshire   *SU38*

On the scarp of the downs west of Wantage an enormous figure is carved in the chalk. It lies close to the Ridgeway, one of the great highways of prehistoric times, and it looks over a great sweep of undulating Oxfordshire countryside. The figure is called the White Horse of Uffington, and it has probably been engraved on the hillside for something like 2,000 years. Throughout that period the horse has been very carefully tended by local people; it would soon have disappeared beneath the grass if it had not been scoured every few years.

Just to the east of the horse is a large Iron Age hill-fort that was probably used by the tribe whose emblem it was. The fort, which is about eight acres in extent, is entered through a single gateway protected by an extension of the perimeter banks. Excavation suggests that the fort's earthen banks were once faced with stone and timber.

Immediately below the White Horse is an oddly shaped knoll called Dragon Hill. Its shape is entirely natural, but it may have been used in ceremonies connected with the horse and it is certainly linked to it in legend.

6m W of Wantage.

WINCHESTER CITY MILL

Hampshire   *SU42*

A mill has stood on this site since at least as early as Anglo-Saxon times, but its continued prosperity was cut short in 1348–9, when the Black Death brought disaster to Winchester. It became a tenement in the Middle Ages, and it was not until 1743 that it was rebuilt and returned to its original purpose. It is this building which can be seen today, though it almost certainly incorporates materials from the old mill. In 1820 the City Corporation sold the mill to John Benham, and his family kept it as a working cornmill for over a hundred years. The mill was put up for sale in 1928, and local benefactors purchased it and presented it to the National Trust. It has been leased to the Youth Hostels Association since 1931.

Open April to Oct (at other times of the year by appointment only). Admission charged. At foot of Winchester High Street by Soke Bridge.

WINKWORTH ARBORETUM

Surrey   *SU94*

Set in the heart of some of Surrey's loveliest countryside, the creation of Winkworth Arboretum was begun in 1938. It was the idea of Dr Wilfred Fox, who did much of the work himself and who made the arboretum solely in order to create a place of beauty that could be appreciated by all. He transformed what had been a wild and uncultivated valley slope into a landscape packed with trees and shrubs that is both an extensive botanical collection and a pleasure garden. Dr Fox was especially fond of the colours and textures of autumn, so the arboretum is full of plant species which are at their most beautiful in October and November, but Winkworth is nonetheless enjoyable at any season. There are two lakes in the valley bottom, and it is from here that the panorama of hillside and trees is best appreciated. Another notable viewpoint is from the pine-clad slope on the south side of the arboretum.

Open all year. Admission charged. Wheelchair access. Refreshments. 3m SE of Godalming.

WITLEY COMMON

Surrey   *SU94*

Witley Common is a heathland area on acidic soils, but it also has other habitats created inadvertently by men. In both world wars it was used as an army camp, and it was partly as a result of materials brought in during those periods that different soils were introduced. This variety of soils has led to an enormous range of wildlife, revealed to the visitor in the Information Centre.

Centre open April to end Oct, limited opening March and Nov. SW of Milford, between A3 and A286.

OTHER PROPERTIES

BEDFORDSHIRE

The Clappers and Roberts Farm, Sharpenhoe. *TL03*
Farm and woodland on the Chilterns. 6m N of Luton.

Dunstable Down, Whipsnade. *TL01*
Chiltern downland. 2m S of Dunstable. Public footpaths.

BERKSHIRE

Ambarrow Hill. *SU86*
Pine-clad hilltop. Between railway and A321, ½m S of Crowthorne Station.

Falkland Memorial. *SU46*
19th-century memorial to 2nd Viscount Falkland who fell in first battle of Newbury (1643). 1m SW of Newbury on A343.

The Goswells, Windsor. *SU97*
Three acres, preserving the view of the castle. Now a recreation ground. Between Thames Street and the river.

Lardon Chase. *SU58*
Downland with views of Chilterns and Thames valley. Just N of Streatley, on W side of A417.

Lough Down. *SU58*
Adjoins Lardon Chase; views over Streatley and the Goring Gap.

Pangbourne Meadow. *SU64*
On S bank of Thames, just below Pangbourne Bridge.

BUCKINGHAMSHIRE

Coombe Hill. *SP80*
Highest viewpoint in Chilterns. 3½m SE of Princes Risborough.

Dorneywood. *SU98*
House (not open) and garden, given to NT as official residence for Minister of State or of the Crown. Garden open Aug and Sept Sat pm by appointment in writing. SW of Burnham Beeches.

Gray's Monument, Stoke Poges. *SU98*
In a field, E of the churchyard in the *Elegy*.

Greenlands Estate. *SU78, 98*
Four small viewpoints, N and S of A4155. NE of Henley on both sides of Thames.

Hogback Wood. *SU99*
1m W of Beaconsfield Station.

Whiteleaf Fields. *SP80*
Opposite the Nag's Head Inn, Monk's Risborough, and extending for about ¼m on both sides of the Icknield Way.

EAST SUSSEX

Ditchling Beacon. *TQ31*
Small area on NE slope with traces of hill-fort rampart and ditch, and views. 6m N of Brighton.

Exceat Saltings. *TV59*
A small piece of the saltings, and land overlooking them. S of Exceat Bridge on W bank of Cuckmere river.

Fairlight. *TQ81*
Cliffland, farmland and woods. 4½m E of Hastings. Access by public footpath only.

Lake Meadow, Battle. *TQ71*
Opposite the Chequers Hotel, preserving the view to the N. Access by public footpath only.

Nap Wood. *TQ53*
Oak wood leased to Sussex Naturalists' Trust and used as a nature reserve. 4m S of Tunbridge Wells on A267.

Wickham Manor Farm, Winchelsea. *TQ81*
Farmland 1m SW of Winchelsea, and much of the town with 1¼m of the Royal Military Canal. Access across farmland by public footpath.

The Warren, Wych Cross. *TQ43*
Woodland 2½m S of Forest Row.

ESSEX

Northey Island. *TL80*
300-acre island which is a Grade 1 site for saltmarsh flora and over-wintering birds, leased to the Essex Naturalists Trust. Access by appointment with warden only. In Blackwater estuary.

Ray Island. *TM01*
Salting in tidal creek between mainland and West Mersea; 2½m of coastline.

Rayleigh Mount. *TQ89*
Site of Domesday castle built by Sweyn of Essex. 6m N of Southend.

GLOUCESTERSHIRE

Chipping Campden
The Coneygree. *SP13*
Meadow land between churchyard and the station road.

Dover's Hill. *SP13*
Natural amphitheatre on Cotswolds; site of Dover's Games. On right of B4035 to Weston-sub-Edge.

Market Hall. *SP13*
Jacobean building opposite police station.

Crickley Hill, The Scrubbs. *SO91*
Part of Cotswold escarpment; views over Severn valley. 6m E of Gloucester, just N of A417.

Ebworth, Blackstable Wood. *SO80*
Fine beech trees. N of B4070, near Painswick. Access by public footpath.

Frocester Hill and Coaley Peak. *SO70*
Part of Cotswold escarpment; of botanical interest. Views to Forest of Dean and Welsh mountains. Near Nympsfield on B4060.

May Hill. *SO62*
969ft, with views of ten counties. 9m W of Gloucester.

Stroud
Besbury Common. *SO80*
Above Golden Valley, 3m SE of Stroud.

Haresfield Beacon and Standish Wood. *SO80*
Hill and woodland on N edge of Cotswolds with prehistoric sites. 2-3m NW of Stroud.

Hyde Commons. *SO80*
Common and waste land in Hyde Village. 3m SE of Stroud.

Minchinhampton Commons. *SO80*
Common land with earthworks. NW of Minchinhampton.

Rodborough Common. *SO80*
Includes early first-century enclosure site. 1m S of Stroud.

St Chloe's Green and Littleworth Common. *SO80*
Common land adjoining Minchinhampton Commons on NW.

Stockend and Maitland Woods. *SO80*
Woodland on Scottsquar Hill. 2m SW of Painswick.

Watledge Hill. *SO80*
Common between Nailsworth and Pinfarthing.

Westridge Woods, Wotton-under-Edge. *ST79*
On escarpment above B4060, 1m NW of town. Access by footpath.

HAMPSHIRE

The Chase, Woolton Hill. *SO46*
Woodlands with chalk stream and small farm; nature reserve. 3m SW of Newbury on W of A343.

Hale Purlieu and Millersford Plantation. *SU21*
Heath and woodland with prehistoric sites. 3m NE of Fordingbridge.

Hamble River. *SU51*
Wood and agricultural land with Roman site; nature reserve at Curbridge, 1m below Botley on A27.

Hightown Common. *SU10*
Common land 2m E of Ringwood.

ISLE OF WIGHT

Borthwood Copse. *SZ58*
Woodland; remaining part of medieval hunting forest. 2m W of Sandown.

St Helen's
Horestone Point, Priory Bay. *SZ68*
Small piece of wooded coastline. Access from foreshore only.

St Helen's Common. *SZ68*
Common land with a cottage, and views over Brading Harbour. 1m NW of Bembridge.

St Helen's Duver. *SZ68*
Wide sand and shingle spit stretching almost across mouth of Bembridge Harbour. Good walking.

KENT

Golden Hill, Harbledown. *TR15*
Intended as a playground for children. 1m W of Canterbury.

Grange Farm, Crockham Hill. *TQ45*
Farmland 2m S of Westerham. Access by public footpath only.

Great Farthingloe, Dover. *TR23*
Farm and cliff midway between Dover and Capel-le-Ferne. Access through Aycliffe along Old Folkestone Road.

Ide Hill. *TQ45*
Wooded hillside overlooking Weald. 2½m SE of Brasted.

Mariner's Hill. *TQ45*
Hillside with views across Weald. 1½m S of Westerham. Access by footpath, and to woodland.

One Tree Hill. *TQ50*
Site of supposed Roman burials; views to south. 2m SE of Sevenoaks.

St John's Jerusalem. *TQ57*
Once Commandery of Knights Hospitallers. 3m S of Dartford. Only chapel (now housing early photographs) and garden open April to Oct, Wed pm.

St Margaret's Bay. *TR34*
Mostly arable land but also clifftop and other walks, including St Margaret's Freedown, common land in middle of Bockhill Farm. Access by footpath.

Sprivers Garden, Horsmonden. *TQ64*
Parkland, orchard and wood with mid 18th-century house (not open) and garden, open April to end Sept, Wed pm only. 3m N of Lamberhurst.

Tudor Yeoman's House, Sole Street. *TQ66*
1m SW of Cobham. Main Hall only open on application to tenant.

Wool House, Loose. *TQ75*
15th-century half-timbered house formerly used for cleaning wool. 3m S of Maidstone. Open on written application to tenant.

Wrotham Water. *TQ65*
Mainly farmland, at foot of North Downs. ½m E of Wrotham. Footpath access.

LONDON

Blewcoat School. *TQ27*
Small 18th-century building with a panelled room. 23 Caxton Street, SW1. Access by written request to Secretary, NT.

Eastbury House, Barking. *TQ48*
16th-century red brick manor house. Access by written appointment only.

East Sheen Common. *TQ17*
Adjoining Richmond Park on N, just S of A305.

Hawkwood. *TQ46*
Farm and woodland between Chislehurst and Orpington.

Petts Wood. *TQ46*
Wood and heath; a memorial to W. Willett, founder of Summer Time. Between Chislehurst and Orpington.

Rainham Hall. *TQ58*
Red brick house (18th-century). 5m E of Barking. Open April to Oct, Wed pm by written appointment with tenant only.

Roman Bath, No.5 Strand Lane.
Remains of a bath, possibly of Roman origin, restored in 17th century. Just W of Aldwych tube station. Not open but interior visible from pathway

Selsdon Wood. *TQ36*
3m SE of Croydon. Nature Reserve.

Wandle
Happy Valley. *TQ26*
Two acres on W bank of river Wandle next to Ravensbury Park.

Morden Hall. *TQ26*
Parkland and meadows intersected by Wandle. On E side of Morden Road (A24) and Mordenhall Road (A297).

Wandle Park. *TQ27*
Millpond Gardens; Two acres behind Royal Six Bells Inn at Colliers Wood.

Watermeads. *TQ26*
Nature reserve on W bank of Wandle; admission only by keys obtainable from Head Warden on payment of deposit and small annual subscription.

SURREY

Abinger Roughs. *TQ14*
Wooded ridge with Hackhurst Farm adjoining. Just N of Abinger Hammer.

Blackheath. *TQ04*
Heather and pineclad land. ½m S of Chilworth.

Cedar House, Cobham. *TQ15*
15th-century house overlooking river Mole. Open on prior application to tenant.

Eashing Bridges. *SU94*
Medieval double bridge over river Wey. 1½m W of Godalming.

Gatton. *TQ25*
Woodland and parkland on N slopes of North Downs, 1½m NE of Reigate.

Hackhurst Down. *TQ04*
Part of nature reserve on S slope of North Downs. ½m NE of Gomshall and Shere station.

Harewoods. *TQ34*
Farms, woods and common land at Outwoods, 3m SE of Redhill. Access to Outwood Common, parts of the woodlands, and by public footpath.

Headley Heath. *TQ25*
Open space and woodland. 4m S of Epsom.

Holmwood Common. *TQ14*
Common and woods. 1m S of Dorking.

Hydon's Ball and Hydon Heath. *SU93*
Heath and woodland; bought as a memorial to NT founder, Octavia Hill. Views. 3m S of Godalming.

John Freeman Memorial, Thursley. *SU93*
Meadowland protecting Thursley Church; the poet John Freeman is buried in the churchyard.

Limpsfield Common. *TQ45*
Common land on greensand ridges SE of Oxted.

Little King's Wood. *TQ04*
Mixed woodland on S escarpment of North Downs above Gomshall. Access by footpaths; no access by car.

Netley Park. *TQ04*
Farm and woodland at E end of Shere (house not open).

Ranmore Common and Denbies Hillside. *TQ15*
Wooded common and land on S slopes of North Downs. 2m NW of Dorking.

Reigate. *TQ25*
Open down, copse and beechwood on summit and escarpment of North Downs. Between Reigate and Banstead Heath.

South Hawke, Woldingham. *TQ35*
Down and woodland and hanging woods on S slope on North Downs, 750ft above sea level. 1½m S of Woldingham.

WEST SUSSEX

Drovers Estate. *SU81*
Farm and woodland including disused railway line. Astride Midhurst-Chichester Road.

Durford Heath. *SU72*
Common and scrub woodland. 2½m NE of Petersfield.

East Head, West Wittering. *SU79*
A spit of land on the E side of Chichester Harbour entrance; 1¼m of coastline with dunes, saltings and sandy beaches. Access on foot from West Wittering or by dinghy.

Lavington Common. *SU91*
Heather and pine-covered land with 3 round barrows. 2m SW of Petworth.

Marley. *SU83*
Common and steep woodland S of Haslemere; also Shottermill Ponds.

Newtimber Hill. *TQ21*
Down and woodland with views of the Weald and the sea; prehistoric sites. Between Pyecombe and Poynings.

Quay Meadow, Bosham. *SU80*
An acre between the church and the creek. 4m W of Chichester.

Shoreham Gap. *TQ27*
Farm and downland with Iron Age and other sites. 2m NE of Shoreham.

Sullington Warren. *TQ01*
Open land with two lines of bowl barrows. ½m E of Storrington.

Warren Hill. *TQ11*
Commonland, woods, a farm and some dwellings (not open). 8m N of Worthing.

Woolbeding. *SU82*
Agricultural estate with farmland, woods and commons. 2m NW of Midhurst. Public access to commons and part of woodlands.

WILTSHIRE

Cherhill Down and Oldbury Castle. *SU06*
Downland with Iron Age fort. On A4 between Calne and Beckhampton; approached by footpaths from A4.

Cley Hill. *ST84*
Chalk hill 800ft high; Iron Age hill-fort. 3m W of Warminster.

The Courts, Holt. *ST86*
Weavers brought disputes for arbitration to the house (not open) until end of 18th century. 3m W of Melksham. Garden only open, April to Oct.

Dinton Park and Philipps House. *SU03*
House, farm and Iron-Age fort. House let to YMCA; open April to Sept only by prior appointment with the Warden. In Dinton village, Little Clarendon, a 15th-century stone house, is open on written application to the tenant.

Figsbury Ring. *SU13*
Iron Age hill-fort. 4m NE of Salisbury.

Pepperbox Hill. *SU22*
Open down with 17th-century folly, and woodland. 5m SE of Salisbury.

Win Green Hill. *ST92*
Highest point in Cranborne Chase with a tree circle on the summit. 5m SE of Shaftesbury.

WALES &
THE MARCHER
LANDS

*St Elvis —
sheltered creeks and rugged cliff scenery in St Bride's Bay*

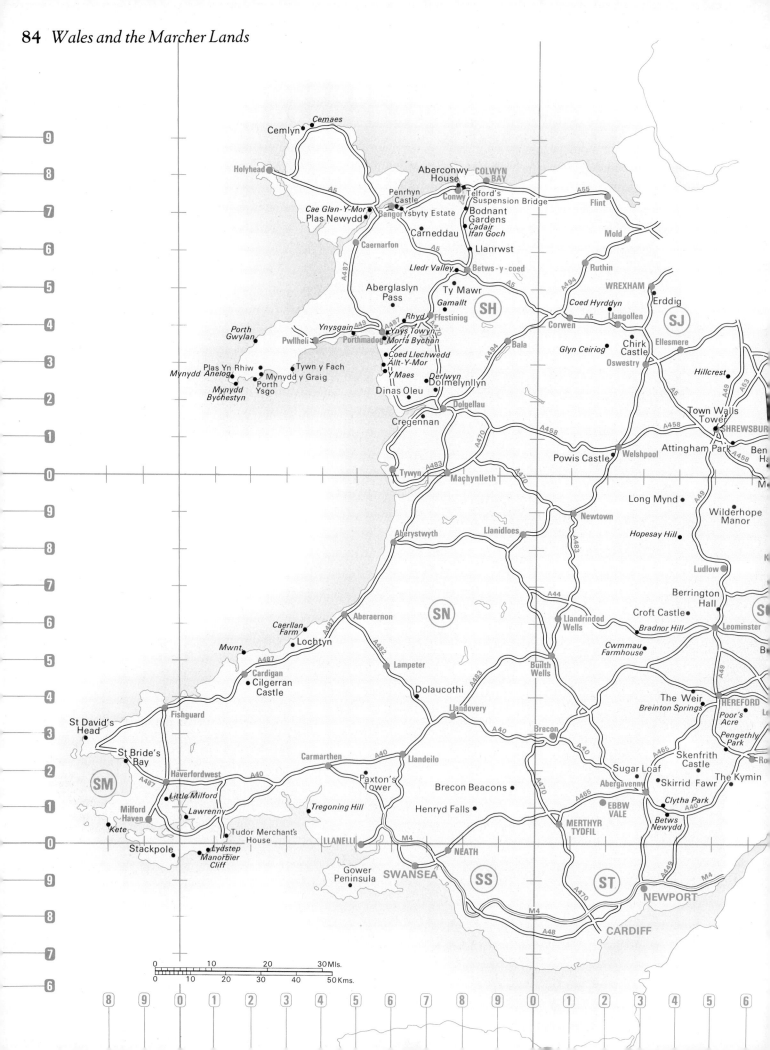

Cemaes
Cemlyn

Holyhead

Aberconwy
House
COLWYN
BAY
Penrhyn
Castle
Conwy
Telford's
Suspension Bridge
Flint
Cae Glan-Y-Mor
Plas Newydd
Bangor Ysbyty Estate
Bodnant
Gardens
*Cadair
Ifan Goch*
Mold
Carneddau
Caernarfon
Llanrwst
Ruthin
WREXHAM
Lledr Valley
Betws-y-coed
Coed Hyrddyn
Erddig
Aberglaslyn
Pass
Ty Mawr
Gamallt
SH
Llangollen
SJ
*Porth
Gwylan*
Ynysgain
Rhyd
Ffestiniog
Corwen
Glyn Ceiriog
Chirk
Castle
Ellesmere
Pwllheli
Porthmadog
Ynys Towyn
Morfa Bychan
A494
Bala
Oswestry
Plas Yn Rhiw
Tywn y Fach
Coed Llechwedd
Allt-Y-Mor
Hillcrest
Mynydd Anelog
Mynydd y Graig
Y Maes
Derlwyn
Town Walls
Tower
*Mynydd
Bychestyn*
*Porth
Ysgo*
Dinas Oleu
Dolmelynllyn
SHREWSBUR
Cregennan
Dolgellau
Powis Castle
Welshpool
Attingham Park
Tywyn
Machynlleth
Long Mynd
Wilderhope
Manor
Newtown
Aberystwyth
Llanidloes
Hopesay Hill
SN
Ludlow
Berrington
Hall
Llandrindod
Wells
Croft Castle
S
Aberaeron
Bradnor Hill
Leominster
*Caerllan
Farm*
*Cwmmau
Farmhouse*
Mwnt
Lochtyn
Lampeter
Builth
Wells
Cardigan
Cilgerran
Castle
Dolaucothi
The Weir
HEREFORD
Breinton Springs
Fishguard
Llandovery
Brecon
*Poor's
Acre*
St David's
Head
*Pengethly
Park*
St Bride's
Bay
Carmarthen
Llandeilo
Skenfrith
Castle
Haverfordwest
Sugar Loaf
The Kymin
SM
*Paxton's
Tower*
Abergavenny
Skirrid Fawr
Little Milford
Tregoning Hill
Brecon Beacons
Clytha Park
Milford
Haven
Lawrenny
Henryd Falls
EBBW
VALE
*Betws
Newydd*
Kete
Tudor Merchant's
House
LLANELLI
MERTHYR
TYDFIL
Stackpole
Lydstep
*Manorbier
Cliff*
NEATH
Gower
Peninsula
SWANSEA
SS
ST
NEWPORT
CARDIFF

0   10   20   30 Mls.
0 10 20 30 40 50 Kms.

ABERCONWY HOUSE

Gwynedd   SH77

Aberconwy House is one of the last surviving timber-framed buildings in Conwy, a town which has preserved its medieval street pattern but few of its ancient houses. This three-storeyed house has oak ceiling joists dated to the 14th century, but it has been added to over the centuries: its leaded casement windows come from a later time, and the notable third floor fireplace is 17th century. The outside staircase to the upper floor is a typical medieval arrangement. An interesting *History of Conwy* exhibition on life in the area from Roman times to the present day is kept here, and the ground floor is used as a National Trust shop.

Open April to end Oct. Admission charged. Castle Street, Conwy, at junction with High Street.

ABERGLASLYN PASS

Gwynedd   SH64

Aberglaslyn is one of North Wales' most famous beauty spots. In the summer months, everyone seems to make for the little stone-built bridge, Pont Aberglaslyn, which spans the tumbling Glaslyn torrent at the southern approach to the pass, causing traffic congestion as they pose for the inevitable photograph.

Hemmed in by cliffs 700ft high the pass was described (rather enthusiastically perhaps) by the 18th-century traveller John Cradock as the 'noblest specimen of the Finely Horrid the Eye can possibly behold . . . 'Tis the last approach to the mansion of Pluto through the regions of Despair'. But do not let that put you off – the countryside and the views are magnificent.

Curiously enough, although Aberglaslyn's precipitous, tree-lined rock faces suggest Snowdonia at its most mountainous, the river Glaslyn was once tidal as far as the bridge. Ships sailed right to the mouth of the pass before the Portmadoc embankment was built early in the 19th century, and there was a thriving boatbuilding industry here. The sea is now six miles away.

Extending S for 1½m from Beddgelert, along both sides of the pass (A487 and A498).

ATTINGHAM PARK

Shropshire   SJ50

The imposing mansion of Attingham, standing in 3,826 acres of parkland, is largely the work of 18th-century architect George Steuart, whose other major works (with the exception of St Chad's Church, Shrewsbury) have disappeared. He was commissioned by Noel Hill, later to become the First Lord Berwick, who had the vision – and the finance – to transform a small Queen Anne house on this site into something far grander – an 18th-century classical mansion.

Behind its shape lies an interesting story. Steuart, an enigmatic figure about whom little is known, was no mere cipher for rich patrons. As part of his contract, he insisted that Tern Hall be saved by incorporating it into his overall design. He achieved this by building his new, classically proportioned central block in front of the existing hall, creating a marriage of old and new through the device of twin flanking pavilions linked by colonnades. Though there is a marked discrepancy in height between front and rear, the overall effect is one of striking, and surprising, harmony.

Lord Berwick hardly had time to enjoy his new residence, for he died in 1789. The Second Lord Berwick, a lover of fine art, commissioned John Nash to build a picture gallery – another rare feature in an early 19th-century English house – and a staircase. Many of the Italianate artefacts which now adorn this well-appointed house belonged to the equally cosmopolitan Third Lord. These three Lords were brothers. In 1842 the estate passed to the youngest of the First Lord's sons, and finally to the Eighth Lord Berwick, who bequeathed the house to the Trust in 1947. The parkland that surrounds the house is largely as it was in the late 18th century, when it was landscaped with the advice of Repton.

Open April to end Sept, limited opening Oct. Admission charged. Free parking. Wheelchair available. Refreshments. 4m SE of Shrewsbury, on N side of the Wellington road (A5).

BENTHALL HALL

Shropshire   SJ60

Benthall Hall is a fine example of a country house built by the English gentry of the 16th century, although some confusion surrounds its precise date of origin. The house as it now stands, built on the site of a much earlier hall, was for some time dated at 1535. Most experts now attribute it to the 1580s. They have plumped for this date partly because of what is known about the Benthall family. They were Catholic sympathisers in a hostile Protestant Elizabethan England, and their 'new' house provided hiding places for priests; there would have been little need for such places in 1535.

Despite – or perhaps because of – the asymmetrical south front, the house has an arresting façade: the mullioned and transomed windows in the two-storey octagonal bays give the house particular appeal, and the building is completed by a gabled roofline and moulded chimneys all in the true 16th-century fashion.

Inside, the decoration is mainly from the first half of the 17th century, the panelling in the dining room originating from around 1610 and the elaborately carved staircase from a little later. The only later additions are the rococo chimneypieces added in the 1760s.

Open Easter Sat to end Sept. Admission charged. Free parking in lane outside. Wheelchair access. 4m NE of Much Wenlock, 8m S of Wellington, 1m NW of Broseley (B4375).

BERRINGTON HALL

Hereford and Worcester SO56

Late 18th-century taste and achievement are both embodied in the pinkish ashlar stonework of Berrington Hall. Thomas Harley, a dynamic banker and government contractor (and, at only 37 years of age, a Lord Mayor of London in 1767), acquired the old Berrington estate in 1775. 'Capability' Brown was immediately set to work on the grounds. He took full advantage of the panoramic position of the site, creating a parkland with an artificial lake of great beauty.

Meanwhile, plans for the house were being drawn up by the eminent architect, Henry Holland (who was Brown's son-in-law). The rectangular-shaped house was built between 1778 and 1781. Although on first impressions almost plain in appearance, it displays all the hallmarks of Holland's elegant style.

In contrast to a certain external austerity, the decoration inside the house is elaborate, with many exceptional features in a superb state of preservation. Among these are the staircase hall – Holland's architectural masterpiece of spatial design – and the ornate plasterwork and painted panels. The Trust has replaced much of the exterior stonework but this remarkable interior remains unaltered since the likes of Brown and Holland gave it their seal of approval.

Open May to end Sept, limited opening April and Oct. Admission charged. Free parking in drive. Wheelchair available. Refreshments. 3m N of Leominster on W side of A49.

BETWS NEWYDD

Gwent SO30

This hilltop site, of 25 acres, looks out across rolling countryside in the Usk valley, only four miles from the little town of Usk itself. Although only a stone's throw from the coal-bearing hills of the so-called 'industrial' valleys of south Wales, the site is surrounded by the rich farmlands characteristic of the England and Wales border country. The Usk valley walk runs along the bank of the river at the foot of the hill, and close by are a number of important historic sites, including the late-medieval ruin of Raglan Castle (not NT).

4m N of Usk (A471), 4m W of Raglan (A449 and A40).

BODNANT GARDEN

Gwynedd SH87

Wales is not famous for its formal gardens, but at Bodnant there is one of Britain's finest. From the garden terraces, begun in 1905, there are commanding views across to the distant Carneddau range and Snowdon. Decoration plays an important part here; fountains, ornaments and balustrading blend with

immaculately tended hedgerows and large numbers of flowering shrubs and plants, carefully introducing and balancing the distant views with the vistas of the garden itself.

Many visitors come to Bodnant in the early summer, when the garden's famous collection of rhododendrons is at its best. Planting and cultivation here have been guided by a desire to grow as wide a variety of plants as possible. Camellias, for example, seem to flourish here, so many varieties have been planted in large numbers. Magnolias, azaleas and conifers also do well. Of particular interest among the various buildings here is a garden house. This was originally constructed in the 1730s in Gloucestershire as a garden house, but was later used as a pin mill. It was brought to Bodnant in 1938 to stand at the end of a mirror-like pool opposite an open air theatre with wings of clipped yew.

Open mid March to end Oct. Admission charged. Free parking. Wheelchair available. Refreshments. 8m S of Llandudno and Colwyn Bay on A470, entrance ½m along the Eglwysbach road.

Bodnant has gradually evolved since the late 18th century to become one of the finest gardens in Britain. Pictured here is the long formal pool called the Canal, which has a mass of water-lilies at each end. The building at the far end is the Pin Mill. Originally the garden house of an Elizabethan mansion at Woodchester in Gloucestershire, it was later used for the manufacture of pins, and then as a tannery. In 1939 it was brought to Bodnant and restored to form a garden feature of great charm

Soft landscapes like this are typical of the Brecon Beacons, which are composed of a sandstone that weathers comparatively readily instead of forming rugged contours. The gentle scenery belies the height of the range, which frequently exceeds 2,000ft and falls only just short of 3,000ft at the highest point, Pen-y-fan. The mountain peaks themselves are wild moorland, but below them the land falls away to the lush pastures of the Usk and Tywi valleys, offering a complete contrast

BRAICH-Y-PWLL

Gwynedd   SH12

This lovely, remote site is out on a limb – quite literally. Braich-y-Pwll consists of 122 acres of headland and cliff scenery perched on the western tip of the Lleyn Peninsula, a crooked limb of land pointing into the Irish Sea. Lleyn's cliff-backed coastline is nowhere wilder than along this exposed headland, which has superb views of Cardigan Bay and Bardsey Island.

Near Aberdaron (B4413).

BRECON BEACONS

Powys   SO02

The Trust goes straight to the top in the Brecon Beacons by virtue of its ownership of Pen-y-fan, at 2,907ft the highest peak in the Beacons National Park and south Wales. This summit is part of an 8,192-acre stretch of the main mountain range owned by the Trust.

Pen-y-fan's profile – gently sloping flanks leading to a flattish, rather indistinct summit – betrays the soft nature of the underlying red sandstone rocks. Appearances, though, can be deceptive. The Beacons may lack the rugged grandeur of Snowdonia, yet they still hold the challenge of difficult and sometimes dangerous upland terrain, much of it above 2,000ft.

The Brecon Beacons National Park, of which Pen-y-fan is the central feature, extends from the England and Wales border across into west Wales, enclosing an area of some 519 square miles. The National Trust holds small pockets of land (including farmland) elsewhere in this park, at Blaenglyn, Cwmoergwm and Cwm Sere, all of which fringe the Pen-y-fan massif.

5m S of Brecon, E of A470.

BREDON TITHE BARN

Hereford and Worcester   SO93

Constructed from local limestone with a stone-shingled roof of exceptional pitch, this 132ft-long barn belonged to the church lands of Worcester until it became Crown property in the 16th century. Ventilation and light came from the many holes and slats in the walls. An external staircase leads to an unusual room, complete with fireplace and chimney, located above the easternmost porch. This was used by the monk responsible for running the barn.

3m NE of Tewkesbury, just N of B4080.

CARNEDDAU

Gwynedd   SH66

The Carneddau, located among Snowdonia's most dramatic landscapes, is a collective name for Wales's second highest mountain range. The effects of glaciation are everywhere to be seen in the cwms and rugged slopes above the Nant Ffrancon Pass to the north-west of Capel Curig.

Ten of Snowdonia's 13 main summits are included within the Trust property here which, with six farmsteads, amounts to some 15,860 acres. Not surprisingly, the area contains some of Britain's most challenging climbing country.

Tryfan, at 3,010ft, is now part of mountaineering lore. The first successful Everest expedition trained here. Experienced walkers often find that peace and solitude are better guaranteed among the peaks of the Glyders or Carnedd Dafydd than on the more popular tracks around Snowdon itself. At Cwm Idwal, with its hauntingly beautiful lake, there is a nature reserve.

8m SE of Bangor, astride A5, near Capel Curig.

CEMLYN

Gwynedd   *SH39*

This 321-acre site lies along Cemlyn Bay on the north coast of the Isle of Anglesey. Cemlyn is typical of the north Anglesey coastline, where some of the oldest geological rock formations in the world are to be found. The sheltered lagoons and the coastline which fringes them provide winter sanctuary for many wildfowl. Part of the site has therefore been designated a nature reserve under the control of the North Wales Naturalists' Trust. However, the cliffs and headland at Trwyn Cemlyn in the north of the property are always open to visitors.

2m W of Cemaes Bay on N coast of Anglesey.

CHIRK CASTLE

Clwyd   *SJ23*

The stately home of Chirk is equipped with an immaculate pedigree. A castle was first built here in the late 13th century by the Marcher Lord Roger Mortimer as part of an overall plan by King Edward I to consolidate his hold on Wales. Quite exceptionally, it has been inhabited ever since. Consequently, it has also been much altered and improved over the centuries, only one tower now retaining any medieval character.

The castle came into the Myddleton family in 1595, when it was bought by Thomas Myddleton, an adventurer who had sailed the Spanish Main with Sir Walter Raleigh. He also became Lord Mayor of London in 1613. At this time, Chirk was described as 'mighty large and stronge castel, with dyvers towers', though following damage in the Civil War the site, by the 1750s, had apparently become a most disagreeable dwelling-house.

Chirk's fortunes changed in the 1760s when its owner, Robert Myddleton, embarked on a programme of wholesale improvement. The superb series of neo-Classical state rooms in the north wing date from this time. Also noteworthy are the Great Saloon and Long Gallery, the latter completed in 1678. The theme of constant evolution was continued into the 19th century, when A. W. N. Pugin, architect of the Houses of Parliament, made additions to the east range.

The many lovely rooms, sumptuously furnished and decorated mostly in elegant 18th-century style, are hung with fine paintings. Perhaps the most curious are those by a supposedly foreign artist showing the Rhayader Falls – with ships sailing over dry land. Legend tells that the artist was asked to include sheep on the hills, and misheard the instruction.

The intricately patterned 18th-century ornamental iron gates guard the entrance to a large, attractive park landscaped in the late 18th century by William Emes.

Open April to Oct. Admission charged. Free parking. Limited wheelchair access. Refreshments. ½m W of Chirk village, off A5, 1½m private driveway to Castle.

HELEN OF WALES

The lady who has earned comparison with the fateful Helen of Troy was Nest, the fiery and beautiful ward of Henry I who married Gerald de Windsor, his representative in Powys.

Her beauty captivated Owain, son of Cadwgan, Prince of Powys. He swore to make her his and, gathering a band of hot-headed warriors to him, attacked Gerald's castle, which stood where the ruins of Cilgerran Castle stand today. His action so enraged the King that he went to war against Owain's blameless father, who lost his hand as a result. Meanwhile Owain, who had relinquished Nest, fled to Ireland.

Years later Gerald met Owain in battle and slew him. Nest survived them both to marry again.

Top left: The magnificent Saloon at Chirk Castle. The 15 ceiling panels are painted with mythological scenes, and on the walls hangs a set of four late 17th-century Mortlake tapestries and portraits by Kneller, Wright, Dahl and Van der Mijn. The harpsichord was made in about 1742

Above: The spectacular position of Cilgerran Castle above the deep gorge of the river Teifi was also a very practical one. It stands at the tidal limit of the Teifi and was accessible by ship from the sea. It is also at the lowest possible crossing place of the river, whatever the state of the tide, and the rocky promontory on which it is built provided a natural defence

CILGERRAN CASTLE

Dyfed   SN14

The romantic ruin of Cilgerran stands on a craggy outcrop above a gorge of the river Teifi. The nature of the site, and perhaps the heroic legends associated with it, have for centuries attracted visitors and inspired artists, including Turner, Wilson and de Wint.

Originally, the castle on this site was probably a simple motte-and-bailey structure. The stone castle, built by the Norman baron William Marshall as part of his conquest of west Wales, dates from 1225. It was deserted by 1275, after the English suffered defeat in this area in 1258. It was repaired eventually, but following attack by the forces of Owain Glyndwr in the Welsh uprising of 1405, the castle was left to ruin.

Although derelict for centuries, the strength and tactical importance of Cilgerran's main feature – its two great circular towers – can still be appreciated.

Open all year. Admission charged. Wheelchair access. 3m S of Cardigan on left bank of the Teifi.

CREGENNAN

Gwynedd   SH61

This beautiful spot lies beneath the northern slopes of the Cader Idris mountain range, 1,000ft above the village of Arthog and the Mawddach Estuary. The views – of the Mawddach, Barmouth and the surrounding Snowdonia National Park – are superb.

The twin lakes of Cregennan are part of this 705-acre property, together with two hill farms and an area of mountainside. Traces of Bronze and Iron Age peoples have been found in this vicinity. In complete contrast a large bungalow on the site (not NT), built in 1897, is one of Britain's first pre-fabricated buildings.

1m E of Arthog (A493) up steep winding road, or can be approached by the Cader Idris road from Dolgellau.

CROFT CASTLE

Hereford and Worcester   SO46

Croft Castle is a testimony to the continuity of lineage: the 'famous and very Knightly family of the Crofts' have lived here, apart from a break between 1750 and 1923, since the 11th century.

Like Chirk on the other side of the Welsh border, Croft was originally a simple castle, square in design with a tower at each corner, and enclosing a courtyard.

This basic configuration, although vastly altered over the centuries, is still evident in Croft as it stands today. Its walls and towers are 14th- or 15th-century in origin, though subsequent modifications have been many. Croft's real transformation from castle to country house occurred in the mid 18th century when the Crofts sold to the Knight family. Under the influence of the 'Georgian Gothick' movement the existing central structure with two elegant bays each side of the entrance hall was built, sash windows were added, and the Gothic theme was continued within, as exemplified by the fine staircase, ceilings, many decorative features and furniture.

The fine park is unusual for being one of the few to escape the attentions of 'Capability Brown' and his contemporaries. Because it has not been landscaped, an ancient avenue of sweet chestnuts still marches half a mile across the park as it has done for 350 years, and Croft can boast some of the country's oldest oaks. In Fish Pond Valley can be seen an example of 'picturesque' gardening, a style which developed in reaction to Brown's 'natural' landscaping. The planting and the arrangement of pools and walks create blatantly contrived vistas of 'picturesque' charm. The Victorian age added the inevitable cedars, wellingtonias and pines, now all fully mature.

Open May to end Sept, limited opening April and Oct. Admission charged. Free parking. Wheelchair access. Refreshments. Signposted from Ludlow-Leominster road (A49).

DINAS OLEU

Gwynedd   *SH61*

The size of this site – a mere 4½ acres – belies its significance. The cliché 'From small beginnings . . .' springs to mind, for this was the first property to be acquired by the National Trust, in 1895.

Dinas Oleu is a cliffland site in a commanding position above the resort of Barmouth at the northern mouth of the Mawddach Estuary. Views across the estuary to Cardigan Bay and the Cader Idris massif are splendid.

Above Barmouth (A496) at its S end.

DOLAUCOTHI

Dyfed   *SN64*

An extensive site of 2,577 acres, Dolaucothi, near the village of Pumpsaint, is famous for its Roman gold mines. Gold was mined here soon after the Roman conquest of Wales and around AD 80, probably to provide bullion for the imperial mints in France and Rome.

The precious metal was mined through opencast workings and shafts sunk into the sides of the hills. A sophisticated system of aqueducts was also constructed, the courses of which can still be seen. Although exploited mainly by the Romans, the mines were worked as recently as 1939. Two short waymarked trails now serve as an introduction to this fascinating site.

Between Llanwrda and Lampeter on A482.

DOLMELYNLLYN

Gwynedd   *SH72*

One of Wales's most spectacular waterfalls, Rhaiadr Ddu, is located on this attractive 1,249-acre estate. The falls, an easy walk from the village of Ganllwyd, are reached through a patch of oak woodland – an unusual feature in these parts, for Dolmelynllyn is virtually encased by the conifer forests of Coed-y-Brenin.

5m NW of Dolgellau, on W side of A470.

DUDMASTON

Shropshire   *SO78*

Dudmaston's name derives from Hugo de Dudmaston, a knight who was given land here in 1170. A house has occupied the present site since the early 18th century. The work of architect Francis Smith of Warwick for Sir Thomas Wolryche, it was probably begun around 1695 and largely completed by the time of Sir Thomas's death in 1701.

Remodelling, carried out by Whig MP William Wolryche Whitmore in the 1820s, included alterations to the roofline with the addition of pediments and a parapet, and the building of a staircase and library.

Given to the Trust in 1978, Dudmaston is surrounded by a landscaped park. From the house, there are fine views of its 3,000 acres of farm and woodland.

Limited opening April to end Sept. Admission charged. Wheelchair access. Refreshments. 4m SE of Bridgnorth on A442.

Erddig's owners, the Yorke family, treated their domestic staff with great respect and affection, which may explain why the house has such an unexpectedly grand kitchen. Its large Venetian window and stylish archway recesses reflect the tastes of the late 18th century, when it was built. Originally it was an entirely separate building from the main house, but a linking block was built in Victorian times

ERDDIG

Clwyd	*SJ34*

Erddig must surely be one of the most intriguing of the National Trust's many properties. This late 17th-century house is unique for the insight it gives into the 'upstairs, downstairs' life of a country estate.

The house was built in the 1680s, though enlarged and refurbished soon after by John Meller, a prosperous London lawyer. Meller's expensive tastes for gilt and silver furniture are still with us today, together with an outstanding state bed in Chinese silk.

Following Meller's death in 1733, the house came into the Yorke family, remaining with them until 1973 when the property, with 938 acres, was given to the Trust. This continuity of ownership, coupled with the Yorkes' reluctance to throw anything away, has made a major contribution towards Erddig's distinctive charm and character.

Splendid though the interior may be, the house is memorable for the view it gives of the master and servant relationship. A range of restored outbuildings, for example, contains a laundry, a smithy, a sawmill and a working bakehouse. The Yorkes would no doubt approve of Erddig's current role, for they held their domestic staff in high regard, even commissioning paintings of successive generations of family servants.

The gardens are also unconventional. The Yorkes, eschewing fashion, kept them in their original form, so what we see today is very reminiscent of their look in the mid 18th century, thanks to extensive replanting.

The Afon Gamlan becomes a rushing torrent at the falls of Rhaiadr Ddu, on the Dolmelynllyn estate. The constant spray from the falls creates ideal damp conditions for the growth of many rare species of ferns and mosses

Erddig, its outbuildings and gardens represent one of the largest restoration projects ever undertaken by the Trust.

Open April to end Oct. Admission charged. Free parking. Wheelchair access to gardens and part of outbuildings only. Refreshments. 2m S of Wrexham, off A525.

FLEECE INN

Hereford and Worcester	*SO25*

This is an unusual site – a country pub in the care of the National Trust.

The Fleece Inn began life as a farmhouse in the 14th century. It was later altered during Tudor and Elizabethan times and became a licensed house in 1848. The description 'licensed house' is most appropriate, for the Fleece Inn was just that. Henry Byrd the owner, sold beer and cider from his home, a tradition continued into the 1970s by his great-granddaughter, Lola Taplin, who continued to run the Fleece Inn until her death in 1977.

Although renovated, the inn is very much as it was in the 19th century, with an original family collection of furniture and ornaments. The worn flagstones, open log fires and exposed timber walls all add to the impression of stepping into the past. It is fitting that traditional beer should be served in such an historic atmosphere, for the Fleece Inn is now leased to CAMRA, the Campaign for Real Ale.

Open during normal licensing hours. 3m E of Evesham, on B4035.

GOWER PENINSULA

West Glamorgan

The Gower Peninsula juts into the Bristol Channel to the west of Swansea. Traditionally, it is the holiday destination of thousands of people from south Wales, but much is remarkably unspoilt.

On the north coast, merging into the waters of the Loughor Estuary, are the salt marshes of Llanrhidian. These desolate acres are the haunt of wading birds like curlews and oystercatchers and are patrolled by patient, sentry-like herons. Further round the coast is Whitford Burrows, a spit composed of more salt marshes and sand dunes. Here the birdlife is more varied and there are exciting wild plants to be found.

Forming the westernmost tip of the Gower is Worms Head, a rocky headland which owes its name to the fact that its outline is said to resemble a recumbent dragon – or worm. It is a breeding ground of birds like guillemots and kittiwakes. The National Trust owns all of Worms Head and much of the great arc of sand which forms Rhossili Bay. Overlooking the bay are the windswept grasslands of Rhossili Downs, dotted with a variety of prehistoric burial chambers. On the south-western coast is the Gower's most famous prehistoric site – Goat's Hole Cave, where in 1823 a skeleton of Cro-Magnon man was discovered. The bones had been dyed red by ochre from the surrounding rocks, and this caused the remains to become known as the Red Lady.

The Trust also owns cliffs and headlands overlooking Port Eynon Bay and Oxwich Bay, as well as a narrow river valley stretching from Bishopston down to Pwlldu Bay. The little river that runs through the valley travels for much of its course below ground. Halfway down are the remains of an Iron Age fort. Inland, several areas of downland and common also belong to the Trust, and these lonely areas are superb spots for walkers and lovers of natural history.

SW of Swansea.

HANBURY HALL

Hereford and Worcester   SO96

This red brick house, built in 1701, speaks of the age of Wren. Hanbury is the quintessential English country squire's residence and still 'seems tucked away in a dreaming Midland world of its own'.

It was the home of Thomas Vernon (1654–1721), a successful barrister. In design, it was copied from the work of William Talman, a prolific builder of country houses. The front of the house has great dignity; its entrance, beneath a porch and between two Corinthian columns, is flanked by the substantial bays of the library and drawing room. Within, the hall and staircase are the most important features. The hall ceiling is painted with a representation of the four seasons, and the stairwell walls and ceiling are decorated with murals by James Thornhill, executed shortly after 1710, depicting a Dr Sacheverell (who was accused of sedition in that year) about to be dismembered by the Furies. The house is furnished with pieces brought in by the Trust, and includes 18th-century English furniture. Displayed in the Long

Dovecotes like the one at Hawford were built to preserve baby pigeons – or squabs – as a source of fresh meat

Projecting almost due west into Carmarthen Bay, Worms Head offers magnificent views at sunset. At the landward end of the headland is Rhossili, the most westerly village in the Gower Peninsula. The Trust owns considerable stretches of Gower's beautiful coastline, and much of it remains an unspoilt haven for wildlife, despite the area's great popularity with holidaymakers

Room is the R. S. Watney collection of English porcelain figures and a beautiful collection of flower paintings.

The formal 18th-century garden has disappeared beneath wide lawns, but the delightful orangery has survived.

Open May to end Sept, limited opening April and Oct. Admission charged. Free parking. Wheelchair access. Refreshments. 2½m E of Droitwich, 1m N of B4090, 4½m S of Bromsgrove, 1½m W of B4091.

HAWFORD DOVECOTE

Hereford and Worcester　　　　　*SO86*

Dovecotes were once an important element in the life of an English village, providing fresh pigeon meat in winter. This dovecote at Hawford Grange is one of the survivors from the thousands that existed 300 years ago. Sixteenth century in origin, the structure is timber framed and square in design. Access is on foot only from the entrance drive.

Open all year. Admission charged. 3m N of Worcester, ½m E of A449.

HENRHYD FALLS

Powys　　　　　*SN81*

These falls, some of the finest in south Wales, tumble for 90ft in the course of the river Llech's progress through a deep, wooded ravine. This beauty spot is located close to the edge of the south Wales coalfield – a thin seam of coal lies exposed in the cliff here. The Trust owns 26 acres of the gorge, which include Graigllech Woods as well as the falls themselves (which are easily accessible from a nearby car park).

Just N of Coelbren Junction, midway between A4067 and A4109.

THE KYMIN

Gwent　　　　　*SO51*

The views across the Wye and Monnow valleys have long been admired from this 840ft hill above Monmouth town. A group of 18th-century gentlemen thought enough of them to form the 'Kymin Club', though their weekly meetings on the summit in summer also involved 'a cold collation, and a dessert of fruits, with wine and other liquors to a certain limitation'.

In 1794 they built their pavilion, or Round House here. This was followed in 1800 by the delightful Naval Temple, in commemoration of Britain's victories on the sea. The temple, set within a walled enclosure, was opened on a summer morning in 1801, amid feasting and dancing. It is decorated with plaques commemorating 15 admirals and their most famous battles. Appropriately enough, Nelson breakfasted here in 1802.

1m E of Monmouth between A466 and A4135.

LLANRWST

Gwynedd　　　　　*SH76*

This, the 'capital' of the Conwy valley, is the home of the Trust property Tu Hwnt i'r Bont, which means 'At the other side of the bridge'. The bridge referred to is 17th century and Inigo Jones's most celebrated Welsh work. On the west bank, right beside the Conwy, stands the pretty stone house of Tu Hwnt i'r Bont, a 15th-century building which was once used as a courthouse. It was later split into two cottages and is now run as a tearoom and shop.

Open Easter to end tourist season. At W end of the old bridge over the Conwy, on main Betws-y-Coed to Conwy road (A496).

LOCHTYN

Dyfed　　　　　*SN35*

This 213-acre site, acquired in 1965, is set amongst south Cardigan Bay's most dramatic cliff and coastal scenery. A remote spot, Lochtyn attracts seals and bird life in abundance. The visitor has to walk, by steep paths, to reach the three beaches and the panoramic viewpoint at Pen-y-Badell hilltop. The Trust property also includes a farm and island.

Immediately NE of the village of Llangranog.

LONG MYND

Shropshire SO49

The name of this impressive stretch of hill country harks back to Britain's warlike past. Although firmly located in present-day England, the Mynd is an abbreviated form of the Welsh *mynydd*, or mountain. In less settled times, Long Mynd was frontier country, separating the Welsh from the English.

Ten miles long by two to four across and rising to 1,700ft, the Long Mynd is still a formidable natural barrier. Roads may now cross it, but the haunting beauty of its moorlands, ridges and secluded valleys is best appreciated on foot.

15m S of Shrewsbury, W of Church Stretton valley and A49; approached from Church Stretton and, on W side, from Rathinghope or Asterton.

LOWER BROCKHAMPTON

Hereford and Worcester SO65

This house is one of the 'grand old fathers' of the black-and-white timbered architecture so common along the Welsh border. The building dates from the late 14th century, and is in an isolated spot, so it is hardly surprising that defences were considered necessary.

Lower Brockhampton exhibits the classic features of this style of timber-framed building – plus something that is almost unique. This is a detached gatehouse, built on the edge of the defensive moat. One of the few surviving timber gatehouses, its precarious appearance suggests (quite incorrectly) that it may not be with us for much longer. The house is part of a 1,680-acre estate in a countryside of rolling hill farm and woods, dotted here and there with orchards.

Hall only open April to end Oct. Admission charged. Wheelchair access. 2m E of Bromyard on Worcester road (A44), reached by rough narrow road through 1½m of woods and farmland.

MALVERN HILLS

Hereford and Worcester SO73

Rising abruptly from the flat Worcestershire plain and the undulating, rich pastoral countryside of Herefordshire, the Malverns look extraordinarily dramatic, although they are nowhere higher than 1,400ft and are only eight miles long and one mile wide. Of these bare, grassy hills, their feet clothed in woodland, the Trust owns several small sites outright, and some 1,200 acres by covenant. The finest property is probably the 26-acre summit of Midsummer Hill, which is encircled by the ramparts and ditches of an Iron Age hill-fort. Traces of hut sites can be seen within the 19-acre enclosure of this fort, which is believed to have been inhabited from about 300 BC until 48 AD, when it was destroyed by the Romans during the invasion of Britain.

3m E of Ledbury, N of the A438.

Moated farmhouses are more often associated with East Anglia than the Welsh Borders, but this 500-year-old example at Lower Brockhampton is one of the finest of its kind in England

MIDDLE LITTLETON TITHE BARN

Hereford and Worcester   SP04

Tenant farmers would once pay their dues, in kind, to the Benedictine monks of Evesham at this tithe barn. This building, 140ft by 32ft, has been described as looking like a large church – certainly, it is one of the biggest and finest of its kind. According to the record books it was built by Abbot Ombersley between 1367 and 1379. However, experts think that it is a good deal older, possibly by 100 years. Its stone tiled roof covers a structure of blue lias and Cotswold stone dressing, with one of the two original wagon porches remaining.

Open all year. Admission charged. 3m NE of Evesham, E of B4085.

MORVILLE HALL

Shropshire   SO69

Morville Hall is an Elizabethan house, rebuilt in the 18th century with the addition of two projecting wings topped by cupolas and decorative weathervanes. The house, situated in pleasant countryside, stands close to the village church.

Open by written appointment only. Near Bridgnorth.

MYNYDD-Y-GRAIG

Gwynedd   SH22

This is another of the remote, dramatic stretches of Lleyn Peninsula coastline acquired by the Trust. The 201-acre site is located on the western flank of Porth Neigwl, or Hell's Mouth, so named for its reputation as a graveyard for sailing ships in times gone by.

The coastline rises steeply here to exposed bracken- and heather-covered slopes and an 800ft summit, site of an ancient hill-fort. Accessible only on foot, it is certainly worth the walk – especially for the views across Porth Neigwl to the distant hills of mid Wales.

W of Porth Neigwl.

PAXTON'S TOWER

Dyfed   SN51

Although celebrated as an architectural folly, Paxton's Tower was built by the banker Sir William Paxton in 1811 as a serious memorial to Lord Nelson. It stands self-confident and supremely conspicuous above the quiet, unspoilt farmlands of the pastoral Vale of Tywi. The tower is triangular, topped by a hexagonal lantern, with a tall, chimney-like turret attached to each corner.

7m E of Carmarthen, 1m S of Llanarthney.

The great tithe barn at Middle Littleton belonged to the Abbey of Evesham, and was used to store tithes – crops paid as rent to the landowner, amounting to one-tenth of the produce grown by each tenant farmer on abbey land. One of the barn's two original porches, big enough to accommodate large farm wagons, has survived almost unaltered, but the second wagon porch has now gone. The inset shows some of the beams which support the barn's great stone-tiled roof

PENRHYN CASTLE

Gwynedd   SH67

Penrhyn is a gigantic sham castle, albeit built in a beautifully executed neo-Norman style. As it stands today, the castle has not yet approached its 200th birthday. It was built for G. H. Dawkins Pennant, who made his fortune from the slate quarrying industry in North Wales.

In location, at least, Penrhyn can claim some authenticity, for the castle occupies a site which dates back to medieval times. Dawkins Pennant commissioned architect Thomas Hopper (1776–1856) to build a residence that tells us much about its first master and the heady spirit abroad in early 19th-century Britain.

Hopper was given total freedom, which extended to interior decoration and the design of much of the furniture. Within, he introduced Arabo-Byzantine elements in creating his lavish interiors, though the recurring use of slate is perhaps the most telling feature. Everywhere it is lavishly moulded into Hopper's version of Gothic decoration. The great hall is floored with it. A full size billiard table is made from it. The state bed is carved from it.

Penrhyn is an outstanding – some would say outrageous – castle. Whatever its faults, strong reactions are guaranteed.

The castle stands in splendid, 47-acre grounds with views of the coastline and mountains of Snowdonia. Penrhyn also has a collection of dolls, kept in a bedroom suite, a National Trust shop in the old kitchen, and the Penrhyn Castle Industrial Railway Museum in the stable yard.

Open April to end Oct. Admission charged. Free parking. Wheelchair available. Refreshments. 3m E of Bangor, at junction of A5 and A55.

PLAS NEWYDD

Gwynedd   SH56

In English, Plas Newydd means 'new place' – hardly an accurate description for a house with a 500-year history. The original house on this site, built by the Griffiths family of Penrhyn, dates from the early 16th century. The Plas Newydd we see and admire today can be traced from a later time – the 1750s – when two towers were added by its owner, Sir Nicholas Bayly.

These towers, in Gothic style, were of crucial influence during the rebuilding of the house which took place between 1783 and 1799. This reconstruction, largely the work of architect James Wyatt and his assistant, Joseph Potter, created the house as it stands today, an elegant building in Georgian Gothic style. The architects' craftsmanship is best seen in the 'new' entrance front on the west of the house and in the stable block.

Further alterations to the house took place in the 1930s. Externally, these amounted to cosmetic changes to the façade, amongst which was the removal of the mock battlements. More significant was the wholesale remodelling of the north wing. In the long dining room built on the ground floor is the striking Rex Whistler mural.

Although the house is of great distinction both inside and out, of equal attraction to visitors is Plas Newydd's situation, set amongst 169 acres of beautiful gardens and parklands overlooking the Menai Strait and the mountains of Snowdonia.

Open April to Oct. Admission charged. Free parking. Wheelchair available, limited access. Refreshments. 1m SW of Llanfairpwll and A5 on A4080.

The huge mock-Norman edifice of Penrhyn Castle stands amid magnificent scenery, overlooking the Menai Strait and backed by the great peaks of Snowdonia. A manor house stood here in the Middle Ages, but all traces of early buildings were obliterated when, in the 1820s, the wealthy and ambitious owner set about spending his fortune on commissioning this huge sham castle – now hailed as a rare masterpiece of Norman revival architecture

The east front of Plas Newydd, overlooking the Menai Strait. At the water's edge is a small private harbour, built at the end of the last century for Lord Uxbridge's steam yacht. He is said to have inspected the vessel every morning, insisting that it be kept constantly prepared to sail – though he never actually went on a voyage in it

The Rex Whistler Mural

Outstanding among Plas Newydd's treasures is the huge mural in the long, narrow dining room. The canvas is 58ft long, and fills the entire length of one wall and a portion of each of the two end walls. It was painted by Rex Whistler, a young artist who was a close friend of the owners of Plas Newydd in the 1930s, the Sixth Marquess and Lady Anglesey.

The painting depicts an estuary, its steep and mountainous shores echoing the view of the Menai Straits and the Welsh mountains seen from the dining room windows. But Whistler's coast is bathed in sunlight, the estuary is dotted with islands, and everywhere rise extraordinary buildings of an imaginary Renaissance city. Some features are recognisable – there is the steeple of St Martin's-in-the-Field's, the Round Tower of Windsor Castle and many other architectural references to famous European buildings. On a more personal note, the young man seen sweeping leaves in the distance is a self-portrait of the artist.

A typical visual joke of Whistler's is the arrangement in the foreground of Neptune's trident and crown leaning against the quayside wall, with wet footprints apparently leading from the sea into the room itself.

Adjoining this room is a Rex Whistler exhibition, where examples of the artist's work as a book illustrator, stage and costume designer reveal his considerable talent, and emphasise the tragic loss suffered when he was killed at the age of 39 in 1944.

PLAS–YN–RHIW

Gwynedd   *SH22*

This old manor house stands in lovely gardens on the western end of Porth Neigwl. The building is medieval in origin, with Tudor and Georgian additions. Having stood derelict for some years, it has now been fully restored by the Trust. The gardens also were reclaimed, and replanted with rhododendron and azalea, yew and fir, and even with sub-tropical shrubs.

The attractive 50-acre gardens and woodlands, which extend to the shore, are part of the much larger Plas-yn-Rhiw estate (416 acres). This includes traditional Welsh cottages, Mynydd-y-Graig (see page 95), and Foel Fawr Mynytho, an old windmill.

Open April to end Sept. Admission charged. Wheelchair access. 10m from Pwllheli on S coast road to Aberdaron.

PORTH YSGO

Gwynedd   *SH22*

This beautiful little bay, a Trust site of some 22 acres, is part of the Plas-yn-Rhiw estate. Locked away among some of Lleyn's most inaccessible cliff scenery, the small beach is reached by a $\frac{1}{4}$-mile walk from Ysgo Farm. The path leads through a sheltered valley, a place of botanical interest and rich in bird life, alongside a stream which ends in a high waterfall tumbling over cliffs close by the beach.

Reached via footpath from Ysgo Farm on Plas-yn-Rhiw Estate, midway between Rhiw and Aberdaron.

POWIS CASTLE

Powys   *SJ20*

Powis started life in medieval times as a border castle, built to bring order to the troubled Welsh Marches, though unlike many of its contemporaries it never became derelict.

The secret of its success is its continuous occupation. Powis is a successful amalgam of architectural styles from across the centuries, a combination of medieval fortress, Elizabethan manor house and 19th-century stately home.

Its square keep and stone hall, although much altered, come from its early period, as does the twin towered gatehouse defended by arrow-slits and, originally, a portcullis. The castle was much altered in the late 16th-century by Sir William Herbert, who bought Powis in 1587 and proceeded to convert it into a comfortable Elizabethan house.

The Herbert family were Powis's most influential and long-standing residents, presiding over many changes in the following centuries, which culminated in the extensive improvements carried out by architect G. F. Bodley at turn of this century.

Within the house, Powis exhibits an almost overwhelming mixture of artefacts, décor and interior design. Its treasures include mahogany and satinwood bookcases, 15th-century weaponry, a superb staircase decorated with murals, family portraits which include a Gainsborough, 17th-century Brussels tapestry, a gilded state bed of theatrical proportions and, perhaps the most ceremonious touch of all, silver toilet sets dated 1700.

Open early April and May to early Oct. Admission charged. Free parking. Wheelchair available, limited access. Refreshments. 1m S of Welshpool on A483.

ST BRIDE'S BAY

Dyfed   *SM72*

Under this overall heading we find some of the most magnificent coastal scenery in the Pembrokeshire Coast National Park. The Trust owns 15½ miles of coastline here, all located on or close to St Bride's Bay.

The property includes farmland in the south, near Marloes, cliffland near the old port of Solva, the rugged coastline around the St David's Peninsula leading to the sands at Whitesands Bay, and St David's Head.

In W Pembrokeshire in the Pembrokeshire Coast National Park.

ST DAVID'S HEAD

Dyfed   *SM72*

The old county of Pembrokeshire is rich in historic and religious influences – nowhere more so than around the tiny cathedral city of St David's, where Wales's patron saint founded his 6th-century monastery.

He was born near St David's Head, a promontory to the north-west of the city overlooking Whitesands Bay. The Trust owns 520 acres of this headland, which displays evidence of Neolithic and Iron Age settlements. Commanding views of shoreline and sea extend, on a clear day, right across to the Wicklow Hills in Ireland.

NW of St David's.

SKENFRITH CASTLE

Gwent   *SO42*

Skenfrith is a border castle, originally founded at the time of the Norman Conquest. Together with nearby Grosmont and White Castles, it forms the 'Three Castles of Gwent', a trio of fortifications constructed to control a strategic route between England and Wales.

The earliest castle here would have been made mainly of timber. Skenfrith as it now stands was the work of Hubert de Burgh, adviser to King John, who rebuilt the castle in stone between 1228 and 1232.

Hubert's bold, simple plan reflected the new

POWIS CASTLE GARDENS

At some time between 1688 and 1722 the four great terraces of Powis, each nearly 200yds long, were built on the pink limy rock on which the castle stands. The site demands an architectural solution if any gardens are to exist, and so these terraces have survived for nearly four hundred years. The castle's owners ignored fashion – even Capability Brown's plans for landscaping them were rejected. The only change has been the addition of a portico to the orangery in the 18th century. Clipped topiary, such an important feature of the original gardens, still survives, but the beds of each terrace have become the home of an astounding collection of plants (each clearly labelled).

From these terraces, elegantly decorated with stone balustrading, clipped yews, statues and urns, there is a magnificent and often reported view across the Severn valley, to the 'dramatic line of the Breidden Hills and also to the gentle chequering of fields over the vast slope of the Long Mountain'.

Known in Welsh as Castell Coch or 'Red Castle' on account of its sandstone façade, Powis Castle stands sentinel over its unusual terraced gardens. Their delightful design was commissioned by the First Marquess of Powis in the 1680s. The castle itself, continuously inhabited since it was built in the 13th century, has gradually evolved from a purely practical border fortress to a handsome and fascinating stately home

military style of the 13th century and was influenced by the castles he had seen overseas whilst waging war against Phillip Augustus, King of France. A well-preserved round keep stands alone on a mound within an enclosure, which in turn is protected by a curtain wall with defensive round towers at each corner, the entire castle surrounded by moat and river.

The castle, on its five-acre site, stands in a rarely visited, pastoral part of Gwent beside the Monnow river.

Open all year. Wheelchair access. 6m NW of Monmouth.

SKIRRID FAWR

Gwent SO31

This knoll rises above the rolling plains of the border to more than 1,500ft, and overlooks the market town of Abergavenny. From its 205-acre summit, there are views across the eastern flank of the Brecon Beacons National Park – in particular, the Black Mountains and the 'twin', though slightly higher, Trust property known as the Sugar Loaf.

3m NE of Abergavenny.

STACKPOLE

Dyfed SR99

Here, amongst the high cliffs and remote bays on the southern part of the Pembrokeshire Coast National Park, is a National Trust property of great diversity. In addition to spectacular headlands and sandy beaches, the site includes freshwater lakes, farmland and other fascinating habitats rich in wildlife.

The Trust's lands, nearly 2,000 acres in all, include eight miles of cliffside and two sandy bays – Barafundle and Broad Haven. This coast is best explored on foot by following the relevant section of the long-distance Pembrokeshire Coast Path. Walkers are rewarded with magnificent seascapes and, in contrast, the possibility of encountering one of the rare plants which grow beside the cliff.

Inland, the area is also rich in natural history, particularly at the lily-covered freshwater Bosherston Lakes (good for coarse fishing) fringed by woods. Stackpole Warren is also interesting: previously an area of exposed sand dune, the Warren now supports unusual flora, such as the curiously named viper's bugloss.

The entire property is centred around the site of Stackpole Court, an 18th-century mansion now demolished.

4m S of Pembroke.

THE SUGAR LOAF

Gwent SO21

A dominant feature of the green hills and vales around Abergavenny in the Usk valley, this extinct volcano rises to 1,955ft. The Trust owns more than 2,000 acres here including attractive, open mountainside, common land and beechwoods. The Sugar Loaf is popular walking country, with a track to the summit (approached up the west side of a farm called the Parc) and many miles of footpath.

1½m NW of Abergavenny.

The Trust owns an eight-mile stretch of the wild and beautiful Pembrokeshire clifflands around Stackpole. Pictured here is Stackpole Quay, whose harbour was carved out of a former quarry. It was one of several landing stages built in remote creeks here in the 18th century in order to keep this comparatively cut-off part of Pembrokeshire supplied with essential items like coal and building stone

TELFORD'S SUSPENSION BRIDGE

Gwynedd SH77

The Conwy estuary, still guarded by the medieval towers and curtain walls of Conwy Castle, was for centuries an effective natural barrier against east-west communications in North Wales. Thomas Telford, the engineering genius who lived during Britain's early industrial age, was the first to arrive at an entirely satisfactory solution with a suspension bridge built across the estuary at the eastern approach to the castle.

The bridge, with a span of 372ft, was built between 1822 and 1826. Its great appeal lies in its decoration. After only 150 years, the bridge seems to be an integral part of the ancient castle which preceded it by several centuries. Its mock military touches are well judged, giving the bridge an overall appearance that belies its functional, industrial origins. Interestingly, Conwy is probably the only suspension bridge to retain its original chains, their immunity against corrosive sea breezes attributable to a hot-dip in linseed oil during manufacture.

Telford's bridge, now open to coast traffic only, served well until the late 1950s, when a new road bridge was opened.

Spanning the estuary of Conwy river, at Conwy Castle.

A True Pioneer

Thomas Telford transformed communications in Britain during the early 19th century by building roads, bridges, canals and docks to a standard never before achieved. In Wales, he carried out some of his most ambitious engineering feats. His superb aqueducts at Chirk and Pont Cysyllte, for example, are masterpieces.

In 1811 Telford was commissioned to survey a route from Shrewsbury to the port of Holyhead on the Isle of Anglesey. Although his road – now the A5 – crossed the rugged difficult terrain of Snowdonia, at no point did the gradient exceed one-in-ten, thus allowing stagecoaches to maintain a regular ten miles per hour. His first important river crossing came at Betws-y-Coed. Here, he built the handsome Waterloo Bridge, decorated with roses, thistles, leeks and shamrocks. It was completed in 1815, 'in the same year the battle of Waterloo was fought' according to its inscription.

His Conwy Suspension Bridge, completed in 1822, was a prelude to one of his greatest works, the Menai Suspension Bridge – built between 1819 and 1826, it links mainland Wales with the Isle of Anglesey. One of the great monuments of the Industrial Revolution, it was the first big iron suspension bridge in the world.

Although Telford never had the benefits of today's sophisti-

cated civil engineering equipment, the soundness of his work has never been in doubt. The Pont Cysyllte Aqueduct still gives canal craft a bird's eye view 121ft above the Vale of Llangollen. The Menai Suspension Bridge continues to carry traffic to and from Anglesey.

THE WELSH BIBLE

Elizabeth I, in an Act of 1563, ordered a translation of the Bible and the Book of Common Prayer into Welsh. She was herself of Welsh descent, and in her fight against Catholicism, realised there had been no replacement for the Latin service since the Reformation, and as her Act states, English was 'not understood by the greatest number of her majesty's most loving and obedient subjects inhabiting the country of Wales. . . .'

In 1507 the New Testament and the Prayer Book were published. But, although they represented great strides in overcoming the problem of finding Welsh words to fit biblical language, they failed to create the new Welsh prose the task demanded. Bishop William Morgan, born in the humble farmhouse of Ty Mawr, achieved this, not only for the New Testament, but for the whole Bible. His translation was published in 1588, and apart from a revision in 1622, it is the Bible which is used in Welsh chapels and churches today.

Telford's bridge at Conwy

TOWN WALLS TOWER

Shropshire   *SJ41*

Shrewsbury, an historic town built on a huge loop in the river Severn, would once have been protected by both a castle and town walls. Town Walls Tower, a remnant from these medieval times, is located in the south of the town overlooking the river. Of 14th-century origin, this is the last remaining of Shrewsbury's watch towers, though throughout this well-preserved old town there are streets and buildings which still display an authentic medieval and Elizabethan flavour.

Not open. Overlooking the Severn, S of town.

TUDOR MERCHANT'S HOUSE

Dyfed   *SN10*

Tenby's medieval seafaring days as a thriving trading port are remembered at the Tudor Merchant's House in Quay Street, just a short walk from the harbour. A three-storeyed building, tall and narrow, it is furnished in authentic style with a suitable air of prosperity.

The house is a fine example of late 15th-century architecture and is particularly noteworthy for the survival of its chimneys, one rectangular, the other circular. Flemish influence can be traced within the house, on the walls. The house's fresco wall paintings

remained undiscovered until the late 1960s, hidden under no less than 28 coats of limewash. These paintings might well have been the work of one of the many Flemish weavers who settled in the Tenby area during the 14th and 15th centuries.

This well-preserved building has its original beamed ceilings, and each floor retains its original fireplace.

Open Easter to end Sept. Admission charged. On Quay Hill opposite Bridge Street.

TY MAWR

Gwynedd   *SH75*

Ty Mawr's unassuming appearance belies its stature within the firmament of traditional Welsh culture. This remote old farmhouse stands on the site of the birthplace of William Morgan, born in 1541, who was later to translate the Bible into Welsh. His work provided the basis for Welsh prose, because most Welsh literature beforehand had taken the form of poetry. His translation made a major contribution to the survival of the Welsh language, now the oldest in Europe.

Ty Mawr as it stands today dates from the 1560s, 20 years after the birth of William Morgan – later Bishop Morgan.

The farmhouse is an authentic, typical example of North Wales rural architecture, with dark, solid undressed stone walls and a slate roof. Within, 17th- and 18th-century oak furniture (on loan from the Welsh Folk Museum, St Fagan's, Cardiff) stands on a traditional stone-slabbed floor.

Open April to end Oct. Admission charged. Refreshments. 3½m SW of Betws-y-Coed.

TYWYN-Y-FACH

Gwynedd   *SH32*

The coastline of the Lleyn Peninsula is, for the most part, an officially designated and protected Area of Outstanding Natural Beauty. The Trust owns considerable individual sections, especially in the remote west where the headland and cliff scenery is at its most dramatic. Here, we have something a little different. Tywyn-y-Fach, just north of the popular little resort and sailing centre of Abersoch, is a 19-acre coastal site of sandhills with a covering of bracken and scrub.

On NE outskirts of Abersoch.

THE WEIR

Hereford and Worcester   *SO44*

Standing next to a loop on the River Wye as it slowly meanders through the English border country near Hereford, The Weir's 254 acres include a late 18th-century house (not open to the public) and riverside gardens.

The house enjoys a fine situation, perched above steep slopes which fall away to the Wye and a famous salmon leap, with views across the river to the hills of Wales.

The gardens on these steep banks are planted with beech and the London plane tree, and are underplanted with spring-flowering bulbs and autumn crocus. The shrubs and bushes here provide shelter for other plants – and prevent the gardens from slipping into the river.

Open April to early May, limited opening May to end Oct. Admission charged. 5m W of Hereford.

WICHENFORD DOVECOTE

Hereford and Worcester   SO75

This 17th-century dovecote stands tall and slightly askew, resembling a giant doll's house. Its striking black-and-white timber-framed architecture with wattle and daub infilling is the traditional building style of the area, and is a familiar sight in these parts, but for a dovecote it represents a considerable rarity.

The gabled roof is topped by what, on first impressions, looks like a chimney – in fact, it is a lantern to admit the birds. Inside are nearly 600 nesting boxes.

Open all year. Admission charged. 5½m NW of Worcester, N of B4204.

WILDERHOPE MANOR

Shropshire   SO59

Wilderhope is a house of the late Elizabethan period, largely unaltered, in isolated Corvedale on the southern slopes of Wenlock Edge. It was built in the late 16th century for Francis Smallman, who lived here until 1599.

One glimpse of Wilderhope's roofline tells us immediately of its origins. Gables and hefty

Wilderhope Manor, with its solid walls of uncoursed rubble, stone-tiled roof and long chimney stacks, has been altered little since it was built in the late 16th century. Its interior, too, retains fine examples of late Elizabethan workmanship, the plaster ceilings, in particular, reflecting the skills of the provincial craftsman of those times

THE MAJOR'S LEAP

The owner of Wilderhope Manor during the Civil War was Thomas Smallman, a major in the Royalist Army. A story is told that he was caught by Cromwell's troops while carrying despatches from Bridgnorth to Shrewsbury, and taken to his own house to be kept prisoner. He escaped through a secret door and fled on his horse, but the fierceness of his jailers' pursuit forced him off the road and over Wenlock Edge. His horse was killed, but a tree halfway down broke his fall. His pursuers assumed he was dead, and once they had left, the major scrambled up and continued to Shrewsbury.

chimney shafts rise over a stone-tiled roof. The classic Elizabethan theme continues underneath, with solid stone walls of local limestone incorporating a three-storeyed projecting porch and bays with mullioned windows.

Although typical of many country mansions of its time, Wilderhope is exceptional for its well-preserved, unaltered state.

Within the house, the initials of Francis, and of his wife Ellen, appear frequently on the magnificent plasterwork ceilings. A circular staircase, each tread made from a single piece of timber, is also original.

There is no garden, although a terrace was added in 1936, but this only strengthens its delightful air of isolation.

Limited opening all year. Admission charged. Free parking. Wheelchair access. 7m SW of Much Wenlock, 7m E of Church Stretton.

YSBYTY ESTATE

Gwynedd   *SH84*

Much of the property within this large estate (41,722 acres) has already been listed as individual gazetteer entries (see Carneddau, Penrhyn Castle and Ty Mawr). The remaining constituent part is Ysbyty Ifan, a beautiful empty upland region of hill, moorland and valley to the west of the village from which it takes its name. Bounded by the B4406 and B4407 scenic roads, the region includes the mountain lake of Llyn Celyn, almost 1,500ft above sea level.

Although located in three different parts of Wales the estate's individual properties originally formed part of a single property, the largest owned by the Trust.

S of Betws-y-Coed, on B4406 and B4407.

OTHER PROPERTIES

CLWYD

Coed Hyrddyn (Velvet Hill), Llangollen. *SJ24*
A hill above the road from Llangollen to the Horseshoe Pass and the Chain Bridge Hotel.

Glyn Ceiriog. *SJ23*
Meadow, with a mile of the Glyn Valley tramway south of Glyn Ceiriog and E of B4500. Now a public walk.

DYFED

Caerllan Farm, Cwmtydi. *SN35*
A small farm with 800 yds of coastline, E of Cwmtydi Inlet.

Kete. *SM80*
Agricultural land with a mile of coastline. Views to Skomer and Skokholm Islands. Car park. Access along coastal path.

Lawrenny. *SN00*
A hanging wood E of Castle Reach on the river Cleddau.

Little Milford. *SM91*
Woodland with three houses; access to land only by public paths. On Western Cleddau, 3m S of Haverfordwest.

Lydstep Headland. *SS09*
Cliff and coast. NT members free parking. Access from car park or by public footpath from Lydstep village. 4m SW of Tenby, 1½m E of Manorbier.

Manorbier Cliff. *SM09*
Clifftop land with red sandstone cliffs. Immediately south of St James's Church.

Mwnt. *SN15*
Coastland about 4m N of Cardigan.

Tregoning Hill. *SN30*
Cliffland and fields; views of Carmarthen Bay. On E headland of Towy estuary.

GWENT

Clytha Park Estate. *SO30*
A house, Gothic castle, parkland and two farms. Castle leased to Landmark Trust, house open by appointment only. 3m W of Raglan.

Coed-y-Bwynydd (Coed Arthur), Betws Newydd. *SO30*
Hilltop with views of Usk valley. 4m N of Usk.

GWYNEDD

Allt-y-Mor, Harlech. *SH52*
Land a mile south of Harlech, with a footpath to the sea.

Cadair Ifan Goch. *SH76*
A rocky promontory on the E side of the Conwy valley. 3m N of Llanrwst.

Cae Glan-y-Mor. *SH57*
Land on the Menai Strait in Anglesey, given to preserve the view over the strait to the Snowdon range. Also Ynys Welltog, a small rocky island in the strait near the Menai Bridge.

Cemaes. *SH39*
Cliff and agricultural land with parts of two small bays, on the E side of Cemaes Bay in Anglesey.

Coed Llechwedd, Harlech. *SH52*
Land north of Harlech with views over the bay.

Derlwyn. *SH62*
Rough heather moorland with part of a small lake. 2m NW of Ganllwyd.

Gamallt. *SH74*
Moorland with parts of two lakes. 3m NE of Ffestiniog. Access on foot only 1¼m from Ffestiniog on Bala road.

Y Maes, Llandanwg. *SH52*
Land surrounding the medieval church of St Tanwg. Access from public car park at Llandanwg.

Morfa Bychan. *SH53*
Golf course with sand dunes and seashore. 1¼m SW of Portmadoc. No public right of access over golf course.

Mynydd Anelog. *SH12*
Land of Aberdaron including some common land. Access along coastal path from Whistling Sands (not NT) where there is a car park.

Mynydd Bychestyn. *SH12*
Common land near Aberdaron between Mynydd Gwyddel and Pen y Cil; public footpath from Pen y Cil.

Porth Gwylan. *SH23*
Land on the Lleyn Peninsula, including Porth Gwylan harbour.

Rhiw Goch, Lledr Valley. *SH75*
Mountainside with views over the valley. On main road between Betws-y-Coed and Dolwyddelan.

Rhyd. *SH64*
Enclosed mountain bordering the village of Maentwrog; fine views over Tremadog Bay. Partly open to the public, except at lambing time.

Ynysgain. *SH43*
Coastland and foreshore with the mouth of the Afon Dwyfon and some farmland. 1m W of Criccieth. Access by footpath from Criccieth.

Ynys Towyn. *SH53*
Small rocky knoll giving magnificent views of Glaslyn estuary and Snowdon hills. On SE side of Portmadoc.

HEREFORD AND WORCESTER

Bradnor Hill. *SO25*
Common land with golf course on summit. ½m NW of Kingston.

Breinton Springs. *SO43*
Farm and woodland with site of medieval village. On left bank of river Wye. Access by public footpath.

Clump Farm, Broadway. *SP13*
Farmland on the Cotswold escarpment; views over Vale of Evesham. ½m SE of Broadway. Access by public footpath.

Cwmmau, Fernhall and Little Penlan Farms, Brilley. *SO25*
Farmland and woods including interesting timber-framed farmhouses. On Herefordshire and Powys border.

Knowles Mill. *SO77*
A mill in 4 acres of orchard. ½m NW of Bewdley.

Pengethly Park. *SO52*
Farm and woodland 4m W of Ross on N side of A49. Access by footpath.

Poor's Acre. *SO53*
Roadside land in Haugh Wood. 1½m W of Woolhope.

SHROPSHIRE

Lee Brockhurst, Hillcrest. *SS52*
Pasture and woodland; part of the Lee Hill. 10m NE of Shrewsbury.

Hopesay Hill. *SO48*
A sheepwalk with footpaths. 3m W of Craven Arms.

CENTRAL &
EASTERN
ENGLAND

Tattershall Castle —
visible for miles around flat Lincolnshire

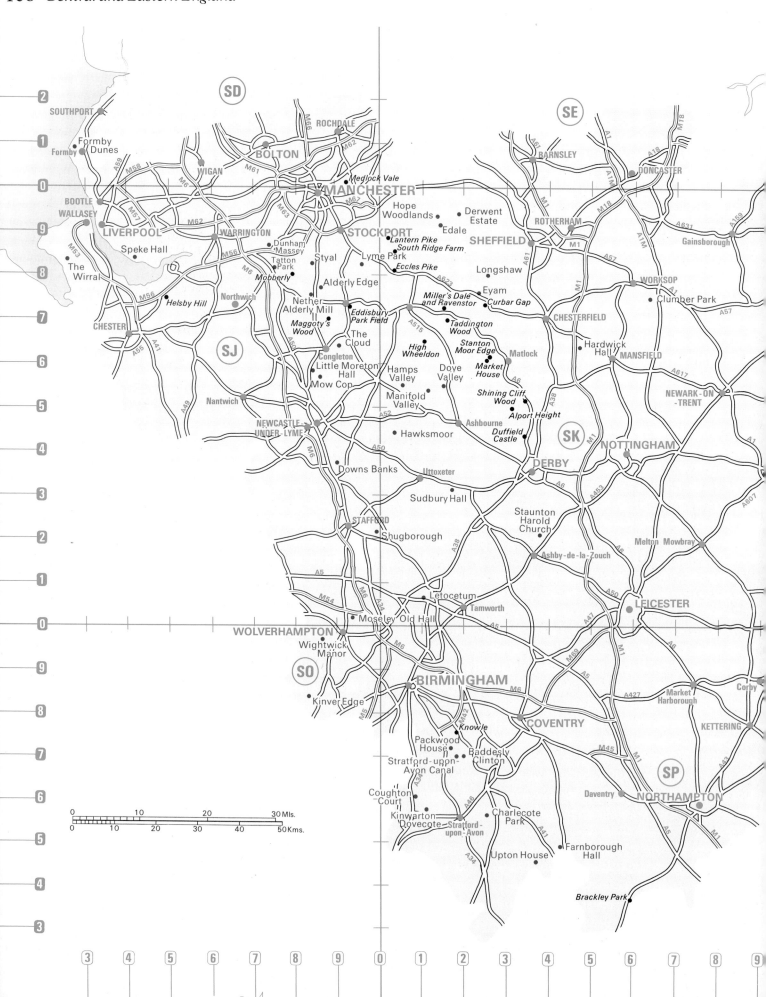

ALDERLEY EDGE

Cheshire   *SJ87*

Alderley Edge is a wooded escarpment of
sandstone around two miles long and rising to
650ft, a place of great natural beauty just a
stone's throw from the Mancunian suburbs. Yet
not so long ago, it was a busy mining area.
Copper was first mined here in pre-Roman
times. Lead and cobalt have also been extracted
from the old levels and shafts which riddle the
hillside.

The Edge is also a place of myth and legend –
hardly surprisingly, for it has been settled since
prehistoric times. Neolithic and Bronze Age
artefacts (including tools and weapons) have
been unearthed here. A beacon on the summit
of the Edge, now marked by a pile of stones, has
been lit since medieval times to signal invasions,
victories or defeats.

4½m NW of Macclesfield, astride B5087.

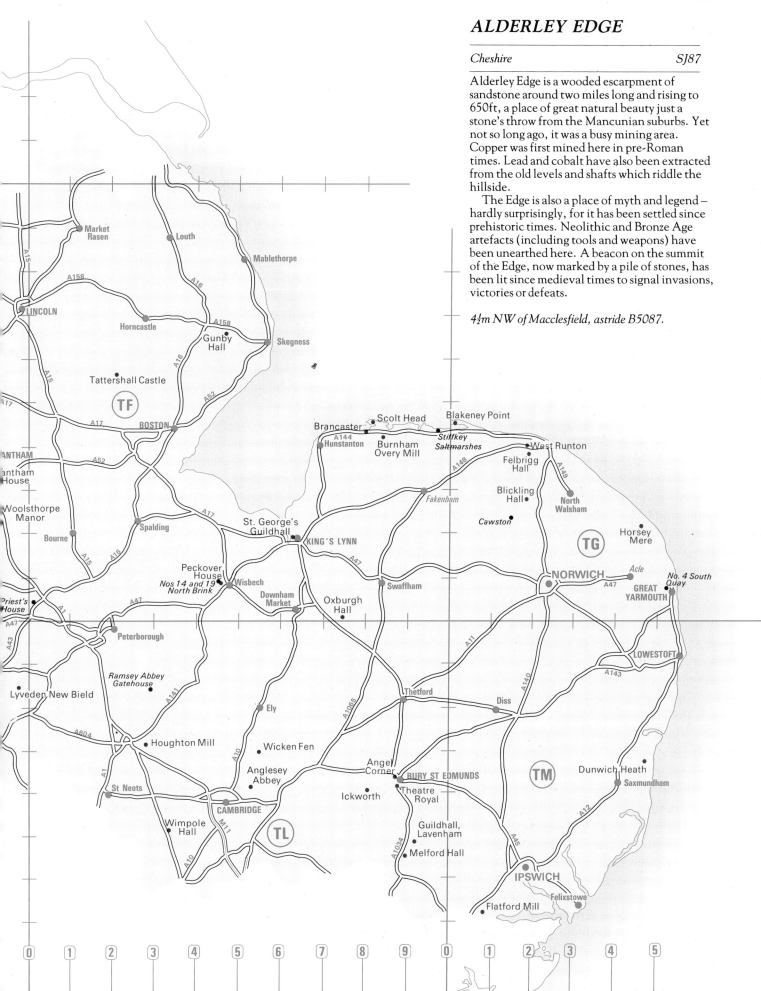

ANGEL CORNER

Suffolk   *TL86*

This historic town still retains its medieval plan, and has many fine old buildings. Amongst these is the Trust's Angel Corner, a Queen Anne house located at No 8, Angel Hill. The excellent Gershom-Parkington collection of clocks, watches and timepieces occupies the ground floor, some dating from as early as the 16th century.

Open all year. On Angel Hill, Bury St Edmunds.

ANGLESEY ABBEY

Cambridgeshire   *TL56*

Anglesey was founded in 1135 as an Augustinian priory, so in the historical sense was never an abbey. It took its name from the nearby hamlet of Angerhale (not the Isle of Anglesey, north Wales), and for the following 400 years continued as a religious house until the Dissolution in 1535.

An uneventful next 400 years are remembered only for the fact that one of Anglesey's many owners was a Thomas Hobson, originator of the phrase 'Hobson's choice'. The house's real history starts relatively recently, in 1926, when it was bought by Huttleston Broughton, later the First Lord Fairhaven.

A man of immense wealth and a dedicated patron of the arts, Lord Fairhaven transformed the old priory to accommodate his extraordinary collection of paintings, tapestries, books, mosaics, bronzes and furniture.

This collection contains pieces from ancient Egypt, renaissance Europe, the Ming dynasty and Constable's England, a range probably unparalleled at any other country house.

Yet the interior of the house, for all its glory, is eclipsed by the gardens, now regarded as Lord Fairhaven's masterpiece. He transformed a dour, difficult fen landscape into a garden described as being 'unique in the 20th century'. The 90 acres of grounds, a blend of formal and free landscaping, rival the best Georgian gardens – with the advantage that at Anglesey they have not yet reached maturity. Their imaginative conception and scale of execution are best displayed in their walks and avenues and the magnificent herbaceous garden, framed by beech hedges.

Open April to early Oct. Admission charged. Free parking. Wheelchair available, access to garden only. In Lode on N side of B1102.

BADDESLEY CLINTON

Warwickshire   *SP17*

A moated building first stood here, probably in the 13th century. The manor as it now stands dates from the time of John Brome, Under Treasurer of England, who bought the estate in

Thomas Hobson, who owned Anglesey Abbey in the early 17th century, left more than what was once an Augustinian priory. He also left his name for posterity, for from it derived the phrase 'Hobson's Choice'. A carrier, he let his horses out without giving the hirers a choice of animal

1438. Substantial improvements were made by Brome and his son Nicholas. This mid 15th-century work can still be seen, particularly in the east (the entrance front) and west ranges.

Through marriage, the house came into the Ferrers family, where it remained for the next 500 years. One of Baddesley's most influential inhabitants was Henry Ferrers 'the Antiquary' (1549–1633). He constructed the great hall about 1580 and was responsible for most of the panelling and chimneypieces.

Baddesley's next phase of development came in the 18th century. The stable and barn yard were constructed, a formal entrance courtyard added, and the south-east corner (housing the present drawing room) was built.

There followed a period of decline and neglect. Baddesley's renaissance came in 1867, when the house was sympathetically renovated, preserving its old character, by Mr and Mrs Marmion Edward Ferrers. Baddesley came to the Trust in 1980. Today, the house still retains, to a remarkable degree, the atmosphere of a medieval manor.

Limited opening April to Oct. Admission charged. Wheelchair available. Refreshments. ¾m W of A41 Warwick – Birmingham road.

BLAKENEY POINT

Norfolk   *TG04*

Blakeney is a long spit of sand and shingle enclosing a vast area of salt marsh, extending roughly north-west into the sea from the north Norfolk coast. This narrow spit runs for almost four miles in all from the mainland at Cley, culminating at Far Point.

Visitors are drawn to Blakeney Point for the wild beauty of its seemingly endless sands. Birds come too – no less than 256 species have been spotted here.

Plant life also thrives among the sand dunes, marshlands, creeks and mudflats at Blakeney. One hundred and ninety species of flowering plants have been recorded, including a type of sea lavender usually found only in the Mediterranean.

Access by foot from Cley or by boat at high tide from Cley or Morston. Wheelchair access (including to an observation hide). 8m E of Wells.

Blickling's impressive red-brick façade is approached by a long forecourt flanked by yew hedges and many interesting gabled outbuildings

BLICKLING HALL

Norfolk   *TG12*

Here is English country house architecture at its most romantic. The south front of the house, looking out across formal gardens, is a Jacobean creation. Domes, towers, chimneys, curved gables and a central cupola adorn the roofline, and the richly modelled red-brick façade contains the fine large mullioned and transomed windows so typical of the period. Blickling was built by Sir Henry Hobart, James I's Lord Chief Justice; work began in 1616.

Although the best of the Jacobean survives in the exterior, much of the interior is Georgian, for the house was considerably altered in the 18th century by a later Hobart, John, Second Earl of Buckinghamshire.

This work is attributable to father and son Thomas and William Ivory. Between 1765 and 1785, they remodelled many of the interiors – including the great hall and staircase – and rebuilt the north and west fronts. As one of their more unusual tasks, they had to design a large neo-classical room which could accommodate an equally large tapestry depicting Peter the Great, a gift brought back from Russia and a reminder of the Earl's times as ambassador at St Petersburg. Jacobean influences have not been entirely removed – the long gallery, for example, is decorated with a fine ceiling from the 1620s.

Later work at Blickling was carried out by another father and son team – Humphry and John Adey Repton. Between them, they built the orangery, enlarged the lake, improved the gardens and added a new clock tower and arcades. The Second Earl died in 1793, before these improvements were finished, an event marked by the construction of a mausoleum in the shape of a pyramid.

The gardens at Blickling are of great interest, displaying evidence of the continual attention they have received over the centuries. The formal layout, dating from the 17th century, but made less formal by landscaping in the 18th century, was re-worked as recently as 1930.

Open April to end Oct. Admission charged. Free parking. Wheelchair available. Refreshments. 3m NW of Aylsham on the B1345.

BRANCASTER

Norfolk   *TF84*

Another section of wild, beautiful north Norfolk coastline in the care of the Trust. The beach and tidal foreshore stretch for some 4½ miles, the 2,150-acre site including sand dunes, salt marshes and a nature reserve. Scolt Head lies just offshore, and is accessible by boat from Brancaster.

Access from the Brancaster beach road, which is submerged at high tide, and also from Brancaster Staithe and Burnham Deepdale. Parking charged. On N coast between Hunstanton and Wells.

BURNHAM OVERY MILL

Norfolk   TF84

This interesting group of buildings gives a fairly complete view of work and life in a village milling community 150 years ago. The attractive red-brick complex includes maltings, a miller's house, mill-workers' cottages and a barn, all built around 1795. Although once a familiar sight in these parts, few such groups of buildings survive today.

The three-storeyed water mill, the largest of the buildings, stands astride the river Burn. White-painted weatherboarded 'lucams' project from its roof; these overhanging structures contain the hoisting gear which raised the grain from ground level to storage lofts on the top floor. A look at Norfolk's milling traditions is completed by a visit to the windmill (also Trust property), built on the hill close by as an addition to the water mill in 1816.

Buildings not open, viewing from outside only. 1m N of Burnham Market.

CHARLECOTE PARK

Warwickshire   SP25

When Sir Montgomerie Fairfax-Lucy gave his house and park to the Trust in 1945, he relinquished hold on a property that had been in the Lucy family since the 12th century, a tenure almost unparalleled in England.

An older house on this site was demolished in 1558 to make way for the present building. Its master was Sir Thomas Lucy, a Justice of the Peace and Knight of the Shires. The gatehouse of pink brick, a much-decorated building with twin octagonal turrets topped with cupolas, is a survivor from his time. So too is the fine, two-storey Renaissance porch, flanked by Ionic pilasters and bearing the arms of Queen Elizabeth to mark her visit to the house in 1572.

In the main, Charlecote's exterior was rebuilt and improved between 1826 and 1867 for George Hammond Lucy. Large-scale alterations were also made inside, between 1823 and 1867, to create an interior now considered as an outstanding example of Elizabethan Gothic.

Charlecote is also interesting for the overall view it gives of life in a large country house around the beginning of the 19th century. The brewhouse, for example, still quite intact, produced considerable quantities of ale (over 4,000 gallons were stored in Charlecote's cellars in 1845). The Victorian kitchens, complete with their original utensils, and the carriages in the coach house are also worth visiting.

The grounds were improved by 'Capability' Brown in the 1760s, but here he was forced to keep the beautiful old avenues of trees, a unique compromise on the part of the famous gardener.

Open May to end Sept, limited opening April and Oct. Admission charged. Free parking. Wheelchair available. Refreshments. 4m E of Stratford-upon-Avon, on N side of B4086.

Shakespeare and Charlecote

England's most famous poet and playwright was fined, possibly flogged and threatened with imprisonment in the hall of Charlecote Park. The young Shakespeare was caught, so tradition has it, poaching deer in the park. Unfortunately for Shakespeare, the owner of Charlecote, Sir Thomas Lucy, was also the local magistrate. In retaliation the poet is said to have scribbled ribald verses about Sir Thomas on the walls of the gatehouse, an act which compelled him to flee to London, where fortune awaited him.

This story has some substantiation in Shakespeare's plays, for it is supposed he used Sir Thomas as the model for the absurd character Justice Shallow, who appears as a figure of fun in *The Merry Wives of Windsor* and in *Henry IV*. The references to a 'dozen white luces' in Shallow's coat of arms corresponds to Sir Thomas's coat of arms, of which he was known to be very proud, and to have remarked whenever they were mentioned 'and a very old coat too'. This phrase and Sir Thomas's excessive pride are both elements of Justice Shallow's character, at whom Shakespeare consistently pokes fun. Whether this story is true or not, it is a very old one, and these and other references give it just enough credibility to ensure it stays a part of Shakespeare's life story.

Mill complexes such as this one at Burnham Overy were once a characteristic part of the Norfolk landscape. The mill itself, the largest building here, was also used for malting and for storing grain

Early 16th-century half-timbered wings flank Coughton Court's magnificent Tudor gatehouse to form three sides of an enchanting courtyard. The east side opens onto the delightful gardens

CLUMBER PARK

Nottinghamshire   SK67

The outline of a vanished building, recently excavated, is all that is left of Clumber House, the seat of the Dukes of Newcastle since the 1770s which was demolished in the 1930s. Although the mansion has disappeared, the beautifully landscaped park which they created is now one of Britain's foremost country parks.

Walking through Clumber Park today, it is difficult to imagine that this was wild, featureless heathland, an enclosed section of Sherwood Forest, until well into the 18th century, when the First Duke set about building himself a great country estate. He employed Lancelot – better known as 'Capability' – Brown, the doyen of 18th-century landscape gardeners, to supervise the metamorphosis of Clumber's flat, unpromising terrain.

The park, split by its long, 85-acre serpentine lake, is a testimony as much to Brown's genius as to the Newcastles' wealth. Its woodlands and tree-lined avenues are particularly beautiful.

Clumber supports a wide variety of plant and animal life. The lake attracts many species of wildfowl; coarse fishing here is excellent – the lake is recognised as one of Britain's best for the sport. Ornithologists also find a rich bird life in the woodland, open grass and heathland within the park.

Among the old buildings that remain – the lodges, two garden temples, a Palladian bridge and the red-bricked stables, is Clumber Chapel, built in 1886 by the Seventh Duke of Newcastle for his private worship. Standing in the middle of the park near the site of the old mansion, it is regarded as a particularly good example of the Gothic Revival style.

Open all year. Parking charged. Wheelchair available. Refreshments. 4½m SE of Worksop, 4½m SW of East Retford.

THE CLOUD

Cheshire   SJ96

Rising, unannounced and dramatic, from the flat farmlands of the Cheshire Plain, this hill's poetic name is a case of justifiable artistic licence. The sombre heather, dark granite screes and uncompromising silhouette contrast strikingly with the gentler surrounding landscape, giving the hill an exaggerated importance.

The Cloud is, in fact, a lovely outpost of the mighty Pennine mountain chain. Views from its 1,000ft summit, on a clear day, extend from industrial Lancashire to the Potteries.

3m E of Congleton.

COUGHTON COURT

Warwickshire   SP06

An unswerving allegiance to Roman Catholicism by its owners has given Coughton a chequered history. The house was originally begun soon after 1518 by Sir George Throckmorton, whose family had inherited the estate in 1409. Coughton's most conspicuous feature – its great gatehouse – survives from this time. Unusually, it does not stand apart from the house, becoming instead Coughton's central feature. It remains a mystery whether or nor he intended to build, in more conventional style, a main house detached from the gatehouse. At any rate, the latter was not long in acquiring its set of wings which were remodelled, in 1780, in Gothic style.

The courtyard contains the first evidence of Coughton's troubled history. Two gabled wings, typical of the early 16th-century half-timbered style, lead incongruously to an empty space. This is the site of the missing fourth wing which, since it contained the chapel, was attacked by a Protestant mob in 1688 and later demolished. Throughout Elizabeth I's reign, although suffering fines and imprisonment, the family continued to hold secret masses and to shelter priests at Coughton. In 1583 there was an abortive 'Throckmorton Plot' to murder Elizabeth and replace her with Mary, Queen of Scots. There was also a connection, albeit tenuous, with the most famous plot of them all, when a group including the wives of those involved in the Gunpowder Plot of 1605 awaited the outcome in Coughton's gatehouse. The present look of the house was determined by the 11th baronet, Sir Charles, who had removed the Jacobean gables on the west front and added battlements by 1835.

He also restored the interior without disturbing its successful blend of influences from the Tudor period onwards. Amongst Coughton's many artefacts is, as one would expect, a superb collection of Catholic relics.

Open May to end Sept, limited opening April and Oct. Admission charged. Wheelchair access. Refreshments. 2m N of Alcester on E side of A435.

DERWENT ESTATE

South Yorkshire SK19

This 6,468-acre estate lies within the Peak District National Park, its treeless, empty moorland heights, cut by deep valleys, rising to 1,775ft along the eastern shoulder of the High Peak.

Man has, however, made his mark on this inhospitable, dramatically beautiful countryside; there are the three earthwork barrows at Bone Low, which have yielded Anglo-Saxon urns. But such obscure remnants are dwarfed by the evidence of modern man – a chain of reservoirs, built around the turn of the century, to supply Sheffield, Nottingham, Leicester and Derby with water.

The Derwent Estate lies to the east of these lakes and the river Derwent, and offers fine views of the flooded dales from the ridges of Howden Moor.

13m W and NW of the centre of Sheffield.

THE DOVE VALLEY

Derbyshire SK15

This wooded, steep-sided valley, in the foothills of the Peak District and just within the southern boundary of the Peak National Park, has been a popular beauty spot for centuries. As early as the 17th century, the 'silver shining Dove' was celebrated in the poems of Charles Cotton.

The sights he saw are still with us today, for the valley remains almost inviolate against the spread of tarmacadam and the assault of the motor car. The village of Ilam is a favourite starting point for walkers. From this point, at the confluence of the Dove and Manifold rivers, they head north through a narrow, steepsided gorge guarded by two hills – Thorpe Cloud and Bunster Hill – at its southern approach.

This is limestone country, and many of the classic features associated with this rock are on display. Reynard's Cavern, for example, is one of a series of natural caverns which riddles the hillsides. The limestone has also weathered into some bizarre shapes, which accounts for the fanciful names ascribed to the various rock features here, such as Lion Face Rock, the Twelve Apostles and Jacob's Ladder.

At Dovedale, the Trust owns a four to seven mile stretch of 1,152 acres on both sides of the valley. The Trust also owns property along the banks of the Manifold at Ilam, including 84 acres of park and woodland, 19th-century Ilam Hall (now a Youth Hostel), Paradise Walk and the Home Farm.

N of Ashbourne.

DOWNS BANKS

Staffordshire SJ93

Downs Bank is an unspoilt oasis surrounded by the industrial and urban developments of Stone, Stoke and the Potteries. Just a stone's throw away from this rural stretch of vale and bracken-covered moorland there stands, for example, the huge Wedgwood pottery works at Barlaston; yet beside the stream of Downs Banks, with only the curlew's haunting cry heard over the wind, and sheep for company, one need never suspect its existence.

1m SE of Barlaston.

The grandeur of Dunham Massey's Garden Front is captured in this waterside reflection. Its approaches open out into the grounds of a formal park. Medieval in origin, the park was already enclosed for deer hunting in Elizabeth's reign, but it was George Booth, 2nd Earl of Warrington, who not only carried out major alterations to the earlier Tudor building and its interior, but was also responsible for planting upwards of 100,000 elm, oak and beech trees

The beautiful valley of the Dove below Thorpe Cloud, where in the 17th century Izaak Walton, author of The Compleat Angler, fished for trout. Despite the well-worn pathways the valley retains its wildness and its grandeur, especially in the higher reaches. It is a haven for all kinds of upland wildlife, such as the dipper, a little bird which feeds under water

DUNHAM MASSEY

Greater Manchester   *SJ78*

By 1721, George Booth, the Second Earl of Warrington, had refurbished the interior of his family's old Tudor house and also established much of the formal park. Work on the exterior of the house continued for the next 30 years under the guidance of architect John Norris to produce the low, plain red-brick house of today. George Booth also collected Huguenot silver and walnut furniture of outstanding quality with which to enrich the house.

Dunham came into the family of the Greys, Earls of Stamford, through the marriage of Henry Grey, the Fourth Earl, to George Booth's daughter in 1736. Henry spent little time at Dunham, but the Fifth Earl added to the house some outstanding pictures collected on his Grand Tour of 1760.

In the early 20th century, the house was again refurbished, this time by architect Compton Hall, who installed the stone centrepiece and dormer windows in the south front. At the same time, extensive sympathetic redecoration work took place inside the house.

Succeeding generations of Stamfords have

protected and conserved the contents, collections and furniture. Until quite recently, most of the rooms were sealed up and their textiles carefully cleaned and stored. The benefits of such a fastidious approach are today evident in the outstanding condition of the house's contents and rooms.

Dunham Massey's 3,000-acre estate includes a fine deer park, and a well-preserved water mill, built in 1616, is one of a number of old buildings standing in the grounds.

Open April to end Oct. Admission charged. Parking charged. Wheelchair access to garden, park and outbuildings only. Restaurant. 3m SW of Altrincham off A56.

DUNWICH HEATH

Suffolk   *TM46*

This heathland of bracken and silver birch is an interesting spot for naturalists and bird watchers (the RSPB Minsmere Bird Reserve forms its southern boundary). Along the sea-front steps lead down 50ft-high cliffs to a mile long sandy beach, where the sea-fishing is reputedly good, and bathing generally safe. Inland, tracks and paths on the heath and in the birchwoods provide enjoyable walking.

S off the Westleton – Dunwich road, ½m before Dunwich.

EDALE

Derbyshire   *SK18*

The Trust owns nearly 2,000 acres of farmland and hill country in the Edale area. Among these are the 819 acres of Mam Tor and the Winnats. The former is a huge lump of Peak District landscape, rising to 1,700ft and looking not unlike a giant quarry. This resemblance helps explain why Mam Tor is also known as Shivering Mountain, so-called after the grit and shale which 'shivers' and slides down its steep western face. From the summit, once rather over-cautiously described as 'very dangerous to ascend', walkers can take in one of the finest views in the Peak District National Park. To the east are Castleton and the ruins of Peveril Castle; to the north is Edale, starting point for the tough, long-distance Pennine Way footpath; and to the north-west, the towering bulk of Kinder Scout. The summit is also interesting in its own right, as the site of an Iron Age hill-fort and ancient earthworks.

The Winnats, or Winnats Pass, is the original road from Castleton to Chapel-en-le-Frith, traversing a limestone gorge to the south of the existing A625. In this exposed, rugged country, its derivation – 'wind-gates' – seems entirely appropriate. Close to its route are the famous Blue John mines, source of the blue crystal spar unique to the area around Castleton.

1m W of Castleton on A625.

EYAM: RILEY GRAVES

Derbyshire   *SK27*

This is surely the Trust's most poignant, heroic site. In the 17th century, with the Great Plague raging, the villagers of Eyam threw up a cordon around their community, not to protect themselves but to contain the infection.

When the plague broke out here, the villagers – inspired by their rector William Mompesson – instead of fleeing to possible safety, decided to remain. This heroic decision cost them dearly, for in a few months over three quarters of the villagers were dead.

Amongst the victims were seven members of one family – the Hancocks, who died between 3 and 10 August 1665. They are buried in the Riley Graves, located on the Righ Led, a steep hillside half a mile from the village.

½m E of Eyam village.

FARNBOROUGH HALL

Warwickshire   *SP44*

Farnborough is a place of great period charm. The home and landscaped gardens, unlike many of their contemporaries, have experienced very little alteration in the last 200 years and survive largely as William Holbech, the owner in the mid 18th century, left them.

William, like all the aristocrats of the time, had undertaken a Grand Tour of Europe from around 1730 to 1745. He returned to Farnborough heavily influenced by Italian art and architecture and proceeded to remodel the old house in the style of a Palladian villa, a home fit for his sculptures and paintings by Canaletto and Panini. The magnificent rococo plasterwork in the hall and dining room and on the staircase dates from the same period.

This remodelling of the house was carried out by architect Sanderson Miller, who was also responsible for landscaping the grounds. The beautiful Terrace Walk, temple, pavilion and obelisk in the grounds were also completed around this time.

The gardens are also notable for their magnificent views, extending across the Warwickshire plain towards Edgehill, Stratford and the Malvern Hills.

Limited opening April to end Sept. Admission charged. Wheelchair access to grounds only. 6m N of Banbury, ½m W of A423.

FELBRIGG HALL

Norfolk   *TQ31*

William Windham built this house in 1620, and of his building the entrance front is a fine example of Jacobean architecture and is particularly outstanding. In the later 1600s, a new brick wing was constructed to the south. Important additions were also made in 1741 by

another William Windham who was sufficiently inspired, on returning from the statutory European Grand Tour, to undertake extensive remodelling work.

These alterations gave Felbrigg a new dining room, staircase and Gothic library – and also somewhere for William Windham to display the many treasures he had acquired during the course of his European tour. The superb Jacobean plaster ceilings in the drawing room and cabinet were, however, retained. Today, we can share something of this glittering past, for the 18th-century rooms are still much as they were during William's time.

Felbrigg's Great Wood of 600 acres was planted in the 17th century. The extensive grounds, which contain an orangery, dovecote and stables, reflect the first William's interest in forestry – we have him to thank, for example, for the beautiful chestnut trees standing in the park. Like the house, the gardens have changed and developed gradually over the years, a process which has given Felbrigg much of its quiet charm.

Open April to end Oct. Admission charged. Wheelchair available. Refreshments. 2m SW of Cromer, off A148.

THE TERRACE WALK

An immense amount of expense and labour was lavished on the landscaping of country house gardens. When the terrace at Farnborough Hall was created the effort was immortalised in a poem by Richard Jago, called *Edge Hill*, published in 1747:

Her spacious terrace, and
   surrounding lawns
Deck'd with no sparing cost of planted
   tufts,
Or ornamental building, Farnborough
   boasts.
Hear they her master's call? In sturdy
   troops,
The jocund labourers hie, and, at his
   nod
A thousand hands or smooth the
   slanting hill
Or scoop new channels for the
   gath'ring flood,
And, in his pleasures, find substantial
   bliss.

Felbrigg Hall's handsome Jacobean south range is complemented by the later buildings to the east which reflect the neo-classical style that gained popularity in the 18th century. The house stands in landscaped grounds laid out by the famous landscape gardener Humphry Repton

FLATFORD MILL

Suffolk TM03

Everyone should recognise this famous site. Flatford Mill appears in many of John Constable's paintings, reproductions of which are a familiar sight in countless homes.

The water-mill and mill house, dating from the 15th century, stand beside the river Stour. They belonged to Constable's father, and the young John spent much of his boyhood here. He first painted this idyllic country scene in the early 19th century – little has changed here since those times.

Another famous building painted by Constable is whitewashed Willy Lott's Cottage, dating from the early 17th century, which stands intact beside the mill.

Grounds and buildings not open. On N bank of the Stour, 1m S of East Bergholt.

FORMBY DUNES

Merseyside SD20

It is an unexpected pleasure to come across these deserted dunes so near the popular sands and seaside resorts of Southport and Blackpool. A gradual silting-up of the coast has led to the establishment of this area of sandy dunes and pinewoods, which is now something of a bird sanctuary – mainly for waders, shelduck and oystercatchers. Unusually, it is also populated by the rare red squirrel.

In 1776 John Constable was born in the mill house which, with the water-mill and the white-painted Willy Lott's cottage, became a favourite subject in many of the great artist's paintings. Countless amateurs have tried to emulate his skill; captured by the camera, the scene takes on an uncanny, strangely unreal, familiarity. Although not open to the public, the buildings are now used by students as a study centre

Its plant life is also unusual. Among the many rare specimens of wild flowers to be found here are some which may well have come from grain ships docking at Liverpool.

W of Formby.

GRANTHAM HOUSE

Lincolnshire SK93

A house was originally built here in about 1380. From the 15th to 17th centuries, it became the home of the Hall family and was for some time known as Hall Place.

Although the central hall originates from Grantham's earliest times and some 15th-century windows survive, the house is mainly a 16th- to 18th-century building, so it displays a mixture of styles and architectural influences, both inside and out.

Externally, its outstanding feature is the well-proportioned garden front, basically late 17th century with original mullioned and transomed windows either side of the doorway. Within, there is evidence of oak panelling from the early 1600s and painted panelling from the following century.

Once a country house, it is now surrounded by town. Its 27 acres of garden and land occupy a peaceful spot, with views of the river Witham and the parish church, in the middle of Grantham.

Limited opening April to end Sept. Admission charged. In Castlegate, E of Grantham Church.

THE GUILDHALL

Suffolk   TL94

This distinctive, timber-framed Tudor building dates from 1529, and is a reminder of the times when East Anglia had a flourishing woollen industry. The carving of rampant lions on the doorpost – the emblem of the Guild of Corpus Christi – identifies the original owners of the Guildhall.

The purpose of the Guild – to regulate the woollen trade – was short-lived, for it was soon dissolved by Henry VIII, who disapproved of its religious associations.

From then on, the building had a chequered life serving, amongst other things, as town hall, prison and workhouse. During World War II, it housed evacuees and later became a restaurant and nursery school.

With so much active service in so many different rôles, the building is inevitably much restored. Nevertheless, many interesting features still remain, including an original oriel window and carved overhang on the first floor. Beams, joists, doorways, panelling and fireplaces also remind us of its Tudor origins. On the first floor there is a museum dedicated to the history of Lavenham and the wool trade.

Open March to end Nov. Admission charged. Wheelchair access. In Market Square.

GUNBY HALL

Lincolnshire   TF46

Sir Henry Massingberd bought the small manor house of Gunby in 1640. His son, Sir William, built his hall here in 1700. The new building was designed in the style of a large town house, rectangular in shape, three storeys high with nine bays. With its rose-red brick façade, it remains a good example of the architecture fashionable during William III's reign.

In 1873, work began on the north wing, built from the main body of the house towards the stable yard.

Gunby's most admired internal feature is its elaborate staircase, built entirely from oak. The portraits by Sir Joshua Reynolds of Bennet Langton and his wife (who were associated with Gunby in the late 18th century) are also outstanding.

The extensive grounds contain a homely mixture of flowers, fruit and vegetables, with little evidence of a formal layout, which gives them a simple charm many find the chief attraction of Gunby.

Limited opening April to end Sept. Admission charged. Wheelchair access. 7m W of Skegness on S side of A158.

HARDWICK HALL

Derbyshire   SK46

Bess of Hardwick, the tenacious, colourful Dowager Countess of Shrewsbury, would be gratified to know that her house is now looked upon as one of the very best, least altered and most authentic of all Elizabethan mansions.

Hardwick Hall was built for this talented woman between 1591 and 1597. The architect, Robert Smythson, was undoubtedly heavily influenced by her in creating a house which is in many ways revolutionary. In design and decoration it is essentially English – a significant rejection of French, Italian and Dutch styles.

Hardwick's great talking point is its façade. Its symmetry is striking; its huge expanse of window area outstanding ('Hardwick Hall, more glass than wall').

The house's two-storey entrance hall, a late Elizabethan equivalent of the medieval great

THE GUILD OF CORPUS CHRISTI

The guilds were first created for religious purposes; for saying masses for the dead, administering charity and financing the improvement of churches. There were also craft guilds, formed by particular trades, which, although modelled on a religious guild, also acted as trade associations, attempting to control wages and prices and set standards of work.

The builders of Lavenham Guild Hall were clothiers, and belonged to the Guild of Corpus Christi. It was named after a holy feast day, which falls on the Thursday after Trinity Sunday. The Guild was responsible for organising the pageantry and festivities of the day, which included a procession and plays performed by members of the Guild. The Guild and the spectacle of Corpus Christi were suppressed at the Reformation because of their religious connections.

In medieval times Suffolk was heavily forested and had little available stone for building, so wood was the obvious choice of building material. By the 15th century, when the Guildhall in Lavenham was built, the construction of timber-framed houses had become a highly-skilled and accomplished process. Floors, walls and roof were built of great oak beams precisely jointed together and strengthened by curved braces to create an extremely strong framework

At the foot of the magnificent bed in the Blue Room of Hardwick Hall is a leather trunk dating back to 1727. It has royal crowns picked out in gilt studs. The set of 16th-century Brussels tapestries, acquired by the legendary Bess of Hardwick when she was mistress of this grandest of all Elizabethan houses, is named The Planets. The bed, with its fine embroidered hangings, belonged to a later occupant, Christian Bruce, whose husband, the 2nd Earl of Devonshire, died 20 years after Bess, in 1628

Bess of Hardwick

The letters ES are silhouetted above each of the six towers of Hardwick Hall, carved in stone as part of the parapet. They stand for Elizabeth, Countess of Shrewsbury.

She was born the daughter of a local squire whose family had owned the Old Hall at Hardwick for centuries. Bess, however, was brought up in near poverty. Her father died when she was a baby, and her elder brother squandered the family's wealth.

A vivacious, red-haired girl of enormous intelligence and wit, Bess found a husband when she was still very young. He was a son of a squire, and died almost immediately after the marriage. She married again, in 1547, to an elderly, wealthy civil servant. They lived happily together for ten years before he died. Her third husband was Sir William St Loe, a favourite of Elizabeth I. Four years later he died. Her fourth and last husband was also the richest. George Talbot, Sixth Earl of Shrewsbury, was one of England's largest landowners.

Bess had become a brilliant and ruthless businesswoman. She owned a glassworks, a leadworks, she was a very successful farmer and had made a fortune out of money-lending. She also had a passion for building. When the Earl died in 1590, Bess became the second richest woman in England, and Hardwick, where she was brought up in such lowly circumstances, was destined to become the grandest of Elizabethan houses, almost a Royal palace, with its own court and ceremony, and Bess as its queen.

hall, is another remarkable feature. It leads to an interior justly famous for its period architecture and contents.

Bess compiled an inventory of Hardwick's important rooms and contents in 1601 and an astonishing number remain much as they were in her day. Its unusually fine state of preservation is explained by its lack of use over the centuries, for after Bess's death in 1608 her descendants made another house – Chatsworth – their principal seat.

There is even a faint memory of Elizabethan times in the gardens, which were untouched by the 18th-century fashion for 'improvement' and landscaping. They are laid out in a series of walled courtyards, with herb, shrub and flower borders.

Limited opening April to end Oct. Admission charged. Wheelchair access. Refreshments. 6½m NW of Mansfield.

HAWKSMOOR

Staffordshire   SK04

These 307 acres, on sloping ground above the river Chumet near Cheadle, are both nature reserve and bird sanctuary. A wide variety of birds are attracted to its woodlands and open spaces, including unusual species such as redstarts, nightjars and some rarer warblers.

Rhododendrons grow in the woodlands, which contain some quite unusual trees – lodgepole pine and red oak, for instance. Specially designed waymarked nature trails, with observation points en route, have been successful innovations on the reserve.

1½m NE of Cheadle on N side of B5417.

HOPE WOODLANDS

Derbyshire   SK19

Some of England's most exposed, challenging moorland terrain can be found within this huge estate of over 16,500 acres. Lying within the Peak District National Park in the centre of High Peak country, its boundaries contain Kinder Scout, at 2,070ft the highest point in the Peak District.

Spectacular views can be enjoyed on foot or four wheels. Walkers can follow sections of the long-distance Pennine Way footpath as it crosses the lofty, but boggy, plateaulands of the High Peak. The motorist has it a little easier, for all he need do is drive the A57 Snake Road for memorable views of Glossop and the Manchester plain to the west and of Ladybower Reservoir to the east.

Grouse are a common sight on the moorlands. Curlews, golden plovers and redshanks are amongst the other birds that can be spotted.

Moorland always accessible except on published grouse shooting days. 12m W of Sheffield, 6m E of Glossop.

HORSEY MERE

Norfolk   TG42

This 120-acre expanse of the Norfolk Broads, separated from the sea by a barrier of sand dunes, is part of a large estate of over 1,700 acres owned by the Trust. Horsey Mere, a shallow broad with brackish water because of the seepage of the sea, is accessible by boat. Its reedbeds are a breeding ground for a number of marsh birds (including the bearded tit), insects and plants. These unusually saline waters also support a grey shrimp known as the opossum.

Farmland, marsh and marrams occupy the remainder of this Trust property. Horsey also has a drainage windmill, built in 1912 on the foundations of an older mill. It was damaged by lightning in 1943 and later restored, though not to working condition.

2½m NE of Potter Heigham.

HOUGHTON MILL

Cambridgeshire   TL27

There has been a water-mill on or near this site beside the river Ouse in deepest Cambridgeshire for around 1,000 years. The present mill originates from the mid 17th century; although its thatched roof has been replaced with tiles, and it was rebuilt in the 19th century, it is believed to be the oldest mill on the river. It is certainly picturesque – a large, four-storey building on an island, it is a long-standing favourite with artists.

Just S of A1123, midway between Huntingdon and St Ives.

ICKWORTH

Suffolk   TL86

This is undoubtedly one of the most unusual houses in Britain, and has little in common with its contemporaries. It was built by Frederick Augustus Hervey, Fourth Earl of Bristol and Bishop of Derry, a rich man with a passion for art and architecture. The Earl-Bishop employed the architect Francis Sandys to assist him with his creation. Work commenced in about 1794 and was not completed until 1830, long after the Earl-Bishop's death (part of the interior is incomplete to this day).

Ickworth's centrepiece is its circular block, three storeys in height, capped with a frieze on the Homeric theme and a grand dome. Intended as the Earl-Bishop's living quarters, it contains large rooms and, in the central, circular hall, a statue – Flaxman's 'Fury of Athens', commissioned in Rome in 1790 for 600 guineas – lit by a skylight 100ft above in the dome.

The Earl-Bishop was a patron of the arts, and planned to house his collection of paintings and sculptures in the two rectangular pavilions connected to the central block by outwardly

curving wings. This never came to pass, for the collection was confiscated in 1798 when the French invaded Italy and by 1803 the eccentric Earl had died of gout.

However, Ickworth is far from devoid of valuable contents. It houses an excellent selection of late Regency and 18th-century French furniture and a number of noteworthy paintings (including works by Gainsborough and Reynolds). We have the First and Second Earls of Bristol to thank for Ickworth's superb collection of silver. They were both avid collectors of pieces from some of the finest silversmiths of their time, and purchased many outstanding examples from the late 17th century onwards.

A formal garden and park, landscaped by 'Capability' Brown, contains the Albana Walk and beautiful cedar woods, evergreen oaks and redwoods.

Open April to Oct. Admission charged. Wheelchair available. Refreshments. At Hominger, 3m SW of Bury St Edmunds.

Arguably the best-known example of half-timbered architecture in England, Little Moreton Hall was planned as an 'H'-shaped house with two wings on either side of an imposing hall. Over the next 100 years, major structural additions were made including a chapel and a long gallery on the second floor. By about 1580 the appearance of the house was much as it is today, and because the Moreton family never quite recovered from the effects of the Civil War, few alterations were made to the fabric. A comprehensive inventory of the contents of the house was completed in 1654, but unfortunately only two or three items have survived

KINVER EDGE

Staffordshire   *SO88*

Iron Age man was the first of many settlers
attracted to Kinver Edge. He built a fort
covering seven acres on the summit, now buried
beneath gorse, broom and silver birches, from
which there are excellent views of Wenlock
Edge and the Clent Hills.

The Edge is remarkable for its cave dwellings.
Possibly first inhabited during the Iron Age,
these have been hollowed out of the soft
sandstone rock along the north face of the hill.
Dwellings in Holy Austin Rock were a place of
hermitage until the Reformation. People
continued to live here in the 17th and 19th
centuries – one cave, at the foot of Nanny's
Rock, has the home comforts of a chimney,
elaborate windows, and traces of plaster on the
walls – some of these houses were still lived in
within the last 30 years.

4m W of Stourbridge, 1½m W of A449.

KINWARTON DOVECOTE

Warwickshire   *SP15*

This simple, circular dovecote has a sturdy,
well-preserved look which belies its age. The
fine ogee arch in the doorway helps to date it to
the mid 14th century.

The tiled roof, with a lantern and dormer
window, protects walls which are 3ft 7ins thick.
Over 500 nesting holes are contained within the
masonry, and each one was served by an
ingenious device called a *potence*.

This rare feature still survives at Kinwarton.
Potence is French for gallows, but as applied to a
pigeon-house it consists of a tall central beam,
pivoted at the top and bottom of the building.
Attached to this rotating beam are two
horizontal supports which in turn support a
ladder. This ladder revolves close to the inner
walls, giving easy access to the nesting boxes.

*Open all year, key can be obtained from Glebe Farm
next door. Admission charged. 1½m NE of Alcester,
just S of B4089.*

LETOCETUM

Staffordshire   *SK00*

In its time, this settlement has had quite a few
names. The Romans called it Etocetum after its
Celtic name, and it later became Letocetum to
the Romanised British.

The town grew up around a posting station on
the important Roman road of Watling Street.
Its most significant remains are those of a
bathhouse, the most complete of its kind in
Britain. The excavations reveal the size and
sophistication of Roman bath-houses, with
their carefully controlled heating and sauna-like
variations in temperature.

Evidence has also been uncovered to indicate
settlement here throughout the entire period of
the Roman occupation of Britain. Finds from
this and the nearby Roman site at Shenstone are
on display at a museum on the site.

*Open all year. Admission charged. 2m SW of
Lichfield, on N side of A5.*

LITTLE MORETON HALL

Cheshire   *SJ85*

The black-and-white half timbered-style of
building is as romantically and traditionally
English as the village green, the maypole and
the duckpond. Of those that survive from the
late medieval period, none is more attractive
than Little Moreton Hall.

The house was started in about 1480 by Ralph
Moreton, but not completed until a century
later. Beyond the moat and gatehouse stands the
much-admired, and much-photographed,
gabled north front, dated 1559 on one of its bay
windows. The whole of the exterior, with its
intricate, heavily gabled roofline, displays 16th-

century timber craftsmanship at its most accomplished.

The rooms, well lit by many windows, are largely empty of furniture and contents. This, however, does allow the skills of the Tudor and Elizabethan carpenters, plasterers, painters and glaziers to be fully appreciated. Little Moreton's long gallery (added in 1570 to comply with the style of the times) and withdrawing room are just two of the many interior features which exhibit workmanship of the highest quality. There is also a chapel, dating from the end of the 16th century.

Open April to end Sept, limited opening March and Oct. Admission charged. Wheelchair available. Refreshments. 4m SW of Congleton on E side of A34.

LONGSHAW

Derbyshire	*SK28*

The rocky outcrops, woods and wild moorlands around Hathersage and Nether Padley may seem a million miles removed from civilisation. Yet Sheffield is only a 15-minute car journey away from this dramatic, and sometimes bleak countryside along the eastern border of the Peak District National Park.

The Trust owns over 1,000 acres of land here along either side of Burbage Brook as it tumbles down from the high moor through a steep valley into the river Derwent. Walkers are rewarded with fine views from the ridges above the Burbage and Derwent of the valleys below, and of the High Peak beyond.

1–3m SE of Hathersage on S side of A625.

LYME PARK

Cheshire	*SJ98*

This house, set in a high, moorland park once famed among huntsmen for its breed of red deer, dates from around 1550, when Sir Piers Legh VII decided to replace the old medieval hall-house with a Tudor mansion. Few external features now remain from this house, although the imposing Tudor gatehouse in the entrance front is an exception.

Major alterations came in 1720, when Peter Legh commissioned the architect Giacomo Leoni, an exponent of the classical Palladian style, to give the old house a facelift. He concentrated on the south front, which overlooks the lake and moorland. His towering Ionic portico, surmounted by giant representations of Neptune, Venus and Pan, is regarded as one of the most ambitious exercises in Palladian architecture in Britain. Early in the following century, Thomas Legh brought in Lewis Wyatt to carry out further alterations, including the addition of the tower above the south front and the dining room.

Not everything from the Elizabethan era has been swept aside. Within the house there is a fine, 120ft-long gallery and a drawing room, both decorated with Elizabethan wainscoting and beautifully-carved stone overmantels.

Sixteenth-century styles mix happily with Leoni's later alterations to the interior. His work is at its most undiluted and impressive in the entrance hall, grand staircase and saloon. This latter room, possibly the most accomplished in the house, has carvings attributed to Grinling Gibbons.

House open end March to end Oct. Park and gardens open all year. Admission charged. Wheelchair access to park and garden only. Refreshments. W outskirts of Disley, S side of A6.

LYVEDEN NEW BIELD

Northamptonshire	*SP98*

This roofless shell of a house is, indirectly, a victim of the Gunpowder Plot. It was never finished because the family of its owner, Sir Thomas Tresham, became involved in the ill-fated plot to blow up Parliament.

Sir Thomas's fierce Catholicism had already landed him in trouble before he started this house in 1600. His adherence to the faith and his interest in architecture are combined in this most fascinating of sites. He wanted to express his religion in bricks and mortar by constructing a dwelling place symbolic of the Passion.

Although Sir Thomas employed architect Robert Stickells to assist him, there can be no doubt where the true inspiration came from. The house was built in the shape of a cross, Sir Thomas taking great care to incorporate into his design emblems and repetitive measurements, all of which had a strong symbolic significance.

The deserted house stands alone in a field, its isolation and abandoned air giving it a compelling sense of mystery.

Open all year. Admission charged. 4m SW of Oundle.

The main entrance to Melford Hall shows original plain, unpretentious mid-Tudor decoration influenced by the Roman Renaissance

Now isolated and abandoned, Lyveden New Bield occupies land which recent excavations established was once a flourishing village

MELFORD HALL

Suffolk   *TL84*

This attractive manor house from the late 16th century still exudes an air of self-satisfied prosperity. It was built by Sir William Cordell, a successful lawyer who became Speaker of the House of Commons and Master of the Rolls. He started the house in 1554 and on its completion in 1578 entertained Queen Elizabeth I here to 'suche sumptuous feastings and bankets as seldom in ani parte of the worlde there hath been seen afore'.

The house was built of red brick with stone decorations. Although later altered in plan from an enclosed courtyard (by the removal of the gatehouse wing) to an open U-shape, much of the original exterior remains untouched. With its decorations of turrets, pinnacles, cupolas and chimneys, it is looked upon as an excellent and typical sample of a late Tudor and Elizabethan manor house.

The house was bought by the Parker family in 1786. A family of distinguished seamen, they decorated the house with naval relics, among them a rare collection of Chinese porcelain captured from a Spanish galleon in the 18th century.

Melford's rooms, unlike its façade, reflect change and continual habitation over the centuries. One of them is now known as the Beatrix Potter Room. The authoress visited Melford Hall on many occasions, and her paintings of the house and grounds can be seen in her room.

Limited opening April to end Sept. Admission charged. Wheelchair available. Refreshments. In Long Melford on E side of A134.

MOSELEY OLD HALL

Staffordshire   *SJ90*

This house is a famous hiding place. King Charles II, on the run after the disastrous Battle of Worcester in 1651, hid here for two days and a night.

Moseley Old Hall, Elizabethan in origin, would originally have been half timbered. Its plain walls now give the impression of the 19th rather than early 17th century; in the 1870s the decaying original façade was covered in brick and the Elizabethan windows replaced.

The original situation of the house would also have been different. When first built, it stood in a remote part of the Staffordshire countryside. Today, it looks out across the suburbs of Wolverhampton.

The house was built around 1600 by the merchant Henry Pitt. We have to look inside Moseley Old Hall for evidence of these early times. Much of the original panelling and timber framing, for example, is still visible. The secret hiding place, designed to shelter Catholic priests but no doubt also used by the fugitive king, can also be seen. This hiding place adjoins a first floor bedroom which still contains the

FAREWELL TO A KING

After the defeat of the Royalist forces at the Battle of Worcester on 3 September 1651, Charles II's flight led him eventually to Moseley Old Hall. Here Thomas Whitgreave hid him from Parliamentary soldiers in a priest's hole. Two days later Charles and Whitgreave said their farewells at the orchard style:

'. . . of which, I acquainted his majestie, hee sent me for my mother to take leave of himm; who bringing with her some raysings, almonds and other sweet meats, which shee presented to himm, some whereof he was pleased to eat, and some took with him. Afterwards, wee all kneeling down, and praying Almighty God to bless, prosper and preserve him, hee was pleased to salute my mother, and gave her thanks for his kind entertainment, and then . . . saying if itt pleased God to restore him, hee would never be unmindful of us, hee took leave . . .'

Five weeks later Charles reached the safety of the Continent.

THE MANIFOLD AND HAMPS VALLEYS

Staffordshire   *SK15*

The waters of the Manifold and Hamps rivers eventually meet with those of the Dove at Ilam. Although these two little rivers are not as well-known as the Dove, they are just as attractive. The Trust owns a number of sites along these two rivers.

The Manifold winds its way in tight loops through rocky gorges and outcrops such as Ape's Tor and Beeston Tor. The caves which disappear into its valley sides have yielded evidence of Roman and Anglo-Saxon settlement.

The Hamps, which joins the Manifold at Beeston Tor, means 'summer-dry' – a giveaway clue for anyone trying to work out the nature of the underlying rock. Both the Hamps and Manifold are known to 'disappear' in the dry summer months. This is a common enough feature in limestone country in the drier months, when a river, reduced in volume, will flow underground through pot holes and passageways in the porous rock, only to reappear downstream. In this case, the waters of the Manifold and Hamps re-emerge near Ilam Hall.

W of Alstonfield.

four-poster bed in which King Charles slept.

The small garden and orchard have been restored to how they may have looked in the 17th century.

Limited opening March to end Nov. Admission charged. Wheelchair access. Refreshments. 4m N of Wolverhampton.

MOW COP

Cheshire and Staffordshire SJ85

Mow Cop Castle sits on top of this rocky escarpment, 1,091ft above sea-level and commanding extensive views across the flat lands around Congleton. It never saw active service, for this is a sham castle, deliberately built in ruinous style in 1750 by Randle Wilbraham. The castle's suitably romantic profile astride the rough ground at Mow Cop's summit must have satisfied Wilbraham as he viewed it from neighbouring Rode Hall.

Mow Cop also has interesting religious associations. Here, on 31 May 1807, an open-air prayer meeting was held, lasting twelve hours, which led to a revival of the non-conformist religion and the establishment of Primitive Methodism.

5m S of Congleton, 1m SE of Mow Cop station.

NETHER ALDERLEY MILL

Cheshire SJ87

There was a mill at Nether Alderley as early as 1290, though no trace of a building that early remains. The present mill has changed little in appearance since it was built in the 16th century. Its red sandstone walls, although over 400 years old, are in superb condition, but the original mullioned windows have been replaced.

Five reservoirs were constructed above the mill to give the small stream the capacity to power the machinery. Originally there was only one reservoir to be replenished by the stream. After a night's fill, the miller could draw enough water off for a normal day's work. The mill is built against the dam of this reservoir, which explains its unusual appearance. This is accentuated by the long slope of the stone roof broken by four dormer windows.

The Elizabethan oak woodwork is the main feature inside, and all the posts and roof framing, with their numbered joints, are original. The machinery would also have been made of wood, but this has long worn out. The present machinery dates from the 1870s, and has been restored to working order.

Open July to Sept, limited opening April, May, June and Oct. Admission charged. 1½ S of Alderley Edge, on E side of A34.

STANDING ON THE FENCE

Packwood House was owned by John Fetherston during the Civil War years. He was unable to make up his mind about whom he should support during the struggle, as he reports in this letter to his brother:

'Good Brother – I am in a great distraction concerning my armour (being altogether to satisfy myself in judgement and conscience what I do) by reason of the general commands of the King and Parliament; my protestation puts me in mind that I am bound in conscience to serve both, and yet there seems now a very great difference between them; which I humbly desire Almighty God, if it be His Will, may be peacably composed and settled for the good of this throne and kingdom.'

It appears he never did make up his mind, because in 1642 General Henry Ireton, Cromwell's commander, slept at Packwood before the Battle of Edgehill, and in 1651 Charles II took refreshment here after his defeat at the Battle of Worcester.

Warwickshire SP17

Packwood probably began life as a modest farmhouse some time between 1556 and 1560. This original building, with its characteristic pointed gables and chimney stacks, now forms the main part of the house. It is also a timber-framed construction, though the external timbers have been rendered over. Additional building took place around 1670, and this later work is easily identified by the plum-coloured Staffordshire brick that was used.

The inside of the house is much altered, though it is still regarded as a fair example of domestic Tudor architecture. Most of the remodelling has taken place this century, when flooring and panelling from other old timber houses was brought to Packwood.

Packwood's great glory, though, are its gardens, particularly the carefully tended Yew Garden. Mid 17th century in origin, the Yew Garden is said to represent 'The Sermon on the Mount'. A single large yew tree stands on top of 'The Mount', close to twelve other yews – 'The Apostles' – and four larger trees representing 'The Evangelists'. Further away, a group of smaller trees form 'The Multitude'. It takes three men a month to prune them. The 113-acre grounds also contain woodland and an attractive flower garden with terraced herbaceous borders and walls which contain unusual 'bee-boles', niches in which bee-hives were kept.

Open April to Sept, limited opening Oct. Admission charged. Wheelchair access. 2m E of Hockley Heath (on A34), 11m SE of central Birmingham.

PECKOVER HOUSE

Cambridgeshire TF40

This elegant Georgian mansion stands beside the river Nene, one of a series of such houses near the centre of town. It was built in 1722 and later acquired by Jonathan Peckover, a prosperous East Anglian Quaker who was the co-founder of the local Wisbech bank.

The exterior is typically Georgian, well proportioned and understated. This is in direct contrast to the elaborate, opulent interior. Every room is panelled, with Georgian fireplaces and carved overmantels. The wealth of rococo decoration in plaster and wood is particularly attractive; so too is the staircase, with its mahogany rail and rich plaster decorations.

The garden layout has survived from Victorian times, with summerhouses, beds, borders and evergreens. Three orange trees in the orangery still give fruit, even though they are rumoured to be 300 years old. The original 18th-century stable block, with its collection of harnesses, still stands in the back yard.

Open early April to mid Oct. Admission charged. Wheelchair access. Refreshments. On N brink of river Nene, Wisbech.

Blending perfectly with its craggy surroundings, Mow Cop is architecturally little more than an artificial ruin; an elaborate sham built for its aesthetic value in the 18th century. But strangely enough, this rich man's folly was to become a place of worship and pilgrimage during the 19th and 20th centuries, when 70,000 people at one time were seen to flock to Mow Cop's 'Holy Mount' to worship and give thanks on the centenary of the birth of their austere religion – Primitive Methodism

An 18th-century wrought iron gate leads into the famous Yew Garden at Packwood House. Originally set out by John Fetherston, probably between 1650 and 1670, the garden is thought to represent The Sermon on the Mount. Crowning what is thought of as 'The Mount', and reached by a spiral path, is a single yew tree known as 'The Master' or 'The Pinnacle of the Temple'. It is probable that this tree and the 12 trees on the raised terrace formed part of John Fetherston's original plan

OXBURGH HALL

Norfolk TF70

This picturesque house is reminiscent from some angles of a medieval castle, from others of a comfortable country manor. Its debt to medieval military architecture is the magnificent gate-house, protected by octagonal turrets rising 80ft from the waters of the moat which surrounds the house. It was built with a drawbridge, which was replaced by a more functional but less romantic bridge of 1710.

The hall was begun in 1482 by Sir Edmund Bedingfeld whose family has lived here ever since. Originally built around a courtyard, the house has been considerably altered over the centuries, though the great gatehouse remains much as it was.

The neo-classical saloon dates from the late 18th century. In the 19th century, the house received the attentions of the architect Pugin. He was evidently most impressed with the 'very perfect shape' of the gatehouse, for he left it unaltered, concentrating on the remainder of Oxburgh. By adding battlements and decorated chimneys he kept the medieval appearance of the place, but remodelled the interior to create dark, richly furnished rooms, which contrast strongly with the lofty rooms of the gatehouse.

From the roof of the gatehouse is a splendid view of the formal French knot garden, laid out in 1845.

Open early April and May to end Oct. Admission charged. Wheelchair available. Refreshments. 7m SW of Swaffham on S side of Stoke Ferry road.

ST GEORGE'S GUILDHALL

Norfolk   TF62

The guildhall dates from the early 15th century (probably 1410–20) following the founding of the Guild of St George in 1736. The Great Hall, 101ft long by 29ft wide, on the upper floor, is still covered by its original roof.

The guildhall has a varied and unusual history. Following the disbandment of the guilds in 1547, it became a courthouse, corn exchange, public meeting place, weapons store, granary and warehouse.

Its closest affiliations, though, have been theatrical. The earliest recorded performance took place here in 1442, and for some centuries theatrical productions continued to flourish on the guildhall's stage; Shakespeare himself is said to have performed here. This all culminated, in 1766, in the construction of a Georgian theatre within the hall. This has been reconstructed, with seating for 367, and is now used for concerts, recitals and performances, and an annual Festival of the Arts.

Open all year. On W side of King Street, close to the Tuesday Market Place, King's Lynn.

SCOLT HEAD

Norfolk   TF84

This island is the most northerly point on the remote north Norfolk coast. The many seabirds which can be seen here include redshanks and greenshanks, oystercatchers and gannets. Particularly populous are the sandwich terns, which breed here in larger numbers than anywhere else in England.

The nature reserve at Scolt Head also supports an interesting marine flora and insect life. Perhaps because it is only accessible by boat (from Brancaster Staithe and Burnham Overy Staithe), this beautiful expanse of sand dune, salt marsh and shingle is the least-visited of Norfolk's nature reserves.

3m N of Burnham Market 1½m N of A149.

Scolt Head seen from Brancaster sands across Norton Creek, the narrow tongue of water which separates this paradise for bird-watchers and botanists from the Norfolk mainland

The Birth of an Architectural Style

Shugborough's grounds are dotted with a bizarre range of structures, some frivolous, some historically significant. Of prime importance are the three neo-Grecian monuments which stand in the park. These were designed by James Stuart – otherwise known as 'Athenian' Stuart – in the mid 18th century and were among the first to be built in this style in the country.

James Stuart returned from Greece in 1775, fired by the Hellenic style of building of which he had made a long and detailed study. Through his writing and his work, he soon established a new, hybrid style of architecture, based on the Greek idiom, which was to remain popular for the next 100 years.

Stuart's most imposing piece in Shugborough's park is the Triumphal Arch, a copy of the Arch of Hadrian in Athens. It was begun late in 1761, but its patron, Admiral Anson, died in the early stages of its construction. The arch then became a memorial to him and his wife, with commemorative sculptures by Peter Scheemakers.

The Tower of the Winds, completed about 1765, was intended as a reproduction of the Horlogium of Andronikos Cyrrhestes in Athens. Its aspirations failed to impress at least one visitor, the

An idyllic corner of the grounds at Shugborough. The Chinese House was completed in 1747, soon after Admiral Anson returned from his round-the-world voyage, which had included a stay in Canton. The ironwork bridge leads to an island on which stands a monument reputed to commemorate the cat which accompanied the admiral on his voyage

SHUGBOROUGH

Staffordshire   SJ92

Although described as a late 18th-century house, Shugborough was begun in 1693. The Anson family – later the Earls of Lichfield – owned this estate for over 300 years from its purchase in 1624, by the prosperous Staffordshire lawyer William Anson, until its acquisition by the Trust in 1966. The present

Earl still lives at Shugborough.

The late 17th-century three-storeyed brick house was inherited in 1720 by Thomas Anson. He greatly enlarged Shugborough by adding flanking, bow-fronted pavilions which were linked to the original central block by single-storey buildings. The delightful plaster ceilings of the dining room and library by Vassali also date from this period. He also devoted his attention to the park, which he decorated with classical temples and monuments.

This was all made possible by his younger brother, George, Admiral Anson the Circumnavigator. A four-year voyage around the world had made him rich and famous, and after his death, brother Thomas inherited his fortune, largely accrued from the capture of a Spanish treasure ship.

The next important building phase came after 1790, when Samuel Wyatt was commissioned by the First Lord Anson to carry out extensive remodelling. Among his additions is the Ionic portico to the entrance front, extending across the full width of the central block. The best of his interior design can be seen in the saloon and red drawing room – the latter especially, with its superior plasterwork by Joseph Rose.

Although most of Shugborough's contents were sold in 1842 by the 'extravagant and imprudent' First Earl of Lichfield, the Second Earl compensated for this by being a collector of fine French furniture. It is thanks to him that the house still contains so much to interest the visitor. His collection includes many excellent 18th-century pieces. Also on display is an interesting range of Chinese artefacts – including mirror pictures and a china service – acquired by Admiral Anson during his travels.

A mid 18th-century stable block, connected to the south end of the house, now houses a county folk museum. At Wyatt's Farm Park, also in the estate, rare breeds of livestock are once again being reared.

Open mid March to mid Oct. Admission charged. Refreshments. Free parking. Wheelchair available. 5½m SE of Stafford on A513.

redoubtable Dr Johnson. Prompted perhaps by his dislike of Admiral Anson, he irreverently wrote:

I praise the grateful wit which this bestows
A temple for the winds by which he rose.

On a small hill overlooking the river Sow is the Lanthorn of Demosthenes, modelled on the Choragic Monument of Lysicrates in Athens. Built between 1764 and 1771, it differs very little from the fourth-century original.

Shugborough's gardens – as distinct from its park – also contain a number of intriguing monuments, but the three described above are unique as an illustration of the birth of an architectural style.

SPEKE HALL

Merseyside   SJ49

Although begun in about 1490, when Sir William Norris built what is now its oldest section, the southern range, it was not until the late 16th century, after his son and grandson had made additions, that this delightful half-timbered building, decked out in traditional black and white, took on its present shape of four wings ranged round a cobbled courtyard, where two ancient yew trees grow. The 17th and 18th centuries passed Speke by, and today it looks much as it did in the reign of Elizabeth I.

Within the house, a point of interest is the modification made to the great hall in 1560, when an ambitiously-designed western bay and overpowering chimney piece were added – an Elizabethan attempt at baronial Gothic. In essence, though the interior is little altered. The

16th-century plasterwork is particularly well preserved; decorative, Flemish-style features abound; and the furnishings (which include Mortlake tapestries), although mainly introduced into the house in the 19th century, are largely 17th-century.

Open all year. Admission charged. Wheelchair available. Refreshments. On N bank of the Mersey, 8m SE of Liverpool centre.

STAUNTON HAROLD CHURCH

Leicestershire   SK32

Behind the inscription on the west door lies the sad story of Staunton Harold Church. It reads: 'In the year 1653 When all things Sacred were throughout ye nation Either demolisht or profaned Sir Robert Shirley, Baronet, Founded this church; Whose singular praise it is To have done his best things in ye worst times . . .'

On reading the inscription, it is not difficult to see why Sir Robert, a staunch Royalist who was not afraid to proclaim his faith, incurred the wrath of Oliver Cromwell. As a direct consequence of building his church with England in the grips of Civil War, poor Sir Robert soon found himself in the Tower of London where he died, only 27 years of age.

He leaves us with a superb church of grand, Gothic design. Staunton Harold is little changed, externally and internally. Within, the magnificently carved woodwork survives complete, together with a very early English-built organ.

Open April to end Oct. 5m NE of Ashby-de-la-Zouch.

STRATFORD-UPON-AVON CANAL

Warwickshire   SP17

This canal was built between 1793 and 1816 to link Stratford with the Grand Union Canal and the Worcester-Birmingham Canal. It was built to allow the exchange of coal from the prosperous Midlands for corn from the decaying agricultural areas around Stratford. The Trust now owns the southern section, between Kingswood Junction (on the Grand Union) and the Royal Shakespeare Theatre in Stratford.

This 13½-mile section, with 36 locks, 26 cast iron bridges and 3 iron aqueducts, is an important link between the river Avon systems, the Grand Union Canal and the Midland Waterway Cruising network. It was leased to the Trust in 1960 and following much restoration work was reopened to craft in 1964, when the canal became Trust property. It offers the best way of seeing Shakespeare's peaceful and rural country.

S from Kingswood junction to the Memorial Theatre garden basin in Stratford.

STYAL

Cheshire   SJ88

Samuel Greg built his mill here, beside the river Bollin, in 1784. Shortly afterwards, buildings were added to house the workers, creating an unusual, self-contained community, consisting simply of a mill, manager's house, workers' cottages and apprentice house.

By 1820, Greg's workforce had grown from 150 to 450. Fascinating records survive from these times, telling us of the conditions of employment (the apprentices, for example, had to work from 5.30am to 8pm, though they did receive the benefits of education and regular medical checks).

The old mill house, known as Quarry Bank Mill, is now a working museum of the cotton textile industry. The industrial and the rural coincide at Styal – this pleasant 252-acre property includes a country park, woodland and quiet riverside.

Open all year. Limited opening Dec to end Feb. Admission charged, refreshments. 1½m N of Wilmslow off B5166, 2m from M56, exit 6.

SUDBURY HALL

Derbyshire   SK13

This house is largely the work of George Vernon, who inherited, in 1659, an estate which had been in his family since 1513. He soon set about rebuilding the old manor house, and over the next 20 years created Sudbury Hall, a brick, E-shaped house with the hipped roof and cupola of a typical Caroline house, which also displays many Jacobean features, such as the style of the brickwork and windows.

The house is remarkable in many ways, not least for its state of preservation. Although threatened with all sorts of unsympathetic

Quarry Bank Mill, the village and estate, were presented to the National Trust in 1939 by Alec Greg, the great, great grandson of the mill's founder. An independent Trust has now been formed to develop Quarry Bank Mill as a study centre for the cotton industry. Five generations of the Greg family were involved in the manufacturing of cotton, and the mill stands as a symbol of their labours, putting the cotton industry in its place in the social and economic history of the north-west of England

Amid the beautiful scenery of north-west Leicestershire, Staunton Harold Church is set on smooth, green lawns above two sweeping lakes. Guarded by giant cedars, the church, dedicated to the Holy Trinity, at first glance gives the impression of a medieval building. The marks of many different masons have been uncovered here, though the identity of the original architect has not been established. Staunton Harold Church was one of the few churches to be built between the outbreak of the Civil War and the Restoration

remodelling in the 18th and 19th centuries, it survives virtually intact. The only 19th-century modification involved the service end of the house and the addition of an east wing, now a delightful Museum of Childhood.

The lavish style of the Restoration is seen in the richly decorated interior. Local craftsmen were initially employed, though the finest work comes from the celebrated London artists whom Vernon subsequently called in. The magnificent plasterwork ceilings are a testament to the stuccowork skills of Bradbury and Pettifer. These are at their most ornate in the drawing room, which also contains beautiful carvings by Grinling Gibbons. Edward Pearce's wainscot and carvings add to the grandeur of the saloon, though Pearce's finest work is undoubtedly the staircase. The hand of the artist Louis Laguerre is also to be seen in the Baroque ceiling paintings and murals.

The state apartments look out over gardens that have changed a great deal over the centuries. Sudbury's 170 acres contain a lake and deer park (late 18th-century) and 19th-century terraces.

Open April to end Oct. Admission charged. Wheelchair access. Refreshments. On A50, 6m E of Uttoxeter.

TATTERSHALL CASTLE

Lincolnshire TF25

It is difficult to miss Tattershall Castle. Its great tower rises 100ft above the flat Lincolnshire plain and is visible for miles around. This imposing keep, together with its double moat, is almost all that is left of an extensive castle, built between 1434 and 1445 by Ralph Cromwell, Treasurer of England.

The castle walls have long since disappeared, victims of decay when Tattershall was abandoned in the late 17th century. Its surviving tower, though, is an important and significant structure, for in architectural terms it represents a break with tradition.

Tattershall was built in the more peaceful late medieval period, when comfort rather than security began to dictate the shape of the great country houses. For all its allusions towards medieval military architecture, Tattershall's great keep is, in essence, a country house. An early and particularly fine example of the craft of the East Anglian brickworker, it rises through four storeys to a roof gallery, with a hexagonal tower at each corner. The large windows in each side are an indication that Tattershall was never seriously intended to be a fortress.

Open all year. Admission charged. Wheelchair access. 3½m SE of Woodhall Spa.

TATTON PARK

Cheshire SJ78

The Egerton family had owned the Tatton estate for 200 years before they came into a great fortune in the 18th century. With this unexpected inheritance William Egerton was able to extensively rebuild the old mansion. The acclaimed architect Samuel Wyatt built the western half, and after both he and his patron were dead, his nephew Lewis Wyatt completed the eastern half for William Egerton's son, Wilbraham. Only the dining room survives from the original house. The result is an elegant, unexceptional neo-classical house, richly furnished and decorated.

The Fourth Lord Egerton, however, was exceptional, and it is he who gives Tatton Park much of its interest. He was the last of his line, and died in 1958.

During his long life he was a pioneer motorist, he won his flying certificate in 1910, he lived with a tribe in the Gobi desert, he farmed in Kenya and assisted in the early development of radio. In the Tenants' Hall, his love of hunting is forcibly expressed – the walls are lined with the heads of his victims shot on his world-wide travels. At the age of 81 he travelled to India to hunt tiger.

The house stands in 54 acres of gardens, largely planned by Humphry Repton in 1791. Additions during the 19th century included the formal terraces by Paxton, the Japanese Garden by the Third Lord Egerton, and extensive planting of azaleas, rare shrubs and trees by the Fourth Lord.

The park extends to 2,000 acres. Repton was also influential here, planning the landscaping and the large lake, Tatton Mere, which now attracts many varieties of wildfowl. The park is populated by rare St Kilda and Soay sheep, and a large herd of deer.

Open all year. Admission charged. Parking charged. Wheelchair available. Refreshments. 2m N of Knutsford, 4m S of Altrincham.

THEATRE ROYAL

Suffolk   TL86

This little playhouse survives from pre-Victorian days. It was built in 1819 by the architect William Wilkins and was a popular venue with the travelling theatre companies of the time. The eminent actor, William Charles Macready, appeared to a packed house of 800 in 1828. In 1892, the world premiere of *Charley's Aunt* was staged here.

The theatre is decorated with a painted frieze, and its pit, boxes and gallery are beautifully proportioned. Although suffering a period of neglect in the earlier 20th century, the interior is miraculously well-preserved and retains an authentic Regency atmosphere.

The theatre was restored in the early 1960s and now holds performances most evenings.

Open all year unless performances are being staged. Wheelchair access. Refreshments. In Westgate Street on S side of A134, Bury St Edmunds.

UPTON HOUSE

Warwickshire   SP34

Works from the British, Dutch, Flemish, French, German, Italian and Spanish schools of painting grace Upton's walls, including masterpieces by Brueghel, Fouquet, Canaletto, Stubbs and Hogarth. The 18th-century porcelain collection contains many rare Chelsea figures and exquisite examples from Sevres. The set of Brussels tapestries depicts *The Hunts of Maximilian*, whilst the furniture includes a fine mahogany suite. All these were collected together at Upton by the second Viscount Bearsted, son of the founder of the Steel Corporation, who bought the house in 1927.

Lord Bearsted altered and extended the rooms to suit his works of art, creating in effect a huge, very plush art gallery. Only the staircase remains from the 17th century. However, he remodelled the exterior in a manner sympathetic to Upton's 17th-century origins.

Upton had originally been built on the site of an earlier house in the reign of James II. Its first occupant was Sir Rushout Cullen, a wealthy London merchant who had aspirations to become a respected country gentleman. The inscription 'RC 1695' on two rainwater heads marks the year of completion.

For the next few centuries, this unexceptional house passed through many hands, without notable incident until its transformation by Lord Bearsted.

Upton's gardens are a delight. On one side of the valley, terraces linked by a balustraded stairway overlook a formal lake. Elsewhere in the 31½ acres of ground there is a water garden in a natural amphitheatre ringed by woods, and a classical temple by Sanderson Miller built above a second, larger lake.

Open April to end Sept. Admission charged. Wheelchair available. 7m NW of Banbury, on W side of A422.

WEST RUNTON

Norfolk   TG14

Although this site contains the highest land in Norfolk, such an accolade in this low, flat county comes without any real altitude. Nevertheless, the views are good – during the Napoleonic Wars, a telegraph station was positioned on the wooded Beacon Hill.

This 71½-acre site, close to the sea, is known locally as the Roman Camp. In Saxo-medieval times there were iron workings here.

Beeston Regis Heath, another Trust property, is a next door neighbour. This 37-acre site of open heath and woodlands offers free access at all times with good views of the nearby coastline.

¾m S of West Runton station.

This painting, entitled St Michael slaying the Dragon *is a rare miniature by Jean Fouquet, and comes from a book of hours made for Etienne Chevalier between 1452 and 1460. It is displayed on a massive gilt pier table near the end wall of the passage gallery at Upton House in Warwickshire*

The Pre-Raphaelites

The conventional view of the Victorian home is turned on its head at Wightwick Manor. This no doubt pleased the Pre-Raphaelites, a group who revolted against the established view of art, craft and design in mid 19th-century Britain.

The Pre-Raphaelite movement was founded by Dante Gabriel Rossetti (1829–1896), William Holman Hunt (1827–1910) and John Everett Millais (1829–1896). Their famous 'Brotherhood', declared in 1848, was a reaction against the staid academic art of the time. They were inspired by a romantic medieval spirit and by the simple naturalism of the Italian Primitive school of painters – Botticelli and Filippino Lippi, for instance – prior to Raphael. They gave their first exhibition in 1848. Not surprisingly, it attracted the contempt of the critics, who regarded Raphael as a great artist. Charles Dickens was amongst the many to voice hostile reactions, though Ruskin defended their work. Although the movement formally came to an end in 1853, it continued to have an important influence on the art movement. Painters such as Ford Madox Brown (1821–1893) and Sir Edward Burne-Jones (1833–1898) were in sympathy with Pre-Raphaelite ideas. So too was William Morris (1834-1896).

Morris is remembered not for his paintings, of which there are only a few. His interests lay in interior design, decoration and handicrafts, in beautifying objects in common use. His designs, quite unlike anything else produced at the time, form the basis of the English revival in decorative art that began around 1875.

WICKEN FEN

Cambridgeshire   *TL57*

These 600 acres of fenland are an undrained remnant of the Great Fen of East Anglia which once covered 2,500 square miles. Natural historians judge this wetland site as one of the most significant in western Europe.

Over 300 species of flowering plants grow amongst the reeds, sedges and dense scrub. Wicken's thriving bird life includes heron, mallard, great crested grebe, bittern, tern, owl and many waders. Around 5,000 insect species have been identified here, a figure which includes over 700 kinds of butterfly and moth.

Wicken Fen survives largely unchanged from centuries ago, though its mere, or open water, was created to attract wildfowl in 1955. A sensitive, delicate environment, it requires constant and careful management.

Open all year. Admission charged. Wheelchair access to parts of Fen. S of A1123, 3m W of Soham.

WIGHTWICK MANOR

West Midlands   *SO89*

This is a deceptive house. Its gables and black-and-white half timbered façade might imply Elizabethan origins. The manor, however, is not yet 100 years old.

Wightwick Manor, begun in 1887, is one of the Trust's most important Victorian buildings. The builder was Samuel Theodore Mander, a Wolverhampton manufacturer with advanced ideas about design, who knocked down the old manor to make way for the new house designed by Edward Ould, a follower of William Morris.

The gabled, half-timbered manor was completed in 1893. In its style of decoration (and its first-class state of preservation) Wightwick Manor is one of the finest monuments to the Pre-Raphaelite movement.

Mander called in Morris and many other craftsmen. Between them, they created an interior of a mixture of styles and influences from many periods, guided by a respect for sound craftsmanship.

Morris was a man of many talents, and all are on display here in the embroidery, wallpaper, textiles, carpets, tiles and books that adorn the interior. The house is also noteworthy for its Kempe glass and de Morgan ware. Paintings and drawings by several of the Pre-Raphaelite movement's founder members also hang here, including works by Dante Gabriel Rossetti and Holman Hunt.

The Pre-Raphaelite influence even extends into the gardens. Laid out by Alfred Parsons, they contain shrubs and plants supplied by Morris, yew hedges and topiary, terraces and two pools.

Open all year except Feb. Admission charged. Free parking. Wheelchair access. 3m W of Wolverhampton off the A454.

WIMPOLE HALL

Cambridgeshire TL35

Wimpole is a place where superlatives apply. It is the largest, most spectacular mansion in Cambridgeshire – an accolade it deserves simply on the strength of the number of famous architects and landscape gardeners who have worked here.

The house dates from 1640–70, when Sir Thomas Chicheley built the original central block (some internal walls still survive). Between 1693 and 1705, the Second Earl of Radnor, a later owner, added a detached service wing and orangery and created the formal gardens.

Wimpole saw much activity in the 18th century. The house again changed hands – and appearance when its new owner, Edward Harley, later the Second Earl of Oxford, built a west wing which joined the main block to the orangery and chapel between 1713 and 1721. He also extended the gardens and in 1730 added the long library designed by James Gibbs.

Further substantial changes occurred from 1740 onwards, when the house became the property of the Earl of Hardwicke. The shape and form of Wimpole as we now see it really dates from these times. The First Earl refaced the central block and carried out extensive internal modifications which included the addition of a long gallery.

The gardens awaited the attention of the Second Earl, who called in the celebrated landscaper 'Capability' Brown in 1767. Humphry Repton made further alterations to the park between 1801 and 1809.

The house contains many remarkable rooms, a reflection of the care and craftsmanship which have been applied lavishly here. Amongst the most exceptional are the unconventional domed Yellow Drawing Room built by Sir John Soane in 1793, Harley's long library and the chapel, finished in 1724 with walls painted by Sir James Thornhill.

Final large-scale alterations were made in 1840 by the Fourth Earl of Hardwicke, when a new east service wing and Italianate towers were added, and the orangery refaced.

Within the 3,000-acre grounds are a group of farm buildings, designed by Sir John Soane in 1792. These have recently been restored to house a farming museum and the rare breeds of livestock which have been introduced into the estate.

Open April to end Oct. Admission charged. Wheelchair available. Refreshments. 8m SW of Cambridge.

The stately façade of Wimpole Hall. The tall central block represents the original extent of Thomas Chicheley's 17th-century building. The lower wings to each side were added by James Gibbs on behalf of Lord Harley between 1714 and 1721. The inset shows Wimpole Hall's elegant book room, started in about 1730 as an anteroom to Lord Harley's new library. Supporting decorated arches, book-cases project into the room on both sides in this unusual design

THE WIRRAL

Merseyside   *SJ28*

Here, on the Wirral peninsula, the Trust owns five separate sites, all in the west, totalling over 230 acres – Burton Wood, Caldy Hill, Harrock Wood, Heswall and Thurstaston Common. These help preserve a countryside now rapidly disappearing in industrial Merseyside.

Burton Wood, above the pretty village from which it takes its name, is an area of Scots pine. Magnificent views can be enjoyed from this site – and also from Caldy Hill, further north, which looks out across the mouth of the Dee to the Point of Air lighthouse five miles away on the far bank.

Heswall, about 40 acres of meadow and arable land, fronts the Dee estuary, and has fine views across to North Wales. This particularly pleasant spot can be reached on foot along the foreshore and the Wirral Country Park, so there is no provision for car parking.

Harrock Wood, quite close to Caldy Hill, is a mixed woodland with water meadow. Also nearby, two miles south-east of West Kirby, is the Trust's largest property here, the 188-acre Thurstaston Common. Thurstaston's open common and gorseland, overlooking the Dee estuary, surrounds a huge rock known as Thor's Stone, which is supposed to have been used by the Vikings as an altar for pagan sacrifices.

S of the Mersey estuary.

WOOLSTHORPE MANOR

Lincolnshire   *SK92*

This small, quite plain house is famous as the birthplace, in 1642, of Isaac Newton, whose family had taken possession of the old manor in 1623.

Isaac's genius soon became apparent, so much so that an uncle observed that it would be wrong 'to bury so extraordinary a talent in rustic business'. He departed for Cambridge in 1662, and although he returned to Woolsthorpe only infrequently, it was here that he formulated his three major discoveries – differential calculus, the composition of white light and the law of gravity.

He came to Woolsthorpe in 1665 and 1666 to escape the plague. In those two years, as he later said, 'I was in the prime of my age for invention, and minded mathematics and philosophy more than at any time since'.

The main feature inside the house is a large upper room with a wainscot partition, erected, so it is said, by Newton himself to give him peace and quiet for his studies.

The celebrated apple orchard stands in front of the house. Here, according to tradition, Newton, watching the apple fall, received his inspiration for the law of gravity.

Open April to Oct. Admission charged. Free parking. Wheelchair access. 7m S of Grantham on the W side of the A1.

ISAAC NEWTON AT WOOLSTHORPE

Newton's phenomenal intellect was perhaps at its height during the period he retreated to Woolsthorpe to avoid the plague. He tells us himself his achievements for 1665:

'1665: the method for approximating series and the rule for reducing any dignity [power] of any binomial to such a series. The same year in May I found a method of tangents and in November the direct method of fluctions [i.e. the elements of the differential calculus] and the next year in January had the theory of colours and in May following I had entrance into the inverse method of fluctions [integral calculus] and in the same year I began to think of gravity extending to the moon.'

Yet shortly before his death, this great man wrote that he seemed to himself 'to have been only like a little boy playing on the seashore.'

OTHER PROPERTIES

CAMBRIDGESHIRE

Nos 14 and 19 North Brink, Wisbech. *TF40*
On either side of Peckover House. May be viewed by NT members only, by written appointment.

Ramsey Abbey Gatehouse. *TL28*
Remains of 15th-century gatehouse of a Benedictine Abbey on SE edge of Ramsey.

CHESHIRE

Eddisbury Park Field. *SS97*
Meadow, 700ft above sea level. 1m E of Macclesfield.

Helsby Hill. *SJ47*
Part of summit, including part of an Iron Age promontory fort. Views over Mersey and Welsh mountains. ½m S of Helsby.

Maggoty's Wood. *SJ87*
In this woodland is the grave of an eccentric 18th-century dramatist and dancing master, Maggoty Johnson. ½m NW of Gawsworth.

Mobberly. *SJ78*
Meadowland, protecting the church. 3m NE of Knutsford. Public footpath from the church.

DERBYSHIRE

Alport Height. *SK35*
Hilltop with views, and a rock called the Alport Stone. 4m NW of Belper.

Curbar Gap. *SK27*
8 acres giving views over the Derwent Valley and the moorlands. ¼m E of Curbar village.

Duffield Castle. *SK34*
The foundations of the Norman keep of a castle destroyed in 1266 by Prince Henry, nephew of Henry III. ¼m N of Duffield Station.

Eccles Pike. *SK08*
Part of the summit; fine views. 1½m W of Chapel-en-le-Frith.

High Wheeldon. *SK16*
Part of the range bounding the E bank of the upper reaches of the river Dove. 5½m SE of Buxton.

Lantern Pike. *SK08*
Moorland hilltop with views. 1½m NW of Hayfield.

Market House, Winster. *SK26*
Late 17th- or early 18th-century stone market house at Winster, 4m W of Matlock, on S side of B5057, in the main street of Winster.

Miller's Dale and Ravenstor. *SK17*
Wooded cliffland astride the river Wye extending to Tideswell Dale. 2m S of Tideswell, S of B6049.

Shining Cliff Wood. *SK35*
On W bank of the Derwent at Alderwasley.

South Ridge Farm, Hayfield. *SK08*
Rising to above 1,000ft; views of Kinder Scout and the Peak. 4m N of Chapel-en-le-Frith.

Stanton Moor Edge. *SK26*
Moorland, 900ft high; views over Derwent Valley. 2m N of Winster.

Taddington Wood. *SK17*
Wooded hillside. 1½m E of Taddington, on S side of Buxton – Bakewell road (A6).

GREATER MANCHESTER

Medlock Vale. *SO90*
Land on banks of river Medlock in the middle of an industrial area; part of a Country Park. 1½m NE of Ashton-under-Lyme.

NORFOLK

Cawston. *TG12*
A duelling stone near the Old Woodrow Inn on B1149, inscribed H.H.; it was set up after Sir Henry Hobart of Blickling Hall was fatally injured nearby in a duel in 1698.

No. 4 South Quay, Great Yarmouth. *TG50*
16th-century building with panelled rooms; 19th-century front. Open weekdays all year; also Sun from June to end Sept.

Stiffkey Saltmarshes. *TG94*
Saltmarsh and 2m of coastline. Access from A149 either side of Stiffkey village. On N coast between Wells and Blakeney (A149) and N of Stiffkey village.

NORTHAMPTONSHIRE

Brackley Park. *SP53*
Open space on E side of High Street, Brackley (A43).

Priest's House, Easton-on-the-Hill. *TF00*
Pre-Reformation priest's lodge. Apply to the Rector for access.

WEST MIDLANDS

Children's Field, Knowle. *SP17*
3-acre field between Kixley Lane and Knowle Church.

THE NORTH COUNTRY

Wastwater —
three miles long and one of Cumbria's smaller lakes

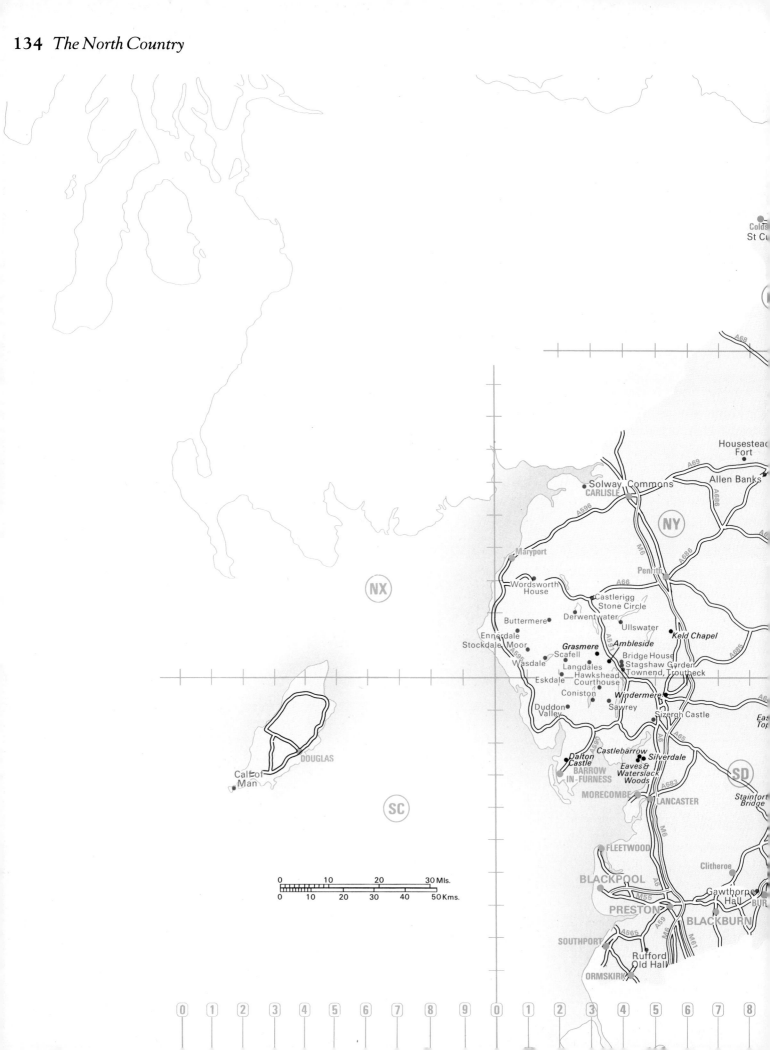

Colds
St Cu

Housesteads
Fort

Allen Banks

Solway Commons

CARLISLE

NY

Maryport

NX

Penrith

Wordsworth
House

Castlerigg
Stone Circle

Buttermere   Derwentwater

Ullswater   Keld Chapel

Ennerdale   *Grasmere*   *Ambleside*
Stockdale Moor
Scafell   Bridge House
Wasdale   Stagshaw Garden
Langdales   Townend, Troutbeck
Eskdale   Hawkshead
Courthouse
Coniston   *Windermere*

Duddon   Sawrey
Valley   Sizergh Castle

Eas
Top

Castlebarrow   *Silverdale*
*Dalton
Castle*
*Eaves &
Waterslack
Woods*
**BARROW
IN-FURNESS**

SD

Stainfort
Bridge

DOUGLAS

Calf of
Man

MORECOMBE   **LANCASTER**

SC

FLEETWOOD

Clitheroe

| 0 | | 10 | | 20 | | 30 Mls. |
| 0 | 10 | 20 | 30 | 40 | 50 Kms. |

BLACKPOOL

Gawthorpe
Hall

BUR

PRESTON   **BLACKBURN**

SOUTHPORT

Rufford
Old Hall

ORMSKIRK

ALLEN BANKS

Northumberland   NY76

This 200-acre site, near the confluence of the rivers Allen and Tyne, is noted for its deciduous woodland of mature beech and oak. These trees grow along the steep-sided slopes of the Allen's riverbank and serve as a habitat for the roe deer and increasingly rare red squirrel.

Walking is popular amongst the hills and crags here, with pleasant riverside trails and more challenging steeper paths. Those who climb the eastern bank of the river are rewarded with fine views northwards across the Tyne to Hadrian's Wall.

3m W of Haydon Bridge, ½m S of A69.

BENINGBROUGH HALL

North Yorkshire   SE55

The late Elizabethan house that once stood on this estate was demolished by John Bourchier in the early 18th century to make way for the present hall, which was completed by 1716. Its exterior and interior layouts are largely intact and original.

William Thornton, a carpenter-architect from York, is thought to have been the builder, but certain exterior features have been credited to a better-known architect, Thomas Archer. The two-storeyed rectangular building of mellow brick has many delightfully controlled Baroque features which enliven what is otherwise a plain exterior. Thornton, however, gave Beningbrough its chief glory; the quite superb decorative woodcarvings which have been compared to those of Grinling Gibbons. Throughout the interior – and especially in the great staircase and two-storey hall – there is evidence of unusually high standards of craftsmanship. The house is therefore a fitting home for a permanent exhibition of nearly 100 17th- and 18th-century portraits, placed here by the National Portrait Gallery in 1978.

The house stands in a 375-acre wooded park, and has a pleasant, mainly modern garden.

Open April to end Oct. Admission charged. Wheelchair available. Restaurant. 8m NW of York, 2m W of Shipton.

BRANSDALE

North Yorkshire   SE69

Bransdale is set among some of the most attractive – and remote – landscape in the North York Moors.

Outdoor enthusiasts will no doubt be glad to hear that this beautiful spot – a small, green valley surrounded by high moorland – 1,900 acres of which are owned by the Trust, is not particularly accessible by car.

6m N of Helmsley in North York Moors, approach from A170 on unclassified road from Helmsley.

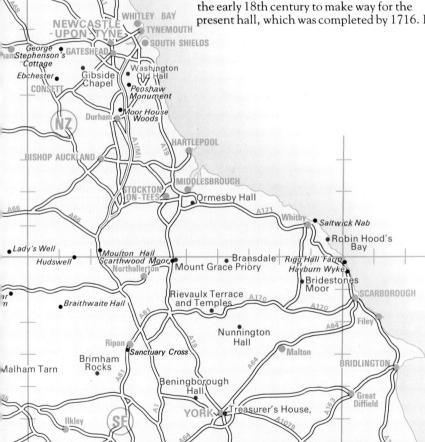

BRIDESTONES MOOR

North Yorkshire SE89

The Bride Stones, standing on this wild, exposed moorland, have a most peculiar look to them. This collection of rocks – the largest have been named the Pepperpot and the Saltcellar – are quite narrow at the base, widening towards the top. The action of the wind and rain on the softer, lower strata produced this curious effect, giving the rocks a precarious-looking profile.

The stones are to be found on an 873-acre site amongst the massive conifer forests of the North York Moors. Grime Moor, part of the Trust's land, contains three groups of barrows. The property is now a nature reserve.

12m S of Whitby, 1m E of A169.

BRIDGE HOUSE

Cumbria NY30

This tiny dwelling – which, it is said, once housed a family of eight – was built in the mid 17th century, probably as a summer house or even an apple store. Originally known as the 'Brig House', it was once part of the Ambleside Hall estate of the prominent Braithwaite family.

This estate was sold in the early 18th century, following which the Bridge House passed through the hands of a succession of owners. Its robust architecture is typical of early stone Cumbrian buildings. In its time, it has served as a dwelling, teahouse, weaving shop and cobbler's shop.

Open as National Trust information centre. On a bridge over the Stock Ghyll, in Ambleside centre.

BUTTERMERE

Cumbria NY11

The long, finger-like waters and high peaks of the Cumbrian Mountains – better known as the Lake District – constitute one of England's most revered landscapes. Buttermere, in the north-west, is located at the head of a valley of which W. G. Collingwood, the author of an early guide to the Lakes, wrote: 'I always think of this valley as made by Heaven for summer evenings and summer mornings: green floor and purple heights, with the sound of waters under the sunset, or lit with the low north-eastern sun into pure colour above, and the greyness of the dew upon the grass.'

Just beyond the lake the road rises into the rocky heights of the 1,176ft Honister Pass. From here, the views across Buttermere, fringed by the forests of Burtness Wood and protected by the rugged Chapel Crags, are spectacular.

The one-mile-long, 230-acre lake and adjoining land is part of over 1,900 acres of Trust property in the Buttermere Valley.

10m SW of Keswick.

CALF OF MAN

Isle of Man SC16

This is the one and only Trust site on the island. It is devoted to conservation, for the Calf of Man is an important nature reserve.

Located on the south-west coast, this islet attracts Atlantic seals and prolific colonies of seabirds, including guillemots, razorbills, puffins and kittiwakes. The views from its high point – 421ft – can safely be described as having international dimensions, extending as they do across to the Scottish uplands, England's Lake District, the peaks of North Wales and Ireland's Mountains of Mourne.

SW of the Isle of Man.

Local folklore once held that Castlerigg Stone Circle consisted of men turned to stone. A stone axe and a 'clublike implement' were found here before 1855. In 1882 an attempt to excavate the site led to a small amount of charcoal being found, but no pottery or other dateable material was uncovered

CASTLERIGG STONE CIRCLE

Cumbria NY22

Stone circles, not an uncommon sight in upland Britain, still generate an air of mystery and speculation concerning the motives of those who built them. This megalithic monument stands on high land to the east of Keswick. Of the original 38 stones which formed the circle – measured at just over 100ft in diameter – only five have fallen. Eight of its unhewn stones are over five feet high, and within the circle a rectangle of stones can be traced.

Castlerigg, against its dramatic Lake District backcloth, makes an impressive sight. The poet Keats must have been impressed, for he recorded his experiences in *Hyperion* following a visit in 1818. Inevitably, the circle has its druidic associations, and is also known as the 'Druid's Circle'.

2m E of Keswick.

The north and west fronts of Cragside seen from the valley of the Debdon Burn. The stream was harnessed by Lord Armstrong to provide the house with electricity – Cragside was the first house in the world to be lit by electric light. The 150ft long footbridge of steel was built between 1870 and 1875, and is unique in its construction

CONISTON WATER

Cumbria　　　　　　　　　　　　　*SD39*

This lake, over five miles long, is flanked by scenery both typical and untypical of the Lake District. The Old Man of Coniston, the most southerly of the great Cumbrian peaks, rises in grand style to 2,635ft from the western shore of the lake. To the east, relatively low hill scenery is clothed with attractive deciduous woodland and the Forestry Commission conifers of the extensive Grizedale Forest.

Coniston's overall character is gentler than that of its lakeland neighbours. Its tree-lined bays are backed by a gradually-sloping landscape of pasture and hillside. The Trust owns over 5,500 acres of land here, both on and off-shore. Peel Island and Fir Island, off-shore from the eastern bank, are part of an estate which includes farm and woodland, open country and mountainside.

The delightful Tarn Hows, just north of the headwaters of the lake, is also within the estate. Although modest in size in comparison to its Cumbrian big brothers, Tarn Hows ('tarn'

comes from the Norse word meaning 'tear drop') rivals them in beauty. Its shallow waters, surrounded by evergreens and larches, contain pike, perch, roach and rudd. Views from this spot, which was partly bequeathed to the Trust by Beatrix Potter, are magnificent, especially looking towards the Helvellyn range and Langdale Pikes.

Coniston Hall is also included within the estate. This is located on the shores of the lake, one mile south of Coniston village.

The original 16th-century hall was probably built by a 'gentleman of great pomp and expense', William Fleming. It is unusual in many respects. First and foremost, the early house would have been quite a grand and comfortable place, not at all typical of the residences built here in the 16th and 17th centuries.

The main living quarters were also, unconventionally, located on the first floor, a sound and sensible arrangement bearing in mind perennial lake mists and occasional floods.

Coniston Hall not open, lake and Hall S of Coniston village on A593.

CRAGSIDE

Northumberland　　　　　　　　　　*NU00*

This well-named house looms above the conifers in the hills near Rothbury, with a Gothic roofline of spires, gables, towers and chimneys. The house belonged to inventor, engineer and arms manufacturer Sir William Armstrong, who originally built a smallish house here between 1864 and 1866 as a weekend retreat and shooting lodge. In 1869, the architect Norman Shaw was commissioned to convert Cragside into a country mansion.

By 1875, the house – perhaps the ultimate example of the romantic mock Tudor and medieval the Victorians so loved – had taken its shape. Inevitably, the work of the architect (good though it was, especially in the grand interiors) was eclipsed by the hand of Sir William himself. Armstrong the inventor gave his house a place in the history books as the first residence in the world to be lit by electricity, the power coming from a water-driven turbine. Arc lights were installed in 1878, to be followed two years later by the incandescent lamp (the original lamps, converted from vases, can still be seen in the library).

He did not stop there, for the house also includes many innovations based on his knowledge of hydraulics and engineering, including the hydraulic lift. Sir William also transformed the surrounding landscape, extending his property from 20 to 1,700 acres, building roads, clearing scrubland, planting trees (over seven million in all) and diverting streams.

This estate, now standing at 2,354 acres, includes a country park.

Open April to Oct. Admission charged. Wheelchair available. Refreshments. 13m SW of Alnwick.

CRUMMOCK WATER

Cumbria   *NY11*

Crummock Water is the largest of the trio of lakes in the Buttermere Valley, all of which are Trust properties. The other two are Buttermere and Loweswater. The entire 623-acre lake, approximately three miles in length, is in the ownership of the Trust together with small parcels of surrounding hill and forest. The only boats on the lake are those let by the Trust for fishing, so little disturbs its peaceful waters.

The Buttermere Valley takes its name from the low pasture, used for cattle grazing, which separates Crummock Water from the neighbouring waters of Buttermere itself. This pastoral stretch, idyllic though it may be, is completely dwarfed by the dark, forbidding slopes of 2,791ft high Grasmoor and Brackenthwaite Fell, which in dramatic contrast rise abruptly from Crummock Water's eastern shore. In the south-west the mountain stream of Scale Beck plunges over Scale Force waterfall (also a Trust property) on its way to the lake, the greatest of many falls in the area.

7m S of Cockermouth.

DERWENTWATER AND BORROWDALE

Cumbria   *NY21*

The many individual areas of land (and water) owned by the Trust around Keswick, the shores of the lake and the mountain hamlet of Borrowdale, add up to over 8,000 acres.

This overall acreage includes many of the Lake District's picture-postcard sites: Ashness Woods, for example, along the south-east shore of the lake with views northwards across Derwentwater to the 3,053ft peak of Skiddaw; the white-washed cottages of Watendlath, a mountain hamlet high up in the fells built round a tarn and shaded by yews; the rocky promontory of Friar's Crag, just one mile south of Keswick, with its panoramas of the wooded shoreline and Derwent Isle, Lord's Island, St Herbert's Island and Rampsholme (all Trust properties); the massive Bowder Stone, a 2,000 ton rock above the narrow defile known as the 'Jaws of Borrowdale'.

S of Keswick.

DUDDON VALLEY

Cumbria   *SD19*

Under this heading we find some of the most remote mountain scenery accessible by car in the Lake District. Over ten individual areas – ranging from farmland to fell, rough pasture to rugged mountain terrain – constitute a total Trust acreage of around 5,500.

All are located in and around the Duddon Valley which runs north of Broughton in Furness. Intrepid motorists can reach the valley from the east and west by driving over the Wrynose and Hardknott Passes. These narrow mountain roads, parts of which run close to some of the Trust land, have some of the steepest inclines which even the most well-travelled motorist is ever likely to encounter.

N of Broughton in Furness.

DUNSTANBURGH CASTLE

Northumberland   *NU22*

Dunstanburgh is one of those castles whose situation is as impressive as its structure. It stands alone on an isolated hill which juts out into the sea, with a sheer sea-cliff of over 100ft protecting its northern approach.

The castle was built in two distinct phases in the 14th century. It was begun by Thomas, Second Earl of Lancaster, in 1316. Following the unfortunate earl's execution in 1322 for treason, Dunstanburgh eventually came into the hands of John of Gaunt, who enlarged it considerably in the 1380s.

The natural protection afforded by this sea-washed site is still self-evident. The man-made defences are less conspicuous, for the castle is in a ruinous state. Its most substantial remnants stand inland, guarding the landward approach. This is the great gateway-cum-keep, consisting of two drum towers at each side of an arched entrance passageway.

Although ruinous, the castle still dominates this lonely, windswept coastline. It is accessible only on foot, across the golf links from Embleton and Dunstansteads, or from Craster to the south. Embleton Links, a 494-acre site of dune and foreshore (including the golf course), are also owned by the Trust.

Open all year. Admission charged. On the coast, 9m NE of Alnwick.

Friar's Crag, Derwentwater. John Ruskin wrote of 'the intense joy, mingled with awe' he experienced as a child 'looking through the mossy roots, over the crag, into the dark lake'

The ruins of Dunstanburgh Castle, seen here from the coast to the south, dominate many miles of Northumberland's seaboard. Perched on a 100ft-high basalt crag – the extreme eastern end of the Great Whin Sill – the most impressive of Dunstanburgh's remains are the twin drum towers of the keep, originally the gatehouse, which were built in 1316

ENNERDALE

Cumbria   *NY11*

The three-mile long Ennerdale Water is the most westerly lake in the Lake District. It is also one of the most inaccessible by car: its cul-de-sac valley can be approached by road only from the west.

The Trust owns substantial portions of land here, amounting to more than 5,000 acres. These lie, in the main, along both sides of the lake and to the north and south of the river Liza which runs into its headwaters.

For the average, car-borne visitor, the rugged Crag Fell rising above the southern shore of the lake will be the most conspicuous Trust property in Ennerdale. The serious walker will be more familiar with the wild terrain further east, towards the source of the river Liza, where the Trust's properties extend as far as Brandreth high in the mountains.

SE of A5086, E of Ennerdale Bridge.

ESKDALE

Cumbria   *NY10*

This small, quiet valley, on the western flank of the Cumbrian Mountains, is accessible for some of the year by miniature railway which runs from the coast at Ravenglass to Boot, near the head of the vale. The 4,000 acres of land in Trust ownership here include the isolated mountain lake of Burnmoor Tarn, a half-way point on the footpath across Eskdale Fell between Boot and Wastwater.

Eskhause, the source of the river Esk, is an even more isolated spot. This is part of the Trust's largest single property here – the 3,328-acre Butterilket Farm – which runs beneath Scafell Pikes and down the valley to Wha House Bridge on the western approach to the spectacular Hardknott Pass, from the top of which all Eskdale can be viewed, and on a clear day the coast and the Isle of Man.

W of Cumbrian Mountains, NE of Ravenglass.

THE FARNE ISLANDS

Northumberland   NU23

The Farnes are a collection of 26 islands, lying two to five miles offshore from Bamburgh in north Northumberland. Although this total sounds impressive, some of these 'islands' are little more than bare rock visible only at low tide. Nevertheless, they are a real hazard to shipping: beacons were kept burning here as far back as medieval times, and in the late 17th century the first official lighthouse was built.

This little archipelago can be divided into two – the 'Outer' Farnes in the north (including Staple Island) separated from the 'Inner' Farnes by the one-mile-wide waters of Staple Sound.

The name derives from the Anglo-Saxon *Farena Ealande* meaning 'Island of Pilgrims'. The Farnes were a place of pilgrimage and hermitage since the earliest days of Christianity in Britain. St Aidan and St Cuthbert were the first saints to travel to the islands in the 7th century. A 14th-century chapel still stands on Inner Farne.

Most visitors to the islands now come for the fauna and flora, for the islands are today an important nature reserve. The variety of seabirds here, all to be seen within a small area, is tremendous. Guillemots, ringed plovers, puffins, razorbills, eider duck, terns and kittiwake are among the species nesting here. The Atlantic grey seal has also made its home in these islands. Botanists travel here for the surprisingly wide variety of vegetation (the soil covering is sparse and there are no trees). Particularly interesting is the *Amsinckia intermedia*, a plant from southern California rarely found elsewhere in Britain.

Inner Farne and Staple Islands open to visitors April to end Sept (accessible by boat from Seahouses). 2 – 5m off the Bamburgh coast.

GAWTHORPE HALL

Lancashire   SD83

This three-storey Jacobean house, probably built by Robert Smythson between 1600 and 1605 for the Shuttleworth family, represents an important milestone in the evolution of English domestic architecture. It embodies innovations in both style and plan. The great hall, for example, contrary to the medieval and early Tudor practice, runs at right angles to the entrance porch.

The Shuttleworths continued to reside at Gawthorpe, and called in Sir Charles Barry in the 1850s to improve the house. External evidence of 19th-century remodelling includes the heightening of the tower and addition of the open-work parapet. Inside, the ceilings and entrance lobby received Barry's attentions, and a new staircase was built. Seventeenth-century decoration still survives, though, mainly in the drawing room with its original plaster ceiling, panelling and fireplace.

The house also contains a unique display of textiles and embroideries, the collection of the late Rachel Kay-Shuttleworth. Gawthorpe Hall is now let to the Lancashire County Council for use partly as a College of Further Education.

Open mid March to end Oct. Admission charged. Wheelchair access to garden only. Refreshments.

GIBSIDE CHAPEL

Tyne and Wear   NZ15

This stately-looking chapel was part of a grand design by Sir George Bowes, a Member of Parliament and influential figure in 18th-century County Durham, for the grounds of his 17th-century house, Gibside Hall.

The orangery, banqueting hall and stable block, built to accompany the chapel, are all in a sad state; so too is the roofless, deserted hall. All that remains is the Palladian-style chapel and a statue to British Liberty (mounted on a column higher than Trafalgar Square's Nelson column).

Designed by James Paine to serve as a family mausoleum, the cruciform chapel was started in 1760, though it remained unfinished until about 1812. Its entrance front, dominated by an Ionic portico and pediment, is its outstanding architectural feature. Exterior and interior detail are superb, especially in its plasterwork.

Open April to Oct. Admission charged, except for first Sun of each month. 6m SW of Gateshead.

THE UNHAPPY COUNTESS

Mary Eleanor Bowes was an extremely rich woman. She inherited the fortune of George Bowes, the creator of the Gibside Estate of which only the chapel remains, in 1760. However, this great wealth earned her the title 'the Unhappy Countess', because in 1776 her money attracted her disreputable second husband, a penniless Irish adventurer named Captain Stowey. This rogue quickly spent her fortune. To pay for an unsuccessful election campaign to become Member of Parliament for Newcastle he felled and sold the estate's fine trees. His cruelty and extravagance forced Mary to seek protection from him, from the Courts, but he defied the law, and following his attempt to force her to sign all her wealth over to him he was caught and imprisoned after a dramatic ten-day coach chase. He spent the rest of his life in prison, from where he waged a fruitless legal battle to obtain his wife's estate.

The exquisitely decorated Gibside Chapel was inspired by Italian architecture. The rare 19th-century mahogany pulpit pictured here, with its inlaid sounding board designed to amplify the speaker's voice stands before the West Apse. The altar is directly beneath the high central dome

The more opulent aspect of the Victorian era is recalled on the Gondola, *a 19th-century steam yacht that now offers pleasure trips along tranquil Coniston Water. First launched in 1859, the boat was a contemporary of the great steamships that heralded a new era in shipbuilding and seafaring. Today, up to 86 passengers can travel in comfort on the boat, which was restored to its former splendour by the Trust in 1980. It moors at Monk Coniston, at the northern end of the lake*

THE MUSEUM AT HAWKSHEAD

Inside Hawkshead Courthouse is a fascinating little museum about life and industry in the Lake District from medieval times to the recent past. It illustrates the day to day home life of the Lakeland people, and displays artefacts from the local woollen, woodland, farming and iron industries.

Some of the farming implements on show were still in use until quite recently. For example, the breast-plough, pushed by the chest or thighs of the ploughman, was still in use in the 19th century, and corn was threshed with a flail up until the turn of the century.

Many dales people were involved in spinning and weaving the coarse wool of the local Herdwick sheep, and old examples of the distinctive Lakeland cloth are on display.

The museum also explains how the coppices in the dales provided charcoal to smelt the iron ore mined from Low Furness, and was later used in another local industry, the making of gunpowder, which stopped only in 1937.

'GONDOLA', LAKE CONISTON

Cumbria   *SD39*

Here we have what is probably the definitive example of the way in which the Trust has diversified and widened its approach to conservation. 'Gondola' is a living piece of Victoriana, a fully-fledged steam yacht operating on the waters of Lake Coniston.

First launched in 1859, 'Gondola' was restored to its former glory by the Trust in 1980. Operating from jetties at Monk Coniston and Coniston Boating Centre, it carries up to 86 passengers in 'the opulence of steam-heated Victorian saloons, peacefully propelled by a steam engine'.

Open Easter to Oct. Admission charged. At Monk Coniston and Coniston Boating Centre.

HAWKSHEAD

Cumbria   *SD39*

The village of Hawkshead stands midway between the waters of Windermere and Coniston at the northern edge of the Grizedale Forest. The Trust owns almost 2,000 acres here, much of it bequeathed by Mr and Mrs W. Heelis, the latter better known as Beatrix Potter.

Hawkshead Courthouse, half a mile from the village, is also Trust property. This largely 15th-century building has a certain rarity as one of the few constructed here in medieval times. Its name may imply something grand and imposing. In reality, it is quite rough-and-ready (possibly like the justice it administered), a robust, rather plain stone-built structure consisting of little more than a single upper chamber. It is now let to the Lake District Museum Trust as a museum.

Courthouse open May to end Sept. Admission charged. ½m N of Hawkshead on B5286.

HEBDEN DALE

West Yorkshire   *SD92*

One of the Trust properties here has a name which would not seem out of place in any Brontë novel. Hardcastle Crags is part of a distinctive vernacular expressed in such books as *Wuthering Heights*. Its alternative name – 'Little Switzerland' – seems altogether too tame for this rocky, pine-clad glen along the northern bank of Hebden Water, a few miles from the picturesque northern town of Hebden Bridge.

The Crags represent 246 of the 400 acres of Trust land here (about five miles, incidentally, from Haworth and so-called 'Brontë Country'). Gibson Wood, opposite the Crags, is owned by the Trust, as are High Greenwood and Black Dean, areas of attractive woodland to the west and south of Hebden Water.

N of Hebden Water.

The Building of the Wall

Hadrian's Wall was begun in 122 AD, to protect Emperor Hadrian's Roman Britain from the barbarian Celtic tribes of lowland Scotland. It was built by Roman soldiers, many of whom were skilled craftsmen and engineers.

Originally the wall was 10ft wide and 15ft high, and it was built of locally quarried stone. To the north it was protected by a deep ditch, to the south by the Vallum, a flat-bottomed ditch with earth ramparts built up on either side. It stretched from Newcastle to Irthing, from where it continued as a 20ft wide turf wall to the Solway, a distance of about 80 miles. At one mile intervals along its length stood milecastles, which housed small contingents of soldiers and guarded gateways in the wall – the Romans did not wish to sever communications with the north, but did want to monitor all contact between the 'barbarians' and the Romano-British in the occupied lands south of the border. Every third of a mile they built a watch-tower.

Seventeen forts in which the Legions were garrisoned were sited on or near the wall. The best preserved of these is Housesteads. Both Housesteads and some of the adjacent wall (one of the finest stretches, incidentally) are owned by the Trust.

HOUSESTEADS FORT

Northumberland   *NY76*

Housesteads is the finest and best-preserved of the forts built at periodic intervals along Hadrian's Wall, the distant northern frontier of the Roman Empire.

This fort still has an air of remoteness about it. It stands dominant, occupying the highest ground along the wall on a strategic crest which was once the confluence of a number of ancient routes.

Meticulous excavations have revealed a substantial, five-acre settlement capable of accommodating 1,000 infantrymen. Within its typically rectangular layout there are well-preserved sections of walling and the remains of a commandant's house and a hospital.

Evidence of a self-contained and surprisingly well-equipped camp can also be seen in the museum, built by the Trust to house the many artefacts found on site. There is also an Information Barn, with a Roman Wall display. (The fort and museum are now under the guardianship of the Department of the Environment.)

The Trust's properties here total around 2,000 acres and include some of the most spectacular stretches of the Wall itself. This runs for some three miles to the west of Housesteads, across rugged Northumbrian terrain past the beautiful waters of Crag Lough.

Open all year. Admission charged. Wheelchair access to Information Barn. Parking charged. Refreshments. 4m NE of Haltwhistle.

The Ship Room in Lindisfarne Castle, designed by Lutyens

The well-preserved stretch of Hadrian's Wall east of Housesteads

THE LANGDALES

Cumbria   *NY20, 30*

The valleys of Great and Little Langdale lie sheltered beneath high mountains right in the middle of the Lake District. The Trust owns well over 2,000 acres in these pretty, glaciated vales. Its holdings include a substantial number of farms.

Great Langdale's eastern approach is protected by the two small lakes of Elterwater and Loughrigg Tarn (the latter also a Trust property). Today, this peaceful sheep-farming valley seems an unlikely manufacturing centre – albeit a prehistoric one, for here Neolithic man had an important axe factory.

W of Ambleside.

LINDISFARNE CASTLE

Northumberland   *NU14*

Lindisfarne Castle stands on an historic island from which it takes its name, off the bleak, wild Northumbrian coast.

Lindisfarne – better known now as Holy Island – is six miles in circumference and is linked to the mainland at low tide by a causeway. From the time of St Aidan in the seventh century, it became a place of religious refuge.

The castle, though, is a relative newcomer. It was built on a rocky crag – the highest point on the island – in the mid 16th century to defend the harbour. Although this border fort saw some active service, by the mid 19th century its former military role had been reduced to that of a coastguard station.

Lindisfarne's renaissance came at the hands of the architect Sir Edwin Lutyens. Edward

Hudson, the wealthy publisher of *Country Life*, bought the dilapidated castle in 1903 and set Lutyens to work on reconstructing it. The architect's style – a sort of cosy medievalism – never fails to enchant most visitors, especially in the castle's creative exploitation of its dramatic position.

Not everyone felt the same, though. One of Hudson's many famous house guests, the irascible Lytton Strachey, found the castle 'very dark, with nowhere to sit, and nothing but stone under, over and round you . . .'

Open April to Sept, limited opening in Oct. Admission charged. Parking charged. On Holy Island, 5m E of Beal.

LORD LONSDALE'S COMMONS

Cumbria   *NY20*

Here is the largest acquisition of land made by the Trust in the Lake District. Its 16,842 acres cover the high ground, fells and mountain tarns in the centre of the Cumbrian massif, stretching from Helvellyn in the north to the slopes of Great Langdale.

This huge area is, not surprisingly, a favourite with those who like their great outdoors undiluted and unadulterated. The challenging terrain includes the Langdale Pikes, their twin summits – The Pike of Stickle and Harrison Stickle – rising to almost 2,500ft above the steep-sided Great Langdale valley – typically glacial scenery.

W of Ambleside.

LOWESWATER

Cumbria   *NY12*

As its name implies, this lake is the lowest of the string of three in the Buttermere Valley. Predictably enough, it is also surrounded by gentler countryside as the high peaks subside to more pastoral lowlands.

The Trust owns some 653 acres here, 160 of which are filled by the waters of the lake. The remainder consists of the conifers and deciduous trees of lakeside Holme Wood and Watering Wood, together with the extensive hillside stretches of High Nook Farm.

5m S of Cockermouth.

MAISTER HOUSE

Humberside   *TA02*

This house, in Hull High Street, is noted in particular for its magnificent staircase hall with delicate wrought-iron balustrading by Robert Bakewell, the famous Derby ironsmith.

It is also important as a reminder of the prosperity of Hull's merchants and traders. At one time, many such houses graced the environs of High Street, close to the wharves and warehouses which brought the mercantile classes their wealth. Maister House, built by Henry Maister on the site of a previous family residence in the 1740s, is one of the finest surviving of its kind.

The staircase hall is, in typical fashion, decorated with ornamental stuccowork of a very high order. This elegant, accomplished interior is a little unexpected, for the façade of the house is finished in dignified Palladian style, interrupted only by a fine pedimented doorcase with Ionic pilasters.

Open all year. Admission charged. In Hull High Street.

MALHAM TARN ESTATE

North Yorkshire	*SD86*

The tarn is a natural lake of 153 acres, surrounded by dramatic Pennine scenery about six miles north-east of Settle. A green, treeless valley dotted with rocky outcrops and strange-looking craters leads south from the lake to this area's other famous landmark, Malham Cove.

The Cove is a huge white limestone cliff, semicircular in shape, which looks like a giant amphitheatre. Its cliff-face, 240ft high with breathtaking overhangs, is said to have inspired – and provided much of the location for – Charles Kingsley's *The Water Babies*.

6m NE of Settle (A65), in Upper Craven.

MARSDEN MOOR

West Yorkshire	*SE01*

The contrast between Britain's busy urban and unpopulated upland environments is nowhere more emphatic than along Marsden Moor. This inhospitable Pennine plateau sits on the divide between industrial Lancashire and Yorkshire, just a stone's throw from the cramped terraced housing of Oldham and Huddersfield.

Peaty, infertile and acidic soils give this place a gaunt, forbidding appearance. Even the sturdy, black-stoned Pennine farmhouses are few and far between on this empty moorland.

Our ancestors must have thought differently about Marsden Moor, for many mesolithic weapons and implements have been found here.

W, S and E of Marsden, astride A62.

MOUNT GRACE PRIORY

North Yorkshire	*SE49*

This priory, the most important surviving Carthusian site in England, reflects a particularly solitary life-style even by monastic standards. Unlike many of the other more

gregarious orders, the Carthusians practised seclusion within the confines of their monasteries, mixing little among themselves.

The Carthusian faith was introduced into England in the late 12th century. Mount Grace was founded in the mid 14th century, receiving its licence from Richard II in 1398.

The priory, dissolved by Henry VIII, was partially converted into a country house in the 1650s. Nevertheless, a great deal remains to remind us of the singular, austere Carthusian regime. Unlike other monasteries, there are no common dormitories here. Each monk lived and slept in his own separate cell, with garden attached, ranged around the cloisters. Each cell contained a lobby, living room and bedroom leading to an upstairs workshop, and had its own piped water supply.

A priory church also stands on this 12-acre site. Mount Grace is now under the guardianship of the Department of the Environment.

Open all year. Admission charged. Wheelchair access. 6m NE of Northallerton.

The lovely setting and daffodil-filled garden of ruined Mount Grace Priory belie its austere history. Rejecting other monastic orders because they were not strict enough, the Carthusian monks who lived here led an almost hermit-like existence, emerging from their solitary cells only to attend church and occasional communal meals in the refectory

Visitors to Nunnington Hall are offered a contrast between the grandeur of the manor house's fine panelled interior and the smaller-scale fascination of the Carlisle Collection. This is a series of miniature rooms, each furnished in detail in the style of its period. Pictured here is the Collection's miniature version of a Palladian hall

NOSTELL PRIORY

West Yorkshire   *SE41*

Nostell, dedicated to St Oswald, was originally founded in the 12th century. The present house, built to the north of the old priory which was dissolved by Henry VIII in the 16th century, dates from the 1730s. The house, started by Sir Rowland Winn, was built in two phases. From 1735–50, the famous architect James Paine worked here. Following Sir Rowland's death in 1765, his successor brought in Robert Adam to complete the house in the neo-classical style.

The elegant state rooms in Paine's block were decorated by Adam, with decorative painting by Antonio Zucchi and plasterwork by Joseph Rose the younger. Thomas Chippendale, who was born at nearby Otley, was commissioned to furnish the house. Almost every room still contains examples of his celebrated furniture.

Open July to end Sept, limited opening April to June and Oct. Admission charged. Parking charged. Wheelchair access. Refreshments. 6m SE of Wakefield on N side of A638.

NUNNINGTON HALL

North Yorkshire   *SE67*

This large manor house has what has been described as 'a confused architectural history'. Although dating largely from the late 17th century, records indicate that a house existed here for some centuries before.

Nunnington's most cohesive architectural feature is undoubtedly its south front, with its classical doorway and beautifully carved stone window surrounds. This was the work of Lord Preston, who remodelled the south side of the house in the 1680s and also laid out the formal walled garden.

This well-proportioned façade fronts a number of rooms decorated in typical late 17th-century style, with moulded panelling and doorcases. A liberal use of oak is everywhere to be seen, from the magnificent panelled hall to the great staircase. The house is also noted for its fine tapestries and china, and the Carlisle Collection of Miniature Rooms, fully furnished in different periods.

Open April to end Oct. Admission charged. Wheelchair access. Refreshments. In Ryedale, 4½m SE of Helmsley.

ORMESBY HALL

Cleveland   *NZ51*

This tasteful, three-storey house was built in the mid 18th century by Dorothy Pennyman, whose family had owned the Ormesby estate since the beginning of the previous century.

Evidence of earlier buildings on site is confined to a low block standing to the east of the Georgian mansion. Although subsequently converted into a kitchen and service quarters, this block still contains an original fine Jacobean doorway.

In its day, Ormesby would have been regarded as a 'middling' house of modest proportions. Nevertheless, it benefited from Dorothy Pennyman's taste and the spendthrift attitude of her successor, Sir James Pennyman.

Sir James moved to Ormesby in 1770 and soon spent nearly £50,000 on, amongst other things, the erection of elegant stables and the redecoration of the dining and drawing rooms. The first floor gallery and some of the bedrooms are also decorated in lavish style with mid 18th-century panelling.

Open April to end Oct. Admission charged. Wheelchair access. 3m SE of Middlesbrough.

RIEVAULX TERRACE AND TEMPLES

North Yorkshire   SE58

This grass terrace, with its classical temples at either end, overlooks the romantic ruin of Rievaulx Abbey, founded by the Cistercians in 1131. Terrace and temples are much younger. They date from 1758 and represent, for many, the high point of 18th-century landscaping.

Thomas Duncombe, their creator, built them to complement a similar set which stood about a mile away at Duncombe Park. Rievaulx's 'noble winding terrace' cuts a path along the edge of a wooded escarpment.

At the far northern end stands the rectangular Ionic Temple with its imposing portico, inspired by the Temple of Fortuna Virilis in Rome. Its classical, rather plain exterior leads to a richly decorated interior with magnificent frescoes. Intended as a banqueting house, it is still furnished in its full glory.

The Doric or Tuscan Temple, in the southeast, is a colonnaded rotunda said to be a scaled down version of the Mausoleum at Castle Howard. The interior of the dome is decorated with rich plasterwork.

Open April to end Oct. Admission charged. Wheelchair available. Refreshments. 2¼ NW of Helmsley.

ROBIN HOOD'S BAY

North Yorkshire   NZ90

The properties here are significant as marking the Trust's first acquisitions of Yorkshire coastline, part of the Enterprise Neptune scheme to protect Britain's coastal heritage.

The 12 acres of cliff and seashore at Rocket Post Field, adjoining the village of Robin Hood's Bay, became Trust property in 1976. This was followed, in 1977, by the 200-acre Ravenscar site which includes one mile of coastline with dramatic cliff scenery.

15m N of Scarborough off A171.

RUFFORD OLD HALL

Lancashire   SD41

The nucleus of this fascinating old house is a black-and-white half-timbered building so typical of the late medieval period. But although founded in the 15th century, Rufford has been substantially altered on two separate occasions by descendants of its original owner, Sir Thomas Hesketh.

The original timber-built great hall was supplemented by a brick wing in 1662. In the 1820s, hall and wing became linked by a 'new' block containing the main staircase and drawing room.

All eyes, though, focus on the practically unaltered great hall. Its solid hammerbeam roof

and decorative features (for example, the windows with moulded timber mullions) are splendid. Even more impressive is the huge movable screen, said to be unique, which separated the hall from the kitchen.

Rufford also boasts a fine collection of 17th-century furniture and a museum of Lancashire life.

Open April to end Oct, limited opening Nov to mid Dec. Admission charged. Wheelchair access. Refreshments. 7m N of Ormskirk.

ST CUTHBERT'S CAVE

Northumberland   NU03

St Cuthbert, the seventh-century Northumbrian saint associated with Holy Island and the hermitage on the Farne Islands died in 684. He was buried on Lindisfarne, but his body was moved by the monks in 875 when the Danes invaded.

There followed a celebrated period of wandering before his coffin found its final resting place at Durham Cathedral. The Trust now owns a 13-acre site around the so-called St Cuthbert's Cave, a natural cavern in the Kyloe Hills. This has been classified, realistically rather than romantically, as 'possibly one of the resting places for the saint's body on its way from Lindisfarne to Durham'.

10m NE of Wooler.

THE CHILD OF GOD

This is how the Venerable Bede referred to St Cuthbert in his writings about this much-loved man. He was born in about 634 AD, and a vision he experienced as a young boy when tending sheep on the Northumbrian hillsides led him to take the vows of a monk at Melrose Abbey. He is known to have preached widely throughout the north of England and southern Scotland before retiring to the rocky islet of Farne. His years of meditation ended there when he was made Bishop of Lindisfarne in 684 AD, a job he threw himself into wholeheartedly for the good of his scattered flock. He was credited with saving a dying baby with a kiss among other miracles, and his gentle but practical nature, knowledge and love of wildlife endeared him to the people. In 687 AD he retired to his retreat on Farne Isle to die. He was buried in Lindisfarne, but his remains were moved to Durham Cathedral to be safe from Viking raids.

SAWREY

Cumbria   *SD39*

A modest, early 17th-century farmhouse near Sawrey, located between imperial Lake Windermere and humble Esthwaite Water, is a place of pilgrimage for all Beatrix Potter fans. Hill Top was, for her, 'as near perfect a place as I ever lived in'; sentiments echoed in her books, for here was the location in which she found the inspiration to write the famous Peter Rabbit series.

Little has changed since her time. The house still contains her furniture, china and pictures – indeed, the look and internal arrangements of this traditional Lakeland cottage will be familiar to devotees of her work. The mahogany chairs, for example, appear in many of her illustrations, as do the balusters and stair-rail.

Beatrix Potter, otherwise known as Mrs W. Heelis, was strongly associated with the early work of the Trust in the Lake District. She left over 4,000 acres of land to the Trust, including – in 1944 – Hill Top, about half the village of Near Sawrey, Castle Farms and the Tower Banks estate. To complete the picture, in 1976 the Trust acquired the Tower Banks Arms (next door to Hill Top), which is now run as a country inn offering accommodation to visitors.

Between Esthwaite Water and Windermere.

SCAFELL GROUP

Cumbria   *NY20, NY11*

Scafell Pike, at 3,210ft the highest peak in England, dominates the scene here. Its summit is surrounded by natural beauty on a grand and uncompromising scale, accessible only to the hardy outdoor enthusiast.

The Trust owns over 2,500 acres here, much of which represents the most rugged mountain

Sweeping views of Rievaulx Abbey are to be had from the specially landscaped Terrace, which is enhanced by two classical temples. One of these, the Ionic Temple, has a lavishly painted ceiling (detail, inset)

Dramatic limestone cliff scenery near Robin Hood's Bay, protected by the Trust's 'Enterprise Neptune'

landscape the Lake District has to offer. To the north of Scafell, around the Styhead pass, the 'group' includes the summits of Lingmell, Broad Crag, Great End, Kirk Fell and Great Gable, all over 2,500ft.

Wordsworth climbed here in 1818. His impression, of 'a stillness . . . not of this world' is still valid today.

Between Borrowdale, Eskdale and Wastwater.

SIZERGH CASTLE

Cumbria   *SD48*

This castle has grown up around its pele (pronounced 'peel') tower, a protective, angular tower built around 1350. In medieval times, pele towers were a common feature in these troubled borderlands. Sizergh, with its massive walls – over nine feet thick at ground level – is one of the largest of them to survive.

In later, more settled times, the castle was improved. A Tudor great hall was constructed in about 1450 (and remodelled both in Elizabethan times and again in the late 18th century). Two Elizabethan wings and a gabled corner block were also added.

Sizergh's interior is noted for its panelling and carved woodwork. Its early Elizabethan decorations are particularly fine, as are its five superb chimneypieces dated before 1580.

The castle has a long – and continuous – association with the Strickland family (they first settled at Sizergh in 1239 and their descendants still live in the castle). They have left a fascinating range of contents, including a 14th-century two-handed sword, early oak furniture and a collection of family portraits.

Sizergh's gardens are not quite so historic. Its rock gardens, made of local limestone with attractive pools and streams, are just over 60 years old. Nevertheless, they contain a much-admired collection of dwarf conifers, many of unusual dimensions.

Limited opening April to end Sept. Garden only in Oct. Admission charged. Wheelchair available, access to garden only. 3½m S of Kendal.

SOLWAY COMMONS

Cumbria   *NY35*

Here we have one of England's last, and least-visited, outposts. The Solway Commons, on the south shore of the Solway Firth, look across a narrow stretch of water to the Scottish hills of Dumfries and Galloway.

This is a lonely, remote coast, on the road to nowhere in particular. The Trust holds around 1,500 acres of common land here, including Burgh Marsh and ten miles of coastline mainly between Bowness and Anthorn. The property is held on a long lease at a peppercorn rent granted by the Seventh Earl of Lonsdale in 1972.

On S shore of the Firth.

STAGSHAW GARDEN

Cumbria   *NY30*

This garden, just half a mile south of Ambleside off the A591, overlooks the northern shores of Windermere. Set into a steep, wooded hillside, with attractive views of the lake, it contains a colourful collection of rhododendrons, azaleas, camellias and spring bulbs.

Open mid March to end June, by written appointment only July to end Oct. Admission charged. Parking at Low Fold car park. ½m S of Ambleside.

STOCKDALE MOOR

Cumbria   *NY10*

This is another remote upland site, on the western fringe of the Lake District, in the hills between Ennerdale Water and Wastwater.

Stockdale Moor must have been of some special significance to our ancestors, for it is liberally dotted with prehistoric cairns and enclosures, including the evocatively named long barrow of Sampson's Bratfull.

4m S of Ennerdale, between Worm Gill and river Bleng.

TOWNEND

Cumbria   *NY40*

Townend's authentic period atmosphere extends to a complete lack of electric lights. Visitors to this 17th-century property are therefore advised to pick a bright, sunny day.

Externally, Townend is a fine example of the 'new' style of housing favoured by the Lake District's wealthier families in the early 17th century, when solid stone structures began to replace the old timber-framed buildings. A local family of small landowners, the Brownes, built Townend in 1623 and continued to live there for the next 300 years.

The house's great charm comes from the unique record it contains of those passing years. Nothing much was ever changed or altered. The family was an intelligent, lively one, accumulating possessions over the centuries, acquiring books, carved oak furniture, local fabrics, paintings and domestic implements. All have been marvellously preserved.

Open April to end Oct. Admission charged. At S end of village, 3m SE of Ambleside.

TREASURER'S HOUSE

North Yorkshire   *SE65*

This house became, in around 1100, the headquarters for a new institution: the Treasurer to York Minster. Appointed by Thomas,

Archbishop of York, the duties of this newly created post were those of a business manager for the church. The office, a prestigious and remunerative one, lasted throughout the Middle Ages until the coming of Henry VIII. The reason for its demise, in 1547, is well documented: the Minster 'being plundered of all its treasure . . . had no further need of a treasurer'.

Between 1628 and 1648 the house was largely rebuilt by Thomas Young. He remodelled the centre range (now the hall) and also gave the garden front its attractive appearance. A century later further improvements were made, including the addition of a William and Mary staircase (in the north-west wing), the remarkable plaster ceiling in the dining room, and the Venetian windows.

By the 19th century, the building had declined in stature and was divided into three dwellings. It was rescued by Frank Green, who undertook extensive restoration work following his acquisition of the property in 1897.

Frank Green also brought to the house a remarkable collection of furniture and other items. This collection – which is as important as the house itself – includes early English china and pottery, 17th- and 18th-century glass, early oak furniture and many examples of French craftsmanship.

Open April to end Oct. Admission charged. Wheelchair access. In Minster Yard, York.

THE TREVELYANS OF WALLINGTON

Eccentrics and country houses often seem to go together; the Trevelyans of Wallington prove the point. Walter Trevelyan inherited the house in 1846. He was a serious man, deeply interested in botany, geology, antiquities, agriculture and the temperance movement; his wife, Pauline, 19 years his junior, was attractive, artistic, and a patron of painters, writers and sculptors. The writer Ruskin, the painter William Bell Scott and the young poet Swinburne were among the guests at Wallington. Although the Trevelyans were very hospitable, the guests varied in their opinion of the eccentric running of the household. Augustus Hare arrived for lunch one day in 1861, which

The Treasurer's House at York as it appears today would be quite unrecognisable by the cathedral's first treasurer, who lived here around 1100. The garden front and the distinctive Dutch-style gables date from the 17th century, when the building was much altered

was as peculiar as everything else (Lady Trevelyan and her artists feeding solely on artichokes and cauliflowers). He also describes the 'endless suites of huge rooms, only partly carpeted and thinly furnished' and wrote that Lady Trevelyan 'never appears to attend to her house a bit, which is like the great desert with one or two little oases on it'. However, the more he stayed the more he liked it. One other guest, David Wooster, stayed for 22 years.

Wordsworth's immortal daffodils still bloom at the edge of Ullswater. The lake's twisting shoreline offers a great variety of views which, together with the mature woodland that surrounds the lake, make the area as enchanting a place to walk in as it was when the poet came here in the early 19th century

TROUTBECK PARK FARM

Cumbria	NY40

The Troutbeck estate forms a large part of the 4,000 acres of land in the Lake District left to the Trust by Beatrix Potter.

This 2,000-acre estate, just east of Ambleside, is one of the most famous sheep farms in the Lake District. The aptly named High Street Roman Road runs within its boundaries, through rugged terrain dominated by the summits of Thornthwaite Crag, Froswick and Ill Bell, all well over 2,000ft.

N of Troutbeck.

ULLSWATER VALLEY

Cumbria	NY31

For those travelling via Penrith, Ullswater is a marvellous introduction to the Lake District. This dog-legged lake, over seven miles long, is fringed by some of the loveliest woodland in Cumbria. The Glencoyne and Gowbarrow estates, running along the north and west shores, contain a mixture of ancient oak woodlands and many exotic trees and beeches planted in the 18th and 19th centuries.

Gowbarrow Park also contains two sites of special importance. The first, near Lyullph's Tower (an 18th-century folly), is now part of our national literary repertoire, thanks to Wordsworth, who saw his much-quoted daffodils here. Nearby is Aira Force, the largest waterfall in the Lake District.

In total, the Trust owns nearly 8,000 acres around the lake and in the narrow, craggy valley leading south to the Kirkstone Pass. This acreage includes Hartsop Hall with its extensive hill sheep farmland and the little lake of Brotherswater.

5m SW of Penrith on A592.

WALLINGTON

Northumberland	NZ08

Wallington, a stately country mansion, had quite humble beginnings. Its site was once occupied by a pele tower, common in these parts in medieval times. Later, a Tudor house was added, though Wallington as it stands today was begun in 1688 by Sir William Blackett, a wealthy Newcastle businessman.

Evidently, his tastes were not those of his successors. Sir Walter Calverley Blackett inherited the property in 1728. Within ten years, major changes were taking place: the entrance front was relocated, the north front rebuilt, windows were altered and the entire interior remodelled.

Yet more changes were made in 1846 by another Sir Walter Calverley – this time with the surname Trevelyan – and his wife, Lady Pauline. These concentrated mainly on the creation of a central hall, by roofing over the open courtyard. The completion of the hall's decoration (by William Bell Scott, a local Pre-Raphaelite painter) in 1868, marks the completion of work on the home.

Wallington's essentially Palladian exterior contains lavish interior decoration, much of it the fine plasterwork of the Francini Brothers, brought in to finish the main rooms in 1740.

Other attractions within include pottery, porcelain and needlework panels and an unusual – and quite delightful – collection of Victorian doll's houses.

The park and gardens, originally laid out by Sir Walter Calverley Blackett, are most attractive. They contain lawns, woodland walks and a walled garden noted for its conservatory with magnificent fuchsias.

House open April to Oct, grounds all year. Admission charged. Wheelchair available. Refreshments. 12m W of Morpeth on the B6342, 6m NW of Belsay.

WASDALE

Cumbria	NY10

Mains electricity was a late arrival here, farms at the head of the dale having to wait until 1977 to be connected. This long delay speaks louder than any adjectives in describing Wasdale's inaccessibility and remoteness, far away from the tourist's Lake District.

Wastwater is a smallish lake by Cumbrian standards, just over three miles long. Nevertheless, its dramatic location, in a mountainous valley leading to the heights of Scafell, rivals that of any of its neighbours.

Motorists can drive along the lakeside, through the Bowderdale woods, to Wasdale Head – but no further. The Trust's properties here, amounting to some 9,000 acres, are scattered around the lake. They consist largely of farmland and include Wasdale Hall (at the foot of Wastwater), let to the Youth Hostel Association.

E of Gosforth (A595) on unclassified road.

WASHINGTON OLD HALL

Tyne and Wear   NZ35

This manor house probably means more to the citizens of the United States than anyone else. Washington Old Hall, 12th century in origin, was the home from which George Washington's family took its name.

Its survival as a shrine to one of the founding fathers of the American Constitution has been a precarious business. Following the sale of the house by the Washington family in 1613, it was partly demolished when a new building was put up on the site. This in turn was almost demolished in the 20th century, by which time the 17th-century house had been reduced to a sorry state as a block of tenements, declared unfit for human habitation in 1936.

The house was saved, appropriately enough, through trans-Atlantic co-operation. A local preservation committee was formed to rescue Washington Old Hall. With funds from both Britain and America, the house was restored and, in 1955, officially opened by the American Ambassador.

Gratifyingly, it was during this restoration that parts of the earlier medieval house (inhabited by the Washingtons and their descendants from 1183–1613) were uncovered.

The ground floor and bedroom have been furnished in typical 17th- and 18th-century style and there is a small, formal garden. Two items of Washington memorabilia are of interest: a bust by Houdon, and the fan given to Martha Washington by Lafayette.

Open March to end Oct, limited opening Nov to end Feb. Admission charged. Wheelchair access. 5m W of Sunderland, 2m from A1 S of the Tyne tunnel.

WORDSWORTH HOUSE

Cumbria   NY13

William Wordsworth (1770–1850) immortaliser of Cumbria's lakes, fells – and daffodils – was born here.

That in itself is enough to guarantee this house the status of a shrine. The fact that he also

FROM WORDSWORTH'S 'THE PRELUDE'

When having left his Mountains, to the Towers
Of Cockermouth that beauteous River came,
Behind my Father's House he pass'd, close by,
Along the margin of our Terrace Walk.
He was a Playmate whom we dearly lov'd.
Oh! many a time have I, a five years' Child,
A naked Boy, in one delightful Rill,
A little Mill-race sever'd from his stream,
Made one long bathing of a summer's day,
Bask'd in the sun, and plunged, and bask'd again
Alternate all a summer's day, or cours'd
Over the sandy fields, leaping through groves
Of yellow groundsel, or when crag and hill,
The woods, and distant Skiddaw's lofty height,
Were bronz'd with a deep radiance, stood alone
Beneath the sky.

OTHER PROPERTIES

CUMBRIA

Ambleside
Bee Holme. *NY30*
A 1½-acre peninsula on W side of Windermere.

Force How. *NY30*
Woodland extending to the southern side of Skelwith Force.

Great Bog. *NY30*
A field beside Lake Road, Ambleside; given to preserve the view.

Kelsick Scar and High Skelgill Farm. *NY30*
Wood, fell and farmland; views over Windermere, Coniston Old Man and Langdale Fells. Footpath from Ambleside or Troutbeck.

Martins Wood. *NY30*
Agricultural land, recently planted with trees. Footpath access.

The Rashfield or Dora's Field, Rydal. *NY30*
Bought by Wordsworth in 1826 and given to the Trust by his grandson. 1½m NW of Ambleside.

Scandale Fell. *NY30*
Grazing and farmland above Scandale Beck. Public footpath access.

Wansfell. *NY30*
Wood and grassland; fine views over Windermere.

Cross Keys Inn, Cautley. *SD69*
Early 17th-century inn.

Dalton Castle. *SD27*
Fourteenth-century Dalton's tower in main street.

Dunthwaite. *NY13*
Farm and woodland, bordering the river Derwent for 1½m. 2m W of N end of Bassenthwaite Lake.

Grasmere
Alcock Tarn, Brackenfell and Chapel Green. *NY30*
Hillside behind Dove Cottage (not NT). Footpath access.

Allan Bank. *NY30*
House (not open) and gardens with park. Wordsworth lived here for three years.

Butterlip How. *NY30*
A viewpoint rising out of the Vale of Grasmere.

Church Stile. *NY30*
Sixteenth-century cottage; now an information centre.

Dunnabeck Paddock. *NY30*
A 1½-acre field.

Easedale. *NY30*
Farm, fell and woodland. Footpath access.

Moss Parrock. *NY30*
½ acre in Grasmere village. Nicholas Wood. Woodland beside footpath from Grasmere to High Close.

Stubdale Cottage. *NY30*
Cottage and land at the foot of Easedale.

Town Head Farm. *NY30*
Farm, and landlord's flock of sheep. At head of Grasmere Valley.

Underhelm Farm. *NY30*
On southern slope of Helm Crag with landlord's flock of sheep.

White Moss Intake. *NY30*
Rough pasture 1m E of Grasmere Village.

The Wray. *NY30*
Meadow and rough pasture and adjoining Allan Bank Park.

Keld Chapel, Shap. *NY51*
Small pre-Reformation building 1m SW of Shap near the river Lowther.

Priory Gatehouse, Cartmel. *SD37*
Last remaining part of an Augustinian Priory; open April to Christmas.

Windermere
Allen Knott and Latter Heath. *NY40*
Overlooking the lake, 2m N of Windermere Station. Latter Heath is ¼m to the east.

Ash Landing, Far Sawrey. *SD39*
Two fields.

Cockshott Point. *SD39*
Lakeshore land with fine views; footpath near the edge of the lake, but the farmland is not open.

wrote about the house and garden when recalling his halcyon childhood days here further establishes this site as a place of pilgrimage for all lovers of his romantic verse.

The house, a substantial but not grand mid-Georgian building, dates from 1745. It retains many original features within, including mid-18th-century softwood panelling, fireplaces, furniture and an elegant staircase.

On a more personal note, pieces of Wordsworth's own dinner service are on view, together with his bureau bookcase and some first editions.

Open April to end Oct. Admission charged. Refreshments. Main Street, Cockermouth.

Some visitors to Wordsworth's birthplace in Cockermouth may be surprised by the elegant interior and rather sophisticated decorations, in view of the poet's lifelong association with the simple, country life. His real attachment during his early years here was to the garden, which he wrote about in some of his poems. Inside the house, his chief interest was his father's well-stocked library, which doubtless encouraged the young poet's literary leanings. Pictured here is the drawing room; the bureau bookcase to the left of the doorway contains some first editions of the poet's works

Common Farm. *SD49*
Farmland on the outskirts of Windermere.

Fell Foot. *SD38*
A country park on the east shore of the south end of the lake.

Ladyholme. *SD39*
A ½-acre island; the site of a pre-Reformation chantry chapel.

Moorhow. *SD33*
Overlooks the lake; magnificent views of the fells.

Post Knott. *SD49*
Rough land above Bowness.

Queen Adelaide's Hill. *SD49*
Lakeshore land; including a cottage and boat landing at Millerground. Given in 1937 to commemorate the Coronation of King George VI. 1m by road W of Windermere station.

Rampholme Island. *SD39*
1-acre wooded island, south of Ferry Nab.

DURHAM

Ebchester. *NZ15*
Woodland on the right bank of the river Derwent.

Moor House Woods. *NZ34*
Woodland with walks by the river Wear.

LANCASHIRE

Silverdale
Castlebarrow. *SD47*
21 acres overlooking Morecambe Bay.

Eaves and Waterslack Woods. *SD47*
Wooded hill and mixed woodland; also Waterslack Quarry. East of Castlebarrow Head.

NORTHUMBERLAND

Buston Links. *NU20*
Half a mile of sand dunes on the coast south of Alnmouth Village. Public footpath access; also by car at Alnmouth Dunes to the north, then foot access only.

Dunstanburgh
Embleton Links. *NY22*
Dunes and foreshore including the golf course; fine coastal walks from Craster to Newton (3½m); plant life and geology. Access also via Embleton and Dunstansteads. 9m NE of Alnwick.

Low Newton-by-the-Sea. *NY22*
Nearly all this fishing village now belongs to the Trust.

Newton Links. *NY22*
Sand dunes and rough grazing south of the Long Nanny in Beadnell Bay. Access on foot from Newton Links House.

Newton Pool. *NY22*
Freshwater pool; a nature reserve. Access by footpath from Newton-by-the-sea or Embleton; bird hide for disabled visitors with wheelchair pathway.

George Stephenson's Cottage, Wylam-on-Tyne. *NZ16*
A stone cottage, the birthplace of the 18th-century inventor. Public access by footpath only.

Lady's Well. *NT90*
A well at Holystone, associated with St Ninian. Always open, free of charge.

Ross Castle. *NU02*
Hilltop with part of an Iron Age hill-fort; views of the Cheviot Hills and Lindisfarne.

St Aidan's and Shoreston Dunes. *NU23*
2m SE of Bamburgh; views of the Farne Islands.

NORTH YORKSHIRE

Braithwaite Hall. *SE18*
Seventeenth-century house, now a farmhouse, and farmland surrounded by high moors. 1½m SW of Middleham.

East Scar Top Farm. *SD98*
Farmland in Wensleydale.

Hayburn Wyke. *NZ09*
High cliffs overlooking a small bay and rocky beach 6m N of Scarborough. Access via Cleveland Way long-distance footpath.

Hudswell. *NZ10*
Woodland on south bank of river Swale, and also on the south side of the Leyburn to Reeth road.

Moulton Hall. *NZ20*
Rebuilt in mid 17th century; open by arrangement with the tenant. 5m E of Richmond.

Rigg Hall Farm, Staintondale. *SE09*
Small farm and 1,000yds of superb cliff. Access via Cleveland Way.

Saltwick Nab. *NZ91*
Cliffland with a low rocky nab jutting out into the sea; 1m E of Whitby. Access by a path near Abbey Farm.

Sanctuary Cross, Ripon. *SE37*
The remains of the only surviving cross which marks the limits of sanctuary attached to St Wilfrid's Abbey. At Sharow, ¾m NE of Ripon.

Scarth Wood Moor. *SE49*
Moorland near the Cleveland Hills.

TYNE AND WEAR

Penshaw Monument. *NZ35*
A Doric temple, commemorating the First Earl of Durham, Governor-General of Canada. Between Sunderland and Chester-le-Street.

SCOTLAND

Glenfinnan Monument —
a tower at the head of Loch Shiel

ANGUS FOLK MUSEUM

Tayside	*NO34*

A row of six early 19th-century cottages with stone-slabbed roofs houses the Angus Folk Museum, one of Scotland's finest collections depicting rural life. Over 1,000 items, illustrating the domestic, agricultural and social history of Scotland over two centuries are packed into these cottages, which have been sensitively converted into a single building. Old cottage crafts such as linen weaving and spinning are vividly recalled, whilst other 'static' rooms depict a Victorian manse parlour and a cottage kitchen, built in 1807. A workbench and lathe from Carmyllie recall the Rev. Patrick Bell, who built the first reaping machine. Another prized exhibit is the copper boiler in which a Forfar merchant, Peter Reid, concocted the celebrated Forfar rock which was to make his fortune. He was then able to finance the building of a public hall, a public park, and a chain of cast iron public lavatories, which he presented as gifts to his beloved home town.

An annexe holds a display of agricultural implements.

Open May to end Sept. Admission charged. Off A94, in Glamis, 6m SW of Forfar.

BACHELOR'S CLUB

Strathclyde	*NS42*

Scots bard Robbie Burns lived near the town of Tarbolton from 1777 to 1784, during which time he founded the Bachelor's Club, a debating society which met in this 17th-century thatched house and was open to any 'cheerful-hearted lad, who, if he has a friend that is true, and a mistress that is kind and as much wealth as genteely to make both ends meet – is just as happy as this world can make him'. Burns was also initiated as a Freemason here in 1781. This marked a change in Burns' life, for here was a social circle to give the young poet a chance to mature. The house now contains a Burns Museum, with relics dating mainly from when the Burns family lived at nearby Lochlea Farm, and it is decorated with period furniture.

Open April to end Oct. Admission charged. In Tarbolton, B744, 7½m NE of Ayr off A758.

BALMACARA ESTATE

Highland	*NG82*

Lowland in the Highlands may sound like a contradiction in terms, but the 5,616 acres of green peninsula that make up the Balmacara Estate come close to that description. Bounded by Loch Alsh, the Inner Sound and Loch Carron, the Estate, given to the Trust in 1946, is composed of mixed woodlands, green fields, rivers and a home farm.

Three crofting townships, an airstrip, the village of Plockton and the Kyle of Lochalsh – a rail terminal and ferryport for Skye – are included within the estate. All around is a staggering variety of landscapes and sea views, by virtue of the mountains, islands, headlands, inlets and bays which border Balmacara. Lochalsh Woodland Garden is another Balmacara property, a delightful place to take a walk in, especially in spring or autumn, when the trees are a kaleidoscope of colour. Lochalsh House is not open to the public, but an interesting natural history display can be seen in the Coach House.

Woodland Garden open all year, Coach House Easter to Mid Oct. Admission charged. Off the A87, adjoining Kyle of Lochalsh.

BANNOCKBURN

Central	*NS80*

This historic site is part of the battlefield where in 1314 Robert the Bruce, King of Scots, defeated the English army. Known as the greatest battle which ever took place on Scottish soil, the Battle of Bannockburn was the result of King Edward I of England's desire to rule the Scottish kingdom. After destroying the Scottish army at Falkirk in 1298 he looked set to achieve his aim; and the execution of patriot leader Sir William Wallace at King Edward's orders in 1305 seemed like just another nail in the Scots' coffin. Scotland was occupied from end to end by the English army, and final surrender seemed imminent. But in 1306 Robert the Bruce was crowned, and in the years that followed the occupied towns and fortresses were re-taken by his armies. Scotland was fighting back. Stirling Castle was the most important stronghold remaining in English hands, and King Robert was determined to retrieve it. When he finally did so on 24 June 1314 on the battlefield of Bannockburn, he became a national hero.

Edward II's 'Great Van', or heavy cavalry, was the instrument by which he won most of his battles, but by clever use of the land (Bruce forced the English to fight in a shallow, boggy valley) and brilliant deployment of his infantry, the Scottish king defeated Edward's cavalry. Edward was also hampered by a need for haste, for he had to relieve Stirling Castle by 24 June – battle was begun on 23 June – as it was promised to surrender on that day. Bruce's victory prevented Stirling from being relieved, and it surrendered.

This historic site, a shrine to the Scots' dream of independence, is now furnished with a Rotunda where objects from the battlefield are kept, and an imposing bronze statue of Bruce mounted on his horse. The Bannockburn Heritage Centre houses a visitor centre and national tourist information centre with shop, snack bar and audio-visual presentation.

Battlefield open all year, exhibition and shop open March to end Oct. Audio-visual presentation charged. Wheelchair access. Refreshments. Off M80/M9 at junction 9, 2m S of Stirling.

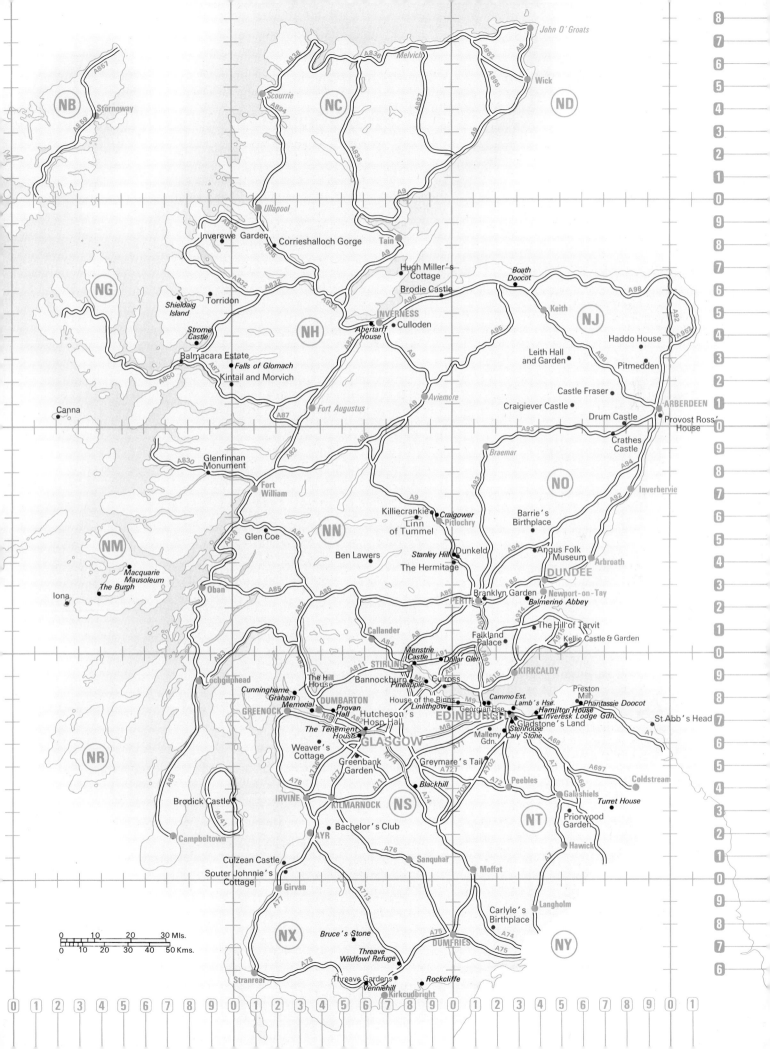

BARRIE'S BIRTHPLACE

Tayside   NO35

Sir James Barrie, creator of *Peter Pan*, was born at 9 Brechin Road, Kirriemuir in 1860. The two-storey building contains a museum where original manuscripts and some of Barrie's personal possessions are on display. Outside, in the old wash-house which the author used as his first theatre, there are drawings on wall plaques of famous characters from *Peter Pan* such as Tinkerbell, Wendy and Captain Hook. Mementoes of actors and producers associated with his plays form a separate exhibition. At his death in 1937 there were moves to transport Barrie's birthplace to the USA, but fortunately, Mr D. Alves bought the site and gave it to the Trust with funds for restoration.

Open May to end Sept. Admission charged. In Kirriemuir, 6m NW of Forfar.

BEN LAWERS

Tayside   NN64

Amid a region of natural wonders is Perthshire's highest mountain. The peaks of Ben Lawers soar 3,984ft above Loch Tay, cut about by glens and affording magnificent views from the Atlantic to the North Sea. Exposed areas of the constituent rocks in the burns and on the hillsides may offer geologists a clue as to why this beautiful mountain is covered with so many exquisite plants, making it Britain's largest and finest rock garden – but nobody really knows. Somehow altitude and exposure have combined to produce a stunning range of Arctic-Alpine flora that has survived from the early post-glacial period. Nourished by an abundance of fresh minerals, a spectacular display of wild flowers, mosses and glowing grassland rich in colour can be seen in June and July. In the Trust's care are 7,667 acres of the Lawers range; the southern slopes noted not only for the Alpine flowers but also for the diversity of wildlife they attract. Birds such as the buzzard, kestrel and red grouse make their home here.

In 1975 the mountain was declared a National Nature Reserve, and information sheets, audio-visual presentations and booklets are on hand at the Visitor Centre.

Centre open early April to end Sept. Admission charged. Off A827, 6m NE of Killin.

BRANKLYN GARDEN

Tayside   NO12

Dwarf rhododendrons are the speciality at Branklyn, often described as 'the finest two acres of private garden in the country'. Husband and wife team John and Dorothy Renton began to establish their garden in 1922 on the site of a former orchard. They experimented with seed from all over the world, and now the gardens are

From Small Beginnings . . .

During the first six years of his life James Matthew Barrie, the third son of a family of ten children, showed no signs of his future genius. He displayed none of the scholarship and ambition of his eldest brother, Alexander. He appeared to be like any other Kirriemuir boy, except that he loved to invent his own entertainment. This passion was sparked off by a toy theatre owned by a school friend called Mills, who was the son of a local bookseller. They played for hours together, pushing the tiny figures on and off stage, and soon they began to experiment. It was not long before the wash-house behind the Barrie's home at No. 9 Brechin Road was turned into an improvised theatre. Here Jamie and his friend acted stories, mostly taken from the Old Testament, and charged the other children of the neighbourhood either 'peeries' (tops) or 'bools' (balls) as an entry fee to see them.

It was not until later, after the family had moved to Forfar, that Barrie's gift for storytelling which spellbound his friends and family became forcefully apparent. But in that wash-house perhaps James Barrie first exercised that extraordinary imagination which produced *Peter Pan*, first staged at the Duke of York's Theatre, 27 December, 1904.

The island of Canna in the Small Isles, which have been designated a national scenic area

blessed with a superb collection, including Japanese orange-skinned birch, conifers and a variety of beautiful small-leaved plants. Bequeathed to the Trust in 1967, Branklyn Garden attracts botanists from all parts of the globe.

Open March to end Oct. Admission charged. On Dundee Road, Perth.

BRODICK CASTLE

Isle of Arran	NS03

Brodick Castle stands on a wooded slope on the Isle of Arran. Part of this castle, the subject of 'many upturnings and rebuildings', dates from the 13th century. Extensions built in 1652 and 1844 helped bring dignity to what was once purely a military base, with wide views across the Firth of Clyde. Until 1895 Brodick Castle was the seat of the Dukes of Hamilton, and the collections of paintings, silverware and porcelain that can be seen in the house today once belonged to the Hamilton family. Mary Louise, Duchess of Montrose, inherited Brodick in 1895, being the daughter of the Twelfth Duke of Hamilton. Her personal apartments are on show, filled with elegant 18th-century furniture. A Sheraton folding-topped mahogany dressing table, a Chippendale tallboy and a George III corner wash-stand are some of the treasures in her dressing room. The bedroom is hung with family portraits and watercolours – some the Duchess' own work.

Dominating the room is a Heppelwhite four-poster bed with a beautiful early Victorian rosewood bed table.

The Duchess of Montrose was responsible for starting the delightful woodland garden in 1923. It ranks as one of the foremost in the world for rhododendrons, and visitors can follow a self-guided woodland walk to its heart.

Castle open May to end Sept, limited opening April and Easter. Country park and garden open all year. Admission charged. Free parking. Refreshments. N of Brodick on the Isle of Arran.

BRODIE CASTLE

Grampian	NS95

The Brodie family was first endowed with its land by Malcolm IV in 1160, and the castle remained in the hands of that family until it was transferred to the Trust, a complicated transaction which was eventually completed in 1980. Most charters and records of the ancient Brodies – one of the oldest untitled landed families in the country – were lost when the house was 'byrnt and plunderit' by Lord Louis Gordon during the Civil War, but it is known that the house and the family had a chequered history. Largely rebuilt after the 1645 fire, disaster struck again in 1786 when the house caught fire once more, causing the death of Lady Margaret Duff, daughter of the Earl of Fife. The present structure is based on a 16th-century 'Z' plan, with additions made in the 17th and 19th centuries. Treasures inside the house include French furniture, Chinese porcelain, 17th-century Dutch paintings and early English watercolours.

A woodland walk takes visitors around the edge of a four-acre lake, with access to a wildlife observation hide. The 'wild' garden and the daffodil collection are delightful seasonal sights.

Open early April and May to end Sept. Admission charged. Free parking. Wheelchair access. Off A96, 4½m W of Forres, 24m E of Inverness.

CANNA

Highland	NG20

Accessible by ferry from Mallaig, Canna is the most westerly of the Small Isles group, and one of the most interesting islands in the Hebrides. A bird sanctuary, sheltering many rare species, including birds of prey, Canna is also of archaeological interest. Stone Age, early Christian, Viking and Celtic remains have been found here. Designated as a site of special scientific interest by the Nature Conservancy Council, this is one of the most interesting and scenic islands to be found off the Scottish coast, although it is only six miles long and half a mile wide.

Lochaber, Highland

CARLYLE'S BIRTHPLACE

Dumfries and Galloway NY28

Thomas Carlyle (1795–1881) exerted a great influence over British literature in the mid 19th century, and on the ethical, religious and political feelings of the time. He was born in an arched house on the main street of Ecclefechan in Annandale, on an ancient river route used by the Roman army to invade Scotland in AD 79. Built by his father and uncle, both master masons, the house incorporates two wings over a covered passage. Carlyle wrote of his father's buildings 'they stand firm and sound to the heart all over his little district' – he was obviously proud of his father's craft. The room where Carlyle was born is now furnished with a collection of the writer's belongings and manuscript letters. Also on show in the house are his crib and box bed and other period furniture.

Open early April to end Oct. Admission charged. A74 in Ecclefechan, 5½m SE of Lockerbie.

CASTLE FRASER

Grampian NJ71

Castle Fraser is one of the most spectacular of the castles of Mar. Built in the native castellated style on the site of what was a plain rectangular tower-house, Castle Fraser's graceful lines and splendid turrets are a monument to traditional grandeur. Michael Fraser began a spate of building work on the old tower about 1575, adding a square tower at the north-west corner. He created a new main entrance with a sweeping staircase leading to a series of small rooms. Two great master masons, Bel and Leiper, took part in the building work, which was completed in 1636, 48 years after Michael Fraser's death. Soon afterwards the lands around the castle were ravaged by Civil War, but the castle itself escaped unscathed. The Trust has set up a 'Castles of Mar' exhibition within Fraser, telling the story of this and other great buildings in the Scottish tradition. The old walled garden has been laid out along formal lines.

Castle open May to end Sept, gardens and grounds open all year. Admission charged to castle, grounds by donation. Free parking. Off B993, 3m S of Kemnay.

CHARLOTTE SQUARE AND GEORGIAN HOUSE

Lothian NT27

Edinburgh is justly famous for its elegant architecture, of which the north side of Charlotte Square is an excellent example. Classed as one of Robert Adam's masterpieces, this block of eleven separate houses, designed in 1791, was 'modernised' during the 19th century. Many of the drawing room windows were lowered in the fashionable Victorian style, front doors were altered and dormer windows added.

The magnificent tower of Crathes Castle, seen from the gardens. These have been described as one of the finest collections of plants in Scotland. They cover about six acres enclosed by a high stone wall and internally divided by hedges and borders

THE SCOTS STYLE

Castle Fraser, Crathes Castle and Craigievar are all impressively tall, turreted and romantic. These slender lines had little to do with defence as the 16th and 17th centuries were comparatively peaceful and prosperous, but had a great deal to do with economics. Stone was plentiful, timber scarce and expensive. So the Scots built tall. Rooms piled one on top of the other could share timber – the floorboards of one could act as the ceiling of another. Similarly roofs could be kept small, and so again use less timber. It was necessity as much as style which created these masterpieces of Scottish architecture.

From 1920 to 1930 the Fourth Marquess of Bute restored the façade to its original Georgian elegance once more. Each house has a basement and four upper floors, strangely enough with no out-buildings (such as stables). The average number who lived in each household was about 15, including a full staff of servants. Number 5 Charlotte Square is the Trust's headquarters, while number 6 serves as the offical residence for the Secretary of State for Scotland.

Number 7 Charlotte Square, known as the Georgian House, provides a complete example of life during the reign of George III. The furnished rooms on show include the dining room, with its Scottish sideboard with thistle decoration, Hamaden carpet and Wedgwood dinner service. The bed chamber is equipped with a medicine chest which boasts, among other things, a monstrous implement used for administering Georgian enemas.

No 7 open April to end Oct, limited opening to early Dec. Admission charged. In Edinburgh city centre.

The waters of the river Droma plummet 150ft over the Falls of Measach in a tumult of noise and spray between the sheer rock walls of Corrieshalloch Gorge. Dwarf rowan, hazel, birch and alder cling to the rocky sides, where ravens have been known to nest

CORRIESHALLOCH GORGE

Highland	NH27

This spectacular box canyon was created when the two summits of Beinn Dearg (3,547ft) and Sgurr Mor (3,637ft) became covered with an ice cap several thousand feet thick in the middle of the Ice Age. As the ice cap melted, the force of the water running down to Loch Broom cut this mile-long chasm out of solid rock. A suspension bridge built by Sir John Fowler, one of the designers of the Forth Railway Bridge, connects the two sheer rock walls of the gorge on a hairpin bend. Below the bridge the waters of the Falls of Measach plunge to a depth of 150 feet. In the crags and crannies in the walls of the canyon five species of fern thrive, and many other

plants now scarce in Scotland since the introduction of sheep. The Trust owns 35 acres around this site, including the rough grass slopes rising from the gorge to the roadside, which are planted with a variety of mixed woodlands such as larch, pine, holly, oak and sycamore.

On the A835 at Braemore, 12m SE of Ullapool.

CRAIGIEVAR CASTLE

Grampian	NJ50

The finest example of its type, this L-shaped tower house stands in a green, hilly countryside, so perfectly sited it appears almost to have grown alongside the mature trees that surround it. The ancient family of Mortimer is said to have begun building the castle towards the end of the 16th century. In 1610 they sold the estate to William Forbes, a successful merchant, who completed the building and interior decoration of Craigievar around 1626. Rising tall, graceful and turreted out of its braeside setting, the six-storeyed castle is an unspoiled example of Scottish baronial architecture. Inside however, the influence of the Renaissance is felt, particularly in the superb plasterwork. Running floral patterns and heroic devices decorate the vault of the great hall, a rare achievement in plaster that expresses the extraordinary mood of optimism in Scotland before the outbreak of the Civil War. Acquired by the National Trust for Scotland in 1963, the castle and its 30 acres of ground have since been extended by an additional 65 acres of farmland.

Open May to end Sept, grounds open all year. Admission charged. Free parking. On A980, 6m S of Alford, 26m W of Aberdeen.

CRATHES CASTLE

Grampian	NO79

Under construction around the same time as Castle Fraser, Crathes Castle was built to replace a swamp-girt tower in the Loch of Leys. On its pleasant, sloping site above the river Dee, this castle's fascination lies mainly within its walls. Making a brilliant display, the painted decoration on the beams and boards of the ceilings give a running commentary on life in the 16th and 17th centuries, complete with proverbs and texts. The Long Gallery is unique in this part of the country in having an oak ceiling decorated with ribs and carving.

The garden is divided into eight separate sections which in turn give marvellous displays throughout the year. The magnificent yew hedges date from 1702. Four nature trails wend their way through the grounds, and there is also a children's adventure playground.

Open early April and May to end Sept. Garden and grounds open all year. Admission charged. Wheelchair access. Restaurant. On A93, 3m E of Banchory, 15m W of Aberdeen.

CULLODEN

Highland   *NH74*

This is the site of the Battle of Culloden, fought on 16 April 1746. A huge memorial cairn marks the spot where a quarter of Bonnie Prince Charlie's Highland army was killed by the Duke of Cumberland's men in the battle which ended the '45 Rising. The English army engineered this spectacular defeat by use of ingenious tactics. Each of the Duke of Cumberland's men bayonetted the exposed side of the Highlander to his right, instead of attacking the man directly in front who would be looking to defend himself with his shield from a frontal attack. In a battle lasting around 40 minutes, 1,200 Scotsmen and 310 Englishmen died. Also in the Trust's care are the Graves of the Clans, simple headstones erected in 1881; the Cumberland Stone, from which the Duke of Cumberland surveyed the scene; Old Leanach farmhouse, around which the battle raged and which now contains contemporary furniture; and a large part of the battlefield. The visitor centre is equipped for audio-visual presentations and contains an up-dated historical display, a study room and a tea-room.

Site open all year, visitor centre open early April to early Oct. Admission charged. On B9006, 5m E of Inverness.

CULROSS

Fife   *NS98*

Culross is a living example of a 16th-century Scottish town. The National Trust for Scotland has restored the old houses with their crow-stepped gables and red pantiled roofs in this harbour town once famous for the manufacture of girdles for domestic baking. Presented with its

The Quelling of the '45

By one o'clock, 16 April 1746, the forces of the reigning monarch, George II, commanded by his son the Duke of Cumberland, were in position and ready for battle on bleak Culloden Moor. About 400–500yds away the army of Prince Charles, for the first time under his direct command, prepared to fight for the Jacobite cause, and re-establish the Stuarts on the English throne.

Prince Charles had marched from the Highlands as far south as Derby before news of superior forces nearby persuaded him to retreat – with London within his grasp just 127 miles away, and, unknown to him, George II preparing to flee. The Battle of Culloden, just four months later, was to decide the fate of the 1745 Rising once and for all.

It was a cold, gale-blown day, threatened with rain and sleet. The Highlanders of the Jacobite army were ill-prepared for a fight on open ground – they preferred the hillsides and glens where Cumberland's cavalry and artillery were less effective. They were also exhausted by a forced march the night before.

The battle began with the Jacobite guns opening fire. They did little damage, and were quickly silenced by Cumberland's answering volley. At last, after perhaps 20 minutes under heavy attack, and as the cold sleet began to fall, the Highlanders were given the order to charge. Almost immediately the Jacobite right wing became entangled with the troop in the centre, who were forced into the right by fierce enemy fire. There was confusion and in the press the Highlanders were unable to discharge their firearms before having to use their claymores. The left wing of the Jacobite charge thus found their right flank exposed and found they had further to charge over rough ground. Before they reached the enemy they could see the centre and right of their army cut to pieces. Prince Charles could not see clearly enough to utilise his reinforcements, and although he and his soldiers exhibited outstanding bravery, the Jacobites were forced to retreat. The day was lost before an hour's battle was fought.

The Memorial Cairn on Culloden Moor, measuring 20ft in height and about 18ft in diameter, stands where the fighting is believed to have been fiercest during the bloody Battle of Culloden in 1746. It was erected in 1881 by Duncan Forbes, 10th Laird of Culloden. The gaps in the rough stonework were originally planted with ferns, and ivy was dug in around the base; but neither would grow

Cumberland pursued his foes relentlessly, cutting down the retreating Highlanders without mercy, killing prisoners and wounded – acts which earned him the unenviable nickname 'Butcher' Cumberland, and which gave a foretaste of what was to happen in the months following the battle, when his army toured the Highlands destroying everything in their path.

Charles, after many adventures, escaped to France five months later, but the Stuart cause, and the Highland clan society which had so devotedly supported it, was lost forever.

For over 50 years the National Trust for Scotland has been gradually restoring the 16th-century township of Culross on the north shore of the Forth. Pictured here is the Study, named after the small, isolated room at the top of its tower. It is only one of several unusual and curiously named houses (all privately occupied) to be discovered among the town's narrow, twisting streets

royal charter in 1588, Culross was one of a chain of towns to enjoy the renaissance of Scottish trade and industry in the reign of James VI, thriving in the trading of coal and salt. The town's appearance today is the result of 50 years of continuing restoration by the Trust. Modern living standards have been achieved, yet the characteristic architecture preserved. Delightful old buildings owned by the Trust include the town house, built in 1626 and the 'study', an 'L' shaped house of the late 16th century, whose rooms were once wholly panelled in oak. Ruined St Mungo's Chapel, built in 1503 at the saint's birthplace, was presented to the Trust by the Earl of Elgin in 1947.

Town house open April to mid Oct, Study mid Oct to end March. Admission charged. Off A985, 12m W of Forth Road Bridge.

CULZEAN CASTLE

Strathclyde NS21

The mighty Kennedy family dominated the land along the Firth of Clyde from the 12th to the 17th century. Culzean was one of about a dozen small castles south of Ayr which formed their chain of command. In 1744 the Ninth Earl of Cassillis, Sir Thomas Kennedy, inherited Culzean, and began a programme of improvement to the building which included the addition of a new wing. When in 1775 David succeeded his brother Thomas as 10th Earl of Cassillis, he called in Robert Adam who added a grand oval staircase and some new rooms to each side of the old square house, enlarged the turrets and added some new ones to give a romantic look. In 1779 a round tower (which housed the brewhouse) and bedrooms were added to the long wing. Adam's plans also involved the demolition of Sir Thomas' wing, built in the 1760s, to accommodate a large round tower on the edge of the cliff. After Adam's death in 1792 various alterations were made to the castle, but it still remains a superb example of the architect's style.

The grounds of Culzean form what was Scotland's first country park, established in 1969. Noteworthy even in the 17th century, the gardens have been constantly improved ever since and they include an aviary, swan pond, camellia house and a home farm designed by Robert Adam.

Castle open April to end Oct, country park open all year. Admission charged. Wheelchair access to country park only. Restaurant. 4m W of Maybole, 12m S of Ayr.

DRUM CASTLE

Grampian NJ70

Built for Alexander III in the late 12th century, the great square tower of Drum dominates the castle to this day. The work of Richard Cementarius, the king's Master Mason, this mighty tower remained the home and stronghold of the lairds of Drum for eight generations. When Scotland's trade flourished in the 17th century, the castle flourished also, and a new house was built alongside the old tower. Another spell of prosperity in the 18th century brought further improvements, with a new arched north entrance by architect David Bryce, a gallery, staircase and reconstituted courtyard. The old hall became transformed into a grand library with heraldic devices in plasterwork on the ceiling.

The grounds contain plantations of conifers, deciduous woodland and an aboretum.

Open May to end Sept, grounds open all year. Admission charged. Free parking. Refreshments. Off A93, 3m W of Peterculter, 10m W of Aberdeen.

DUNKELD

Tayside	*NO04*

The Trust has owned 20 houses in High Street and Cathedral Street, Dunkeld, since 1954. The properties date in the main from the rebuilding of the town after the Battle of Dunkeld in 1689 between Jacobite forces (supporters of James VII) and William III's army. Known as the 'Little Houses', they have been well restored by the Trust and retain their authentic, 17th-century appearance. The wall of one house in the square bears an upright ell – a unit of measurement which is the Scottish equivalent of a yard – and is the site for the recently-opened Ell Shop, run by the Trust. Nearby is Hermitage Bridge and the Falls of Braan, in a picturesque wooded area. Stanley Hill, an artificial mound raised by the Duke of Atholl in 1730, provides a six-acre wooded backdrop to Dunkeld village.

Ell Shop open April to end Dec. Off A9, 15m N of Perth.

FAIR ISLE

Shetland Islands

Home of the beautiful and intricately-patterned jumpers, Fair Isle is the most isolated inhabited island in the British Isles. Situated midway between Orkney and Shetland on one of the major migration tracks, this small island (3m long and only half as wide) is a natural bird sanctuary with its own observatory and hostel. Over 300 species have been noted, and seabirds that breed here include the storm petrel, fulmar, shag, eider, gull, kittiwake, gannet and puffin.

In order to stem depopulation the Trust has encouraged improvements in housing, water supply and electricity – the latter provided by a chain of small diesel-powered generators now superseded by an aero-generator (windmill) giving electric power 24 hours a day for the first

The ancient, high square tower of Drum Castle overlooks the low, spacious extension of 1619, built when the expense of timber for roofs and floors was no longer a governing factor

Remote Glen Coe offers excellent opportunities to both the casual walker and the serious climber. Its stark grandeur is best seen in May and June, when the weather is most likely to be settled

LITTLE HOUSES

The Little Houses Improvement Scheme, run by the National Trust for Scotland, recognises the need to preserve the ordinary houses of centuries past. Small properties of architectural or historical merit are bought and then resold to a private owner who will either employ his own architect or the Trust to restore the house. Alternatively the Trust will restore the property at their own expense before selling. In every case the property is restored under the control of, or with the approval of, the Trust, and the owner must guarantee the integrity of the building in perpetuity. In this way the Trust ensures the survival of valuable buildings, and, through donations and the sale of such properties, the means by which further properties in need of their care can be purchased.

time on the island. A new airstrip, improved radio links and fire fighting equipment have also been installed by the Trust.

Fair Isle lives up to its name; it really is a beautiful island, especially in summer, when wild flowers transform the sandstone cliffs into a riot of colour.

Bird Observatory open Mar to end Nov. Access is by mailboat; the Good Shepherd III, *which sails twice weekly in summer, or by plane with Loganair. Between Orkney and Shetland.*

GLADSTONES' LAND

Lothian   NT37

Gladstones' Land is a six-storey tenement block in Edinburgh's Royal Mile. Owned by merchant Thomas Gledstanes for about 14 years, the 17th-century property contains some remarkable painted ceilings – and preserves Edinburgh's last arcaded ground-floor. After purchasing the site in 1617 from the Fisher family, Gledstanes was able to alter it architecturally to comply with fashionable taste. He added a new façade the depth of a room and a staircase to the front of the 'L'-shaped building. Inside, the wooden ceilings bearing painted designs of flowers and fruit, with the date 1620 are perhaps the site's most noteworthy feature, and enough to ensure that their benefactor's name lives on. The rooms have been refurbished in period style. At street level the building is furnished with reconstructed shop booths, in which replicas of 17th-century goods are displayed.

Open April to end Oct, limited opening Nov to early Dec. Admission charged. In the Lawnmarket, Royal Mile, Edinburgh City Centre.

GLEN COE

Highland   NN15

The spectacular mountain wilderness known as Glen Coe comprises some of the finest climbing and walking country in the Highlands. Although now popular enough in summer to cause conservation worries, Glen Coe was once cursed with an image of gloom and misery. 'Glen Coe itself is perfectly terrible' wrote Charles Dickens during an 1841 tour of the Highlands. This lingering feeling of distaste felt by many in the 18th and 19th centuries is no doubt due to the Massacre of Glen Coe, an atrocious piece of butchery that shocked contemporary opinion in the 1690s.

The MacDonald Clan of Glen Coe had failed to swear allegiance to King William within a prescribed time limit set by the Government, so the King's troops were sent in to the glen with the barbaric order 'do not trouble the Government with prisoners'. For almost a fortnight the troops were billeted upon the neighbourhood of Glen Coe, enjoying the hospitality of the unsuspecting people, before turning on their hosts in a bloody massacre in which men, women and children were slaughtered, houses were burnt down and livestock driven away.

The inaccessibility and remoteness of the area contributed much to the glen's sinister atmosphere, until the advent of roads towards the end of the 18th century made Glen Coe more accessible to travellers.

Today the 14,200 acres in the Trust's care support wildlife such as red deer, wildcat, golden eagle, dotterel, golden plover, ptarmigan, mallard and teal, although shelter is scarce.

Visitor Centre open early April to early Oct. Admission charged. Free parking. Lochaber, Highland, A82.

GLENFINNAN MONUMENT

Highland   NM98

Erected in 1815, the monument that stands at the head of Loch Shiel is a tower enclosed within a grassy, walled area, surmounted by a kilted figure added in 1834. It was built in memory of the clansmen who followed Prince Charles Edward Stuart in the third and last, unsuccessful attempt to reinstate the Stuart kings on the British throne. Symbolically the statue is dedicated to all men who fought and died for the Highlands and their Prince. The figure's sculptor was John Greenshields of Carluke, Lanarkshire.

Three large plaques, inscribed in Gaelic, English and Latin tell the story of the monument, which is said to stand on the exact spot where the Prince raised his standard in 1745.

Open early April to early Oct. Admission charged. Refreshments. A830, 18½m W of Fort William.

GREENBANK GARDEN

Strathclyde NS55

A typical Scottish walled garden, Greenbank's two and half acres surround an elegant Georgian house built for a Glasgow merchant in 1763. A public appeal for the establishment of a Gardening Advice Centre resulted in Greenbank being accepted by the Trust in 1976 and turned into a kind of outdoor gardening school, with regular classes and demonstrations. Greenbank has special appeal to owners of small gardens.

Open all year. Admission charged. Wheelchair access. S of Glasgow city centre, off Mearns Road.

GREY MARE'S TAIL

Dumfries and Galloway NT15

Descriptively named, Grey Mare's Tail is a rippling waterfall that cascades from a height of 200ft to join the Moffat Water in a torrent of white foam. Around the waterfall rare and beautiful wild flowers grow, and a herd of wild goats crop the grass. Information boards by the roadside give notes on the flora and fauna of the area. Acquired in 1962, the Trust's one and only property in the southern uplands is traversed only by steep, sometimes dangerous paths, and visitors are advised to take the greatest of care when walking in this 2,383-acre area.

10m NE of Moffat off A708.

HADDO HOUSE

Grampian NJ83

Designed in 1731 by William Adam for William, Second Earl of Aberdeen, Haddo House was built between 1732 and 1735 on the site of the old fortified House of Kellie. Adapted from the Palladian style of Italy, the house is designed on the *piano nobile* plan. The north wing was originally designed as stables and granaries, the south as kitchens and servants' quarters. Most of Earl William's entertaining would have been carried out in the centre block's elegant first and second floor rooms, with the ground floor reserved for offices and the children's nursery. This basic composition remains unchanged.

Haddo House is renowned for its Choral Society, founded in 1945, and boasts an international reputation for concerts, opera and drama which attracts top performers from around the world.

When in 1978 Haddo House and grounds came into the care of the Trust, 180 acres of adjoining parkland were given to Grampian Regional Council for the establishment of a country park. A network of enchanting woodland paths wind through an area of varied scenery which attracts all kinds of wildlife. At the centre of the park is a bird observation hide, and hundreds of geese and ducks roost on the middle lake.

Open May to end Sept (except 15–16 May) Admission charged. Wheelchair access. Refreshments. Off B999, 4m N of Pitmedden.

THE CURSE OF GIGHT

On the Haddo estate are the ruins of Gight Castle. It had been the home of the Gordons for centuries until debts forced the family to sell in 1786. Centuries before the Seer, Thomas the Rhymer, had cursed the house when the owner had refused him hospitality.

When the heron leaves the tree
The laid o'Gight shall landless be
At Gight three men a violent death
*   shall dee*
And after that the lands shall lie in lea.

The 1786 sale fell through, but the resident herons left to settle at Haddo. Next year the land was bought by Lord Haddo. In 1791 he was killed at Gight in a riding accident. A few years later a farm servant met a similar fate, then in 1856 a third man was killed by a falling wall. The wise man's prophecy was finally fulfilled.

The drawing room at Haddo House was designed by William Adam in 1731. This room is situated on the first floor, with other elegant rooms used solely for entertaining. The front door originally opened on to this floor, which made this room cold and draughty despite its luxurious appearance; perhaps that was one of the reasons why the front entrance was brought down to ground level in 1880

The 18th-century house at Greenbank is the attractive focus for a series of small gardens displaying flowers, shrubs and vegetables as part of a garden advice centre for amateur gardeners. The interior of the house is not normally open to visitors

THE HERMITAGE

Tayside   NO04

The Hermitage, a charming 18th-century folly in a picturesque setting on the river Braan, was originally the centrepiece of a wild garden. Built in 1758 as a summer house placed to give the most dramatic view of the cascading waterfall below, the Hermitage was also known as Ossian's Hall and belonged to the Duke of Atholl. The rectangular building with its slate roof and circular look-out platform is surrounded by 37 acres of interesting woodland, including some Douglas fir, through which winds a nature trail.

Parking charged. Off A9, 2m W of Dunkeld.

HILL OF TARVIT

Fife   NO31

A gem from the Edwardian era, this interesting mansion was designed by Sir Robert Lorimer for F. B. Sharp, a connoisseur who wanted each room to become a harmonious backcloth to his works of art. The oak-panelled central hall contains two 16th-century Flemish tapestries, and in the airy drawing room elegant pieces of 18th-century French furniture by J. C. Saunier

and Adam Weisweiler stand. The dining room is the background for heavier English furniture, while superb quality paintings by Raeburn and Ramsey, and Chinese porcelain and bronzes decorate other rooms. A restored Edwardian laundry is a major point of interest, and visitors may take a woodland path to a hilltop toposcope.

House open Easter, then May to end Sept, grounds open all year. Admission charged. Off A916, 2½m S of Cupar.

THE HILL HOUSE

Strathclyde   NS28

Successful publisher Walter Blackie bought some land in fashionable Helensburgh in 1902. He then commissioned Glasgow-born architect Charles Rennie Mackintosh to design him a family villa on the crown of a hill – hence the name of what became one of the architect's most spectacular houses. Complete unity of design has been achieved in the Hill House, meaning that Mackintosh included in his plans the shape, space, lighting, decoration, furniture and smallest details of every room. Perhaps the most striking feature of the house is his use of inlaid coloured glass, adding an extra dimension by the way it catches the sun at various times of

the day. Other themes include the contrast between light and dark throughout the house, and the geometric and curvilinear patterning on doors, walls, carpets and chair backs.

This architecturally complex house has many ultra-modern features, yet many which were inspired by ancient Scottish architecture. Mackintosh designed the house integrally within a formalised garden setting, including everything down to the arrangement of roses in the flower beds.

Open all year. Admission charged. Upper Colquhoun Street, Helensburgh, Strathclyde.

HOUSE OF THE BINNS

Lothian NT07

Astride the western slopes of twin hills (called binns or bynnis in old Scots) is the historic house of the Dalyell family. Bought in 1612 by Thomas Dalyell, and enlarged and redecorated by him up until 1630, the house stands today as an example of changing architectural tastes. In Thomas's day it was a tall, grey, three-storeyed building with small windows and twin stair turrets. His son, General Tam Dalyell, created a 'U' shaped building around a cobbled courtyard with the addition of a west wing, and in the 1740s Sir Robert Dalyell, the Fourth Baronet, made further additions, and so did his son. The result, after a complete refacing of the building by architect William Burn in the 19th century, is a Regency style country mansion. The beautiful moulded plaster ceilings which survive from the early 17th century are the outstanding architectural feature of the house.

Open Easter, May to end Sept. Admission charged. Off A904, 15m W of Edinburgh.

HUGH MILLER'S COTTAGE

Highland NA76

Geologist, editor and author Hugh Miller was born in this thatched cottage at Cromarty on 10 October 1802. A booklet is available to guide visitors around the small museum dedicated to the life of the stonemason who became an

GENERAL TAM OF THE BINNS

General Tam Dalyell, the son of the founder of the House of the Binns, was by all accounts an outstanding character. The legends attached to his name seem only to confirm this. A popular myth is that he played cards with the Devil. He usually lost, but on one occasion, he managed to win a game, which so enraged the Devil that he threw the card table at Tam's head. Fortunately it missed, and was said to have fallen into nearby Sergeant's Pond. Strangely enough, in the dry summer of

The House of The Binns was built by Thomas Dalyell, an Edinburgh butter merchant, who through marriage became Deputy Master of the Rolls under James I

1878, a heavy, carved marble table was recovered from the mud of the same pond, where it had lain for 200 years. The table is on show inside the house.

The General's boots are also kept at the Binns. Water poured into them is said to boil, and if they are taken from the house, they walk, restless to return home. John Dalyell, the General's son, took them to his home at Lingo, in Fife. But every night, when he took them off, they woke the household with their walking, and had to be sent back to the Binns.

The remote little island of Iona – the cradle of Christianity in Scotland and an ancient seat of Celtic culture. The restored abbey can be seen in the background

eminent geologist and man of letters. The house, built in 1711 for John Fiddes, Miller's seafaring grandfather, is the town's only surviving 18th-century building. Miller's geological collection and some of his ltters are on display inside.

Open May to end Sept. Admission charged. A832 in Cromarty, 22m NE of Inverness.

HUTCHESONS' HOSPITAL HALL

Strathclyde NS67

This 19th-century building, designed by David Hamilton, who also designed the Royal Exchange in Glasgow, was completed in 1805. Records note that in December, 1804, George Johnston was paid £2 2s 0d for fixing the weather vane on top of the steeple. The building was administered by the Hutchesons' Educational Trust, and comprised a hall with schoolrooms above. In 1876 the architect John Baird did away with the schoolrooms, and raised the ceiling of the hall to give it its present

impressive and elegant proportions. It is now used as the Trust's Glasgow offices, and houses a visitor centre and a shop.

Open all year. S of Musselburgh (A6124), 1588 Ingram Street, Glasgow.

INVEREWE GARDEN

Highland NG98

Three people were instrumental in creating Inverewe Garden. The first was Osgood Mackenzie, who bought the estate in 1862 and worked on it until his death in 1922. The second was his daughter, Mrs Mairi T. Sawyer, who devoted her lifetime to the garden, passing it over to the National Trust for Scotland in 1952, a year before her death. Third was Dr J. M. Cowan, one of Scotland's most respected horticulturists in the 1950s, who instigated improvements and plant introductions at Inverewe until 1960.

The close proximity of the Gulf Stream provides Inverewe with the warmth necessary for thriving plants, and harsh frosts are rare. Rainfall averages nearly 60ins a year; much of it is caught and conserved by the trees – of which there is a large variety at Inverewe – and released slowly so that it does not erode the soil, but keeps it moist. The trees also help to maintain the equability of temperature which is so necessary for the plants and shrubs. Plants from many lands flourish in this sheltered, fertile spot which was once nothing more than a barren headland on the shores of Loch Ewe. Eucalyptus, rhododendron and many colourful Chilean and South African plants are represented, together with Himalayan lilies and giant forget-me-nots, making a spectacular all-year-round display.

Open all year. Admission charged. Wheelchair access. Restaurant. On A832 by Poolewe, 6m NE of Gairloch.

IONA

Strathclyde NM22

This tiny Inner Hebridean island was colonised by St Columba and his followers from Ireland in AD 563. They came to establish a monastery and convert Scotland to Christianity, spreading the gospel as far as the North of England. St Columba died in AD 597 and his remains were taken back to Ireland. Iona became a place of pilgrimage and many kings and clan chiefs were buried here including King Duncan, whose reputed murder by Macbeth in 1040 was the subject of one of Shakespeare's best-known tragedies. The Abbey and other sacred buildings belong to Iona Cathedral trustees, but the rest of the 1,897-acre island is in the care of the National Trust for Scotland.

Access is by ferry from Fionnphort on Mull. Off the Isle of Mull.

KELLIE CASTLE AND GARDEN

Fife   *NO50*

The history of Kellie Castle reaches back to the 13th century, when the family of Siward had a small castle or tower on the site. The Siwards came to Scotland at the time of Macbeth, and were mentioned in the Shakespeare play. The first extension was made in 1573, when a new tower was built about 50ft away from the old one. At the turn of the new century, building work began to join the two towers by inserting a modern mansion house in between. The castle and estates were sold in 1613 to the family of Erskine, who, during the Civil War, were staunchly Royalist. After the Restoration some elaborate plasterwork was added to the ceilings in four of the rooms. A good example of the domestic architecture of Lowland Scotland, Kellie is now host to an exhibition of the work of architect Sir Robert Lorimer, whose family played a great part in restoring the castle.

Open mid April to end Sept. Garden open all year. Admission charged. Wheelchair access to the garden. On B9171, 3m NNW of Pittenweem.

KILLIECRANKIE

Tayside   *NN96*

Queen Victoria was amused by the Pass of Killiecrankie; she admired this famous beauty spot in 1844. Fifty-four acres around the picturesque wooded gorge are owned by the Trust and are now treasured for the wealth of wildlife found here. But in 1689 Killiecrankie was the site of a bloody battle when King William's troops were defeated by the Jacobite army led by John Graham of Claverhouse – Viscount Dundee, the 'Bonnie Dundee' of the Scots ballad. Dundee was killed at the moment of victory, and a stone marks the spot where he fell. A steep footpath leads to Soldier's Leap, where a trooper is said to have jumped the gorge across the river Garry to escape the Royalist Highlanders. The history and natural history of the Pass are clearly explained in the Visitor Centre.

Visitor Centre open early April to mid Oct. Admission charged for adults, free for children. Refreshments. A9, 3m N of Pitlochry.

KINTAIL AND MORVICH

Highland   *NG01*

A profusion of mountains, lochs, glens and rivers make this one of the most scenic areas in Scotland. The pride of the West Highlands are the steepest grass-sloped mountains in Scotland. Known as the Five Sisters of Kintail, four of the chain of five pointed peaks top 3,000ft. The highest, called Scour Ouran, is a celebrated viewpoint. The area abounds in highland wildlife; red deer, wild goats, merlin, black-throated diver, short-eared owl, greenshank, golden plover and ptarmigan can be seen here, and flora such as mountain azalea, saxifrages, cloudberry and marsh marigold – even 3,000ft up. Morvich, off the A87 at the east end of Loch Duich, is the best point of access to the mountains. At Morvich Farm is a National Trust for Scotland information centre.

Information centre open June to end Sept. Admission free. N of A87, 16m E of Kyle of Lochalsh.

LEITH HALL AND GARDEN

Grampian   *NJ53*

Leith Hall is the centrepiece of this 236-acre estate owned by the Trust. From 1650 it was the home of the Leiths, a family of the Scots lairds who were among those to engineer the change from poverty to prosperity in rural areas by their pioneering attitude towards agriculture. The house is typical of many built during the first half of the 17th century; a rectangular block enclosing a courtyard. Inside are the personal possessions of the successive lairds of Leith, most of whom were in military service. The grounds are a mixture of farm and woodland, with two ponds, a bird observation hide and three countryside walks. Interesting features include a flock of Soay sheep, an ice house where ice was kept before the invention of refrigerators, a 17th-century stable block and an informal rock garden.

House open May to end Sept, grounds open all year. Admission charged. 1m W of Kennethmont.

The garden of Kellie Castle, like the house, was rescued from years of neglect in 1878 by Professor James Lorimer and his wife. She described the state of the garden: 'The garden, still encircled by a tumbledown wall, was a wilderness of neglected gooseberry bushes, gnarled apple trees, and old-world roses, which struggled through the weeds, summer after summer, with a sweet persistence.' Today the 16 acres of gardens, including the fine walled rose garden, are fully restored

The pointed peaks of the Five Sisters, in the heart of Kintail country, rise abruptly from the waters of Loch Duich to heights in excess of 3,000ft. The National Trust for Scotland cares for about 15,000 acres of this dramatic countryside

LINN OF TUMMEL

Tayside   NN86

A fascinating and unusual flora and fauna are the attractions of the Linn of Tummel, 50 acres by the banks of twin rivers Tummel and Garry. The Linn, meaning 'pool' in Gaelic, was created when the Loch Faskally reservoir was built by the North Scotland Hydro-Electric Board. An early example of a 'fish pass' can be seen beside the Linn, where fish enter a 40ft tunnel in order to avoid the cruel torrents of the falls.

2½m NW of Pitlochry.

MALLENY GARDEN

Lothian   NT16

The Trust's gardening advice centre operates at Malleny Garden. Children from local primary schools come here to learn about plant life in a practical way, sowing seed and watching the progress of plants through the seasons. A woodland garden and a fine collection of shrubs are to be found at Malleny. The 17th-century house is not open to the public.

Open May to end Sept. Admission charged. Wheelchair access. In Balerno, Edinburgh, off A70.

PITMEDDEN

Grampian   NJ82

Sir Alexander Seton designed Pitmedden's
Great Garden, inspired by the formal gardens of
the French. When the Trust took over the
property in 1952 little of the original design
remained, due to a fire in 1818. Only an
architectural skeleton was still intact – the
pavilions, walls and stairs which framed the
garden. Dr James S. Richardson HRSA,
formerly Inspector of Ancient Monuments in
Scotland, and other experts were brought in to
restore the garden to its former glory. The
elaborate floral designs take the form of four
formal parterres. Three of them were probably
modelled on the gardens of the Palace of
Holyroodhouse, Edinburgh, in 1647. The
fourth is a heraldic design based on Sir
Alexander Seton's coat of arms. Sir Alexander
planned a high retaining wall with viewing
terraces to the north and south, so that the
intricate patterns could be viewed from above.
Only the north terrace remains; a low wall marks
the spot where the southern one stood.

The maintenance of the Great Garden is a
major task. Forty thousand annual plants,
nurtured in greenhouses and planted each May,
provide the colours of the four parterres. A herb
garden has recently been added to the upper part
of the Great Garden.

Also on the 100-acre estate are a Museum of
Farming Life, with a collection of agricultural
and domestic articles bequeathed to the Trust in
1978, and several rare breeds of livestock.

*Open all year. Museum and other facilities open
May to end Sept. Admission charged. Wheelchair
access. Refreshments. 1m W of Pitmedden village.*

PRESTON MILL

Lothian   NT67

This 16th-century mill ground its last sack of
oatmeal in 1957. It is the oldest mechanical
water-driven mill in Scotland, and was once an
abundant producer of Scotland's traditional
fare. Artists delight in the mill's romantic
setting, the conical-roofed kiln and red pantiled
outbuildings reflected in the waters of the river.
A short walk away is Phantassie Doocot, given
to the Trust in 1961 by William Hamilton of
Phantassie Farm. Five hundred birds once
nested within this massive stone structure with
its sloping, southern facing roof.

*Open all year. Admission charged. Off A1 in East
Linton, 5½m W of Dunbar.*

PRIORWOOD GARDEN

Borders   NT53

Only flowers suitable for drying are grown at
Priorwood, a small but special garden formally
designed with herbaceous and everlasting

annual borders. An attractive orchard boasts a
special walk entitled 'Apples through the ages',
and sweet-smelling dried flowers are on sale in
the Trust shop.

*Open April to mid Dec. Admission by donation.
A6091, in Melrose*

PROVOST ROSS'S HOUSE

Grampian   NJ90

Built in 1593, Provost Ross's House is
Aberdeen's third oldest building. Probably the
work of master mason Andrew Jamesone, the
house is a fine example of early Scottish
domestic architecture with its dormer windows,
projecting tower and arcading. There are plans
to open the property as a maritime museum in
Spring 1984.

Shiprow, in Aberdeen city centre.

ST ABB'S HEAD

Borders   NT97

Described as the 'most important location for
cliff nesting seabirds in south-east Scotland', St
Abb's Head is a spectacular 192-acre headland.
Smugglers once hid their booty in caves within
St Abb's 300ft cliffs. Colonies of guillemots,
kittiwakes, razorbills, shags, fulmars and herring
gulls make their nests here, while migrants use
the headland as a staging post. This Grade 1 Site
of Special Scientific Interest also has

*Stac Lee, west of Boreray, St Kilda, is
the home of the largest gannetry in the
world*

*Box hedges and 40,000 bedding plants
recreate superb 17th-century
parterres at Pitmedden*

considerable botanical and archaeological attractions, and the sea off the coast has been declared a marine nature reserve in recognition of its rich underwater life. The headland was named after St Ebba, daughter of a king of Northumbria.

Parking by donation. Off A1107, 2m N of Coldingham.

ST KILDA

Western Isles

The most westerly group of islands in Britain, the St Kilda archipelago lies 110 miles out in the Atlantic. Until over 50 years ago the main island of Hirta was inhabited, but in 1930 the islanders asked to be evacuated. They had eked a living on the island by crofting, fishing, keeping sheep and fowling among the great colonies of sea birds. The islands have their own sub species of mouse, wren and sheep, plus numerous fulmars and puffins. Boreray and Stacs together form the world's largest gannetry. Each year volunteers join Trust working parties to restore and maintain Hirta's primitive dwellings.

Western Isles.

The Birds of St Kilda

The St Kilda group consists of four islands and many awesome rocky outcrops. The largest island is Hirta, whose 1,575 acres rise to nearly 1,400ft and include the highest sea cliff in Britain – the Ard Uachdrachd buttress of Conachair (1,397ft). This cliff and those on the western face of Boreray are the best for seabirds in the country.

The largest gannetry in the world is on St Kilda, where 44,000 pairs of gannets breed annually. To see these great white birds, with wing spans over 6ft, dive from 100ft for fish they have spotted in the sea below, is a spectacular sight. Forty thousand fulmars nest on St Kilda, and also large numbers of toy-like puffins, storm petrels (like sea-going house-martins), nocturnal Leach's petrels and Manx shearwaters, which only visit land once a year under cover of darkness to breed. Other species include guillemot, black guillemot, kittiwake gulls and the soft-downed eider duck. St Kilda's very own bird is the St Kilda wren, a unique sub-species of which about 100 pairs breed on Hirta.

The birds of St Kilda provided the crofters who lived here until 1930 with valuable income. They ate their eggs, caught young gannets for fresh meat, puffins for feathers and meat, and fulmars for oil. The birds also fertilised the sparse grasslands on which the primitive Soay sheep graze, thought to be similar to those farmed by our neolithic forebears.

Today, St Kilda is a National Nature Reserve, a status it achieved in 1957 when it was handed to the Trust and when it was repopulated as a missile-tracking station by the Department of Defence.

SOUTER JOHNNIE'S COTTAGE

Strathclyde   *NS20*

This 18th-century thatched cottage once belonged to the village cobbler, or 'souter', John Davidson. Robert Burns immortalised the character which he based on Davidson and called Souter Johnnie in his ballad *Tam O'Shanter*. The cottage is now a Burns museum and life-size stone figures of the poet's characters can be seen in the garden.

Open April to end Sept. Admission charged. On A77 in Kirkoswald, 4m W of Maybole.

THREAVE GARDEN

Dumfries and Galloway   *NX76*

Threave Estate came into the hands of the National Trust for Scotland in 1948. Since then, it has been the Trust's policy to integrate farming, forestry and a refuge for wildlife as part of the same estate. A school of gardening was opened here in 1960, designed to give young people training in all aspects of horticulture. The students enrol for a two-year residential course, staying at Threave House, which has been converted into a hostel and is not open to the public. The garden is of interest throughout the year, but it is particularly pretty in April and May when daffodils and other spring flowers

In the garden of Souter Johnnie's Cottage sit the lifelike stone figures of the Souter, Tam o' Shanter, the innkeeper and his wife; all characters from Robert Burns's immortal ballad Tam o' Shanter. *They were sculpted by James Thom of Tarbolton*

OTHER PROPERTIES

BORDERS

Turret House. *NT73*
Dominant feature of Abbey Close, opposite Kelso Abbey. Just off A698, in Kelso. Not open.

CENTRAL

Cunninghame Graham Memorial. *NS37*
Cairn to the memory of R. B. Cunninghame, the distinguished Scottish author. Off A81 in Gartmore, 2½m SW of Aberfoyle.

Dollar Glen. *NS99*
A wooded glen with an attractive walk to Castle Campbell. Path can be dangerous when wet. Under the guardianship of the Scottish Development Department. Off A91, N of Dollar.

Menstrie Castle. *NS89*
Birthplace of Sir William Alexander. Not Trust property, but Trust devised Commemorative Rooms open to public. In Menstrie on A9 5m NE of Stirling. Limited opening to end Sept.

The Pineapple. *NS88*
Extraordinary house shaped like a pineapple. N of Airth, 7m E of Stirling off A905, then off B9124. Let to Landmark Trust, who rent it as a holiday home. Not open.

DUMFRIES AND GALLOWAY

Bruce's Stone. *NX57*
A granite boulder which marks the spot where Bruce defeated the English in 1307. 6m W of New Galloway on A712.

Rockcliffe
Mote of Mark and Rough Island. *NX85*
An ancient hill-fort and an island which is an important nesting site for seabirds. It is requested that the island is not visited during May and June.

Muckle Lands and Jubilee Path. *NX86*
Rough coastline between Rockcliffe and Kippford.

Threave Wildfowl Refuge. *NX76*
Roosting and feeding place for many species of geese (including 1,500 greylag geese) and duck beside the river Dee. Access Nov to March. Off A75, 1m W of Castle Douglas.

Venniehill. *NX65*
Viewpoint to be installed. On A75, in Gatehouse of Fleet. Not yet open.

FIFE

Balmerino Abbey. *NO32*
Ruins of a Cistercian monastery founded in 1229. Picnic area. Visitors may not enter the buildings but can view them from the grounds. Off A914, in Balmerino, 5m SW of Newport-on-Tay.

HIGHLAND

Abertarff House. *NH64*
A 16th-century town house. Let to An Comunn Gaidhealach (The Highland Association). Church Street, Inverness. Not open.

Boath Doocot. *NJ26*
A 17th-century doocot on the site of an ancient motte. In Auldearn on A96, 2m E of Nairn.

The kitchen at Weaver's Cottage, Kilbarchan. Andrew, John and Jenet Bryden built the house in 1723; they left their initials carved into the lintel above the front door. The cottage was lived in by handloom weavers until 1940, and it is now a museum of the local weaving industry

TORRIDON

Highland   *NG93*

Some 16,000 acres of the Torridon are owned by the National Trust for Scotland, including some of Scotland's finest mountain scenery. The mouth of the great sea loch of Torridon splits into upper Loch Torridon and Loch Shieldaig as it progresses inland, and spectacular red sandstone mountains capped with white quartzite rise in the north. Beinn Eighe (3,309ft) and seven-peaked Liathach (3,456ft) are sculpted from sandstone 750 million years old, and contain some very early fossils. In addition to their scenic splendour the mountains are remarkable for their wildlife. Red and roe deer, mountain goat, mountain hare, wild cat and the rare golden eagle can be found here. At the Trust countryside centre at the junction of A896 and the Diabeg road there is a red deer museum and an audio-visual presentation of local wildlife.

Deer museum and display open June to end Sept. Admission to museum charged. N of A896, 9m SW of Kinlochewe.

WEAVER'S COTTAGE

Strathclyde   *NS46*

This 18th-century cottage contains all the trappings of a handloom weaver living in the 1700s. Looms, weaving equipment and domestic utensils can be found inside the cottage, and weaving demonstrations take place on certain days. The attractive cottage garden is also open to visitors.

Open April to end Oct. Admission charged. Refreshments. In Kilbarchan, 8m SW of Glasgow.

bloom in the woodlands. In summer shrub roses steal the show and in winter the holly collection is particularly festive. Other features of the garden are the nursery, the vegetable garden, the pond and herbaceous beds, arboretum, heather garden and rockery.

A roosting and feeding place for wild geese and duck is one mile from the garden on the river Dee.

Open all year. Admission charged. Wheelchair access. Refreshments. Off A75, 1m W of Castle Douglas.

Falls of Glomach. *NH02*
One of Britain's highest waterfalls. N of A87, 18m E of Kyle of Lochalsh. Access by Glen Elchaig, as far as Killilan Square, then 5m on foot; or by Dorusduain on foot starting 2m NE of Kintail Lodge Hotel.

Shieldaig Island. *NG85*
A 32-acre island covered with Scots pine. In Loch Torridon, off Shieldaig.

Strome Castle. *NG83*
Ruins of a castle, destroyed in 1602. Off A896, 4½m SW of Lochcarron.

LOTHIAN

Caiy Stone. *NT26*
A 9ft sandstone monolith. Off B701, Oxgangs Road, Edinburgh.

Cammo Estate. *NS17*
100 acres now feued to the City of Edinburgh District Council for public open space. Off A90, Cramond Brig, Edinburgh.

Hamilton House. *NT37*
A 17th-century house. Off A198, in Prestonpans, 8½m E of Edinburgh. Open only by prior arrangement with the tenant.

Inveresk Lodge Garden. *NT47*
Garden of a 17th-century house with plants for the small garden. A6124, S of Musselburgh, 7m E of Edinburgh. Admission charged. Garden limited opening all year, house not open.

Lamb's House. *NT27*
House and warehouse of a prosperous merchant of the late 16th or early 17th century. Used as an old people's day centre. Off A199, Leith, Edinburgh. Open by appointment only.

Linlithgow. *NS97*
Two typical 16th- or early 17th-century houses. Nos 44 and 48 High Street, Linlithgow. Not open.

Phantassie Doocot. *NT67*
Doocot which once held 500 birds, near Preston Mill (see page 170). Off

A1, in East Linton, 5½m W of Dunbar.

Stenhouse Mansion. *NT27*
Home of a 17th-century merchant. Let to the Scottish Development Department. Just off A71, Gorgie Road, Edinburgh.

STRATHCLYDE

Blackhill. *NS84*
Cairn fort with views over the Clyde valley. Between A72 and A74, Stonebyres, 3m W of Lanark.

The Burg. *NM42*
1,525 acres of the Isle of Mull, with high cliffs known as the 'Wilderness'. 5m W on track from B8035 on N shore of Loch Scridain, Isle of Mull. Cars not advisable beyond Tiroran; from here a tough 5m walk.

Macquarie Mausoleum. *NM53*
Mausoleum of Lachian Macquarie, born at nearby Ulva Ferry in 1761 and known as 'the Father of Australia'. Off B8035, in Gruline, Isle of Mull.

Provan Hall. *NS47*
Probably the most perfect pre-Reformation mansion house in Scotland. Auchinlea Road (B806), Easterhouse, Glasgow. House not open, park and gardens open all year.

The Tenement House. *NS56*
Victorian tenement furnished in period. Admission charged. 145 Buccleuch Street, Garnethill, N of Charing Cross, Glasgow. Admission by pre-booked ticket from NTS Glasgow office (see page 157).

TAYSIDE

Craigower. *NN96*
A beacon hill with splendid views from the summit. Small car park and path to the top. Off A924, 1½m N of Pitlochry.

Stanley Hill. *NO04*
A wooded artificial hill above Dunkeld. Off A9, 15m N of Perth.

NORTHERN IRELAND

White Park Bay —
where Ireland's first inhabitants settled

ARDRESS HOUSE

Co Armagh   H95

In 1760 Sarah Clarke, the heiress to Ardress, had the good sense to marry a successful Dublin architect, George Ensor. Had she not done so Ardress might never have become the graceful Georgian country house it is today. In ten years Ensor completed the transformation by building two wings on to the original simple manor house. These wings have carved screen walls with Palladian style alcoves containing marble busts. The additional rooms in the new wings include a picture gallery with a collection of magnificent paintings on loan from the Earl of Castlestewart, and an elegant drawing room. This room is one of the most perfect late 18th-century interiors in Ireland with outstanding plasterwork in Adam style by Michael Stapleton, the eminent Dublin stuccoer. The other rooms are smaller and simpler with good examples of English and Irish 18th-century furniture.

    The distinctive pale pink washes of the façades were probably introduced by Ensor, and the house overlooks unspoilt natural grounds, with a terrace garden on one side and beech trees on the other. The farmyard has livestock and a display of farm implements.

Open April to end Sept. Admission charged. Wheelchair access. On Portadown – Moy road (B28), 7m from Portadown.

THE ARGORY

Co Armagh   H85

The MacGeough family's links with the Argory began when the property was leased to Joshua MacGeough in 1741, but the present neo-classical house was probably built in the 1820s by his grandson, Walter McGeough Bond. It gives a fascinating glimpse into the way Irish gentry lived in the early 19th century and retains much of the original contents, including Regency mahogany furniture.

    Perhaps the most interesting aspect of the Argory is that it continues to be lit by its own power provided by the acetylene gas plant in the stable yard. There are bronze gasolier lamps in all the major rooms, and in the central staircase hall is a splendid cast-iron stove. Musicologists will be intrigued by the early 19th-century cabinet organ by Bishop of London, probably the most important of its kind in existence. The mechanical works may be seen in the room behind the organ lobby.

    The house is set on a hill overlooking a curve of the river Blackwater, with a walled pleasure garden to the north and a lovely Victorian rose garden with a central sun dial. To the north-east of the house are a series of interesting outbuildings surrounding the coach yard.

Open April to end Sept. Admission charged. Wheelchair available. On Derrycaw road, 4m from Moy.

BLOCKHOUSE AND GREEN ISLANDS

Co Down   J20

Lying off Greencastle and Cranfield Point at the entrance to Carlingford Lough, these two islands total only two acres; yet they provide important nesting sites for common, Arctic and roseate terns. The islands were given to the National Trust in 1968 as a contribution to the Enterprise Neptune coastline appeal, and are leased to the Royal Society for the Protection of Birds, from whose Belfast office viewing permits may be obtained.

At the mouth of Carlingford Lough.

CARRICK-A-REDE

Co Antrim   D04

Carrick-a-Rede means 'the rock on the road'. The road is that taken by the salmon on their way to northern rivers, and the rock is a small basalt stack with two salmon fisheries. This stack is separated from the mainland by a chasm which is 80ft deep and 60ft wide, and is spanned during the summer fishing season by a swinging and seemingly flimsy rope bridge which is taken down in bad weather. Although a great tourist attraction, this is a working bridge used to carry the fishermen to and from the island. It now has

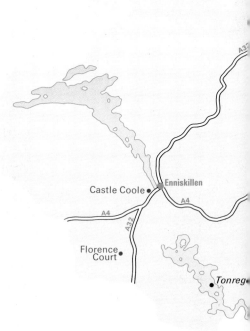

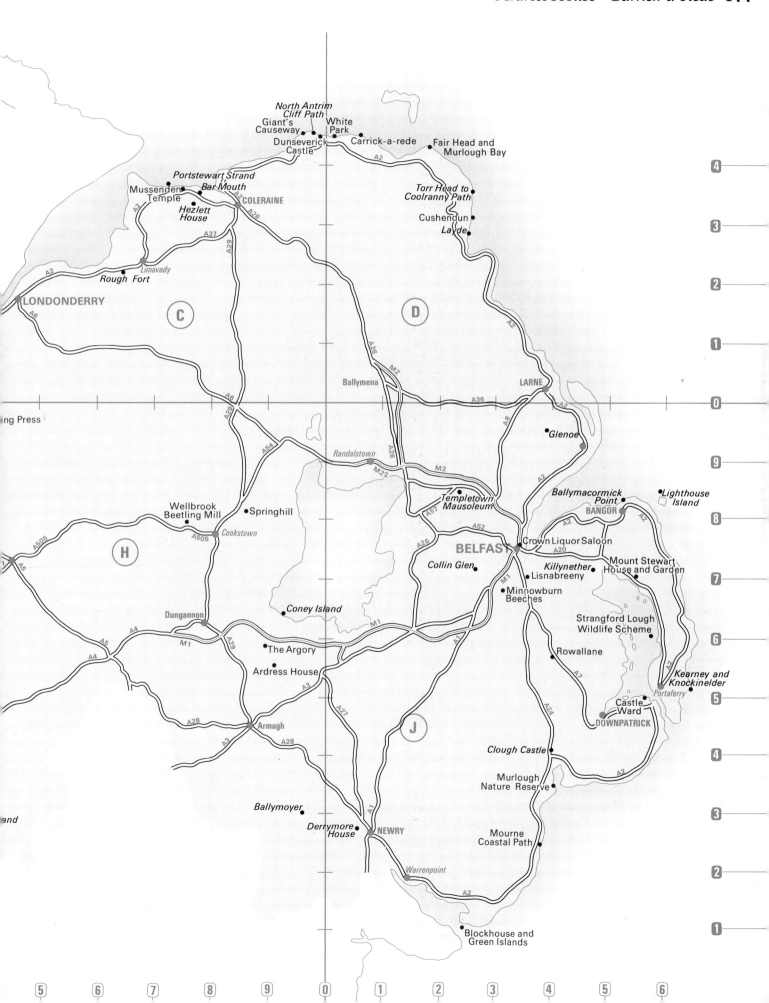

North Antrim
Cliff Path
Giant's
Causeway
White
Park
Carrick-a-rede
Dunseverick
Castle
Fair Head and
Murlough Bay

Portstewart Strand
Bar Mouth
Mussenden
Temple
Torr Head to
Coolranny Path
Hezlett
House
Cushendun
Layde

COLERAINE

A2
A26

A37
A29

LONDONDERRY

Limavady
Rough Fort

A2
A6

C

D

A2

A26

A2

Ballymena

M2

LARNE

A36

A2

Glenoe

A8

A2

Randalstown

M22

M2

Templetown
Mausoleum

Ballymacormick
Point
Lighthouse
Island

BANGOR

A2

Wellbrook
Beetling Mill
Springhill

Crown Liquor Saloon

A505

Cookstown

A52

A26

BELFAST

A20

A2

Killynether

Mount Stewart
House and Garden

H

Collin Glen

Lisnabreeny

A57

Minnowburn
Beeches

Dungannon

Coney Island

M1

Strangford Lough
Wildlife Scheme

A5
A4

A29

M1

A1

Rowallane

Kearney and
Knockinelder

The Argory

A3

A7

Portaferry

Ardress House

A27

Castle
Ward

Armagh

A28

J

DOWNPATRICK

Clough Castle

A24

A28

A2

Murlough
Nature Reserve

Ballymoyer

A1

*Derrymore
House*

NEWRY

Mourne
Coastal Path

Warrenpoint

A2

*Blockhouse and
Green Islands*

two handrails – in time past only one existed and even now the second is regarded as unnecessary by some of the older fishermen! Even when the bridge is not in operation the visitor to Carrick-a-Rede is rewarded by outstanding views along a vast stretch of the northern Irish coastline. On clear days Islay, and the Paps of Jura on the Scottish mainland can be seen. More recently the Trust has also acquired 58 acres of coastline at Larrybane, adjoining the Carrick-a-Rede land, and including a disused basalt quarry and limeworks.

5m W of Ballycastle.

CASTLE COOLE

Co Fermanagh	H24

Built between 1789 and 1795 for the first Earl of Belmore, Castle Coole is the acknowledged masterpiece of the architect, James Wyatt. It may be considered the finest neo-classical house in Northern Ireland, if not in the British Isles. The assurance of its design is particularly remarkable in that Wyatt was working from an earlier design by the Irish architect Richard Johnson. The Portland stone for the superbly constructed and carved exterior was brought from a specially built quay on the coast. The joinery and plasterwork inside the house are of the highest quality with ceilings by Joseph Rose (the elder) and chimney pieces by Richard Westmacott. No expense was spared. An Italian expert in scagliola (imitation stone) was imported here, and joiners were brought from England to make the doors and shutters. The house is filled with fine Regency furniture including a magnificent state bed in flame-coloured silk.

The lawns of the park slope gently to the waters of Lough Coole, the home of a flock of greylag geese, first introduced in about 1700. Their presence is said to ensure the continuance of the Belmore family at Castle Coole. The picturesque parkland providing so worthy a setting for this beautiful house is largely the achievement of a mid 19th-century landscape gardener, James Fraser, probably working under the direction of the Second Lord Belmore. This is an example of the contribution made by successive generations of the family to the development of the estate over the 300 years in which they have lived on this land.

Open April to end Sept. Admission charged. Wheelchair access. 1½m SE of Enniskillen on A4.

CASTLE WARD

Co Down	J74

Castle Ward's peculiar diversity of style came about because the owner and his wife could never agree and in the design of their house were forced into a curious compromise. The owner, Bernard Ward, later First Viscount Bangor, favoured a classical approach while his wife,

Lady Anne Magill preferred the more elaborate 'Strawberry Hill' Gothic style. The house was eventually built with strongly contrasting west and east fronts embracing both styles. This division is continued inside, with Gothic decorations in the saloon, morning room and Lady Anne's boudoir, while the hall, dining room and Lord Bangor's library reflect a more conventional Palladian taste. Not surprisingly the couple separated shortly after the house was finished!

Unusually, it seems that with the possible exception of a valet and lady's maid none of the servants slept in the house. Their living quarters and essential domestic offices were in a courtyard reached by an underground passage. The laundry in this courtyard is fully equipped with an impressive array of irons, ironing boards, mangles and examples of laundered

The laundry at Castle Ward is a delightful period piece. Displayed alongside intricately worked linen and items of clothing are some of the implements once used to keep them neat and in good repair

Lavish decoration is the hallmark of Castle Coole, one of Ireland's grandest stately homes. It was designed by famous architect James Wyatt for Lord Belmore in the late 18th century. Pictured here is the state bedroom

NATIONAL TRUST INFORMATION

For details of opening times and further information about properties in Northern Ireland, contact the Regional Information Officer at the following address:

Rowallane House, Saintfield, Ballynalinch, Co Down
BT24 7LH
Tel. Saintfield 510721

linen and period clothes. The National Trust has recently created a small theatre in part of the large barn in the stableyard.

Castle Ward is splendidly sited with enchanting views over Strangford Lough. The mild, wet climate has encouraged the growth of giant oaks and beeches and rarer foreign plants. In the spring the glades are at their best, with daffodils, bluebells, azaleas and rhododendrons. An imaginatively placed little knoll overlooks Temple Water, the small formal lake or canal, which is the home of a collection of wildfowl, representative of the species to be found on Strangford Lough. The nearby walled garden allows visitors to study the birds at closer quarters and is intended as an introduction to the Strangford Lough Wildlife scheme (see page 186).

Open April to end Sept. Admission charged. Wheelchair available. Refreshments. 7m NE of Downpatrick, 1½m W of Strangford village on S shore of Strangford Lough.

THE CROWN LIQUOR SALOON

Belfast   J73

On the corner of Great Victoria Street and Amelia Street stands perhaps the finest existing example of a High Victorian public house or 'gin palace'. The ground floor façades are faced with brightly glazed ceramic tiles flanked by columns and pilasters. It is, however, the sheer exuberance of the interior that takes the breath away – a fantasy of engraved and painted glass, mirrors, plasterwork garlands and festoons, tiles and mosaics. Elaborately carved and inlaid 'snugs' with tall red oak partitions provide complete privacy for their occupants. With so few genuine examples of this style of public house now in existence it is pleasing that the National Trust has been able to preserve the Crown for future generations.

Open every day except Sundays, during normal licensing hours. Wheelchair access. Refreshments.

CUSHENDUN

Co Antrim   D23

The Ulster Land Fund gave 62 acres of this picturesque village and bay on the east Antrim coast to the National Trust in 1954. The name Cushendun means 'the foot of the Dun', the beautiful salmon river which runs through the village. Each season brings new beauties to an area surrounded by some of the best of Ulster's scenery – golden whin and white bog cotton in spring give way to purple heather and fuchsia hedges in summer and autumn, followed by brightly berried hollies in winter. Some of the cottages may appear foreign to this area; they were designed and built in the Cornish style by Clough Williams Ellis, creator of the village of Portmerion in North Wales.

23m N of Ballymena.

DUNSEVERICK CASTLE

Co Antrim	*C94*

Gazing at the peaceful scene which is Dunseverick today, with its profusion of wild flowers and seabirds, it is difficult to remember that it was once the most strongly fortified castle in all Ireland. Deirdre of the Sorrows (Ireland's Helen of Troy) is said to have landed at this point on the North Antrim coast on her return from exile in Scotland 2,000 years ago. In the 5th century St Patrick consecrated Olcan, the first Irish bishop, at the well, still known as St Patrick's. In the 9th and 10th centuries the Vikings stormed and held Dunseverick for brief periods. The ruined watch tower and curtain wall which are all that now remain, are part of the 16th-century castle which was razed by Cromwell's troops a century later. The National Trust also owns four acres of Dunseverick Harbour and surrounding land.

3m E of Giant's Causeway (B146).

FAIR HEAD AND MURLOUGH BAY

Co Antrim	*O14*

This beautiful stretch of the North Antrim coast includes sandy beaches, cliffland, woodland and wilderness areas containing much of interest to the geologist and botanist. The scarped headland of Fair Head rises 636ft above the sea; the first 300ft is formed by huge basalt columns. From the summit of Fair Head are extensive views northwards to the Mull of Kintyre.

3m E of Ballycastle.

FLORENCE COURT

Co Fermanagh	*H13*

Florence Court was named after the wife of its first builder and owner, Sir John Cole, but his early 18th-century house has long since disappeared. His son John built the present main house in about 1750, and in 1771 long colonnades and wings were added to extend the façade to 350ft in length. The house has an elaborate Baroque entrance front; inside, the staircase, dining room ceiling and the Venetian Room on the first floor are a riot of rococo plasterwork. Following a disastrous fire in 1955, which gutted much of the interior, extensive restoration was carried out, and the present splendid appearance of the rooms is a tribute to the skill of 20th-century craftsmen.

The house looks west to the mountains of Cuilcagh over wild and romantic scenery. 200-year-old beeches, oaks and sycamores grow in the pleasure grounds, together with the famous Florence Court yews.

Open April to end Sept. Admission charged. Wheelchair access. 8m SW of Enniskillen.

GIANT'S CAUSEWAY

Co Antrim	*C94*

It is fascinating to reflect that the Causeway was not 'discovered' until 1692, by the then Bishop of Derry, but it was very remote, and a visit to the North Antrim coast in the 18th century was an expedition through primitive countryside with few passable roads. Indeed Dr Johnson was to remark that although the Causeway might be worth seeing it was not worth going to see. It is acclaimed as one of the most extraordinary natural phenomena in the world, with a peninsula of faceted columns of basalt rock stretching out into the sea.

Legend has it that the Causeway was built by the Irish giant, Finn MacCool, so that he could travel dry-shod across the sea to Scotland, but in fact these rocks were shaped by volcanic activity some 60 million years ago. A large formation on the cliff side closely resembles the pipes of a

The extraordinary basalt columns of the Giant's Causeway reach out into the sea for nearly half a mile. About 40,000 such columns, mostly hexagonal, form the fantastic headland. Bright red bands in the cliffs mark lulls in the volcanic eruptions which created this geological oddity 60 million years ago

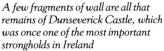

A few fragments of wall are all that remains of Dunseverick Castle, which was once one of the most important strongholds in Ireland

massive organ. Apart from their geological interest the Causeway cliffs have much to offer botanists and ornithologists. One of the most common seabirds present nowadays is the fulmar, which first nested here as recently as 1948. Rabbits, many of them black, are plentiful in the bays and in late evening groups of the Irish hare congregate in the fields behind the cliffs, 96 acres of which are owned by the Trust.

Bus service from car park to Windy Gap. Refreshments. 9m from Portrush.

GRAY'S PRINTING PRESS

Co Tyrone   *H39*

Strabane was an important publishing centre in the 18th century with ten printing concerns and two newspapers. Several of its townsfolk emigrated to America and became successful printers and publishers there. Among them was James Wilson, Grandfather of President Woodrow Wilson, and also John Dunlap who launched the United States' first newspaper in 1771. By 1776 he was printer to the 'Continental Congress' whose members drafted the American Declaration of Independence. It is traditionally supposed that Dunlap served his apprenticeship at Gray's Press before joining his uncle in Philadelphia.

The printing works, now arranged as a printing museum, contain three 19th-century presses, two of which are American inventions. The museum, in the building's upper storey, illustrates the development of print techniques over sixty years. Below the museum, behind a bow fronted window is an 18th-century stationer's shop, now a National Trust Information Centre.

Press open April to end Sept. Shop all year. Admission charged. 49 Main Street, Strabane.

LISNABREENY

Co Down | J37

In this peaceful spot, just two miles south of the centre of Belfast, the Trust owns a glen and waterfall with views over both Belfast and Strangford Loughs.

Near Newtownbreda.

MINNOWBURN BEECHES

Co Down | J36

Along the banks of the Minnowburn and Lagan rivers the Trust has acquired 128 acres with river walks in an area of Outstanding Natural Beauty. Remarkably the property is only 3½ miles from Belfast's centre, at the south end of Shaw's Bridge on the river Lagan.

S of Belfast on river Lagan.

MOUNT STEWART

Co Down | J57

Lord Castlereagh, Foreign Secretary from 1812 to 1823, grew up in this 18th-century house on the east shore of Strangford Lough, home of the Stewart family – later Marquesses of Londonderry.

The present building is the work of three architects. James Wyatt designed the west front which was originally the entrance front, and also an attractive entrance hall – now the breakfast room – for the first Marquess in the 1780s. In 1790 Robert Stewart, later Lord Castlereagh, was elected to Parliament at a cost to his family of £60,000, which brought a temporary halt to the building at Mount Stewart! When it was resumed in the early 19th century George Dance contributed the spacious staircase, and began the new north entrance front. The final form of this façade with its large Ionic pedimented portico, was completed in the 1820s, probably by Vitruvius Morrison, working

The Shamrock Garden at Mount Stewart. The central flower bed, in the shape of a hand, is intended to recall a legend involving the McDonnells, ancestors of the late Edith, Marchioness of Londonderry, who created the garden. A race from Scotland to Ireland was held between two rival Scottish clans, it being agreed that whoever touched Ireland first would possess the land. The McDonnell, seeing he was about to lose the race, cut off his hand and threw it on the shore to stake his claim

The quiet, unspoilt coastline of the Trust's Murlough Nature Reserve is an area of considerable scientific importance, where certain areas are only accessible by permit. Those with less serious interests, however, are well catered for as there is free public access to a magnificent beach

snuff boxes given to him by the Pope and no fewer than fifteen European kings and queens. The house also contains the famous Stubbs painting of the racehorse Hambletonian, and notable silver gilt and porcelain.

Edith, Lady Londonderry, replanted and redesigned the famous garden this century. The estate's close proximity to the Gulf Stream enables the garden to support many rare and sub-tropical trees and plants which cannot be grown successfully elsewhere in Northern Ireland.

In the grounds on a promontory overlooking Strangford Lough is the elegant octagonal Temple of the Winds, acknowledged one of James 'Athenian' Stuart's finest buildings, and his only one in Ireland. He designed this charming little temple in 1782–3 for the first Marquess.

House and Temple open April to end Sept, garden April to end Oct. Admission charged. Wheelchairs available. Refreshments. 5m SE of Newtownards on N side of A20.

MOURNE COASTAL PATH

Co Down J32

The path is in two sections; one runs south along the sea from Bloody Bridge at the foot of Slieve Donard (at 2,796ft the highest mountain in the Mourne Range) past the site of St Mary's Ballaghanery, an early Celtic church. The second part leads up the valley of the Bloody River towards the mountains. The Northern Ireland Government sponsored an unemployment relief scheme by which the path was created.

Car park and foot access from Bloody Bridge.

MURLOUGH NATURE RESERVE

Co Down J43

At the foot of the Mourne mountains near Newcastle the Trust has established Ireland's first nature reserve. The development of the dunes which form the coastline began 8,000 years ago after the last Ice Age. The oldest dunes are at least 5,000 years old while new dunes are still being formed along the beach. The varied nature of the soil, which ranges from lime-rich to acid, is reflected in the wide variety of plants, with their splendidly evocative names. On the beach, sea rocket and prickly saltwort may be found while inland on the richest soil bird's foot trefoil grows alongside less common plants such as the pyramidal orchid. On the acid soil large areas are covered by plants like dune burnet rose and primroses. On the more heathlike land, ling and bell heather predominate with tormentil and lady's bedstraw. In summer the extensive areas of spring sea buckthorn are host to a variety of nesting birds like the stonechat, reed bunting and whitethroat, while the parasitic

for the Third Marquess, Castlereagh's half-brother. Further extensive additions were made to the east end of the house in the middle of the century, and the interior was largely refurnished and redesigned a century later by Edith, Lady Londonderry, widow of the 7th Marquess. Much of the fine furniture and other contents have strong associations with Castlereagh. His full-length portrait by Thomas Lawrence hangs above the Empire desk at which he wrote his dispatches from the Congress of Vienna. On the desk is a massive inkstand fashioned from gold

A blaze of colour in the Spring Garden at Rowallane. The acid soil and damp climate here are especially well suited to azaleas and rhododendrons, of which Rowallane can boast hundreds of varieties. The earliest rhododendrons bloom in March, with the later varieties and the azaleas following on in April and May

The white roughcast front of Springhill is notable for its simple, symmetrical design. The two long, low flanking outbuildings were used by the servants; the one on the left by senior staff, and the other, where the stables were also situated, by junior staff

cuckoo haunts the dunes. Later in the year the buckthorn's orange berries attract large numbers of wintering birds, especially thrushes and finches, to the reserve. Murlough's wild life is further enhanced by the presence of both large and small mammals, and of the only Irish reptile, the common lizard, together with many common and rare moths, butterflies and other insects. Slatted walks provide easy access for visitors in wheelchairs and the Warden organises guided walks for blind visitors.

2m N of Newcastle on T2 Dundrum Road.

MUSSENDEN TEMPLE

Co Londonderry	*C73*

Frederick Hervey, Bishop of Derry and 4th Earl of Bristol, known as the Earl-Bishop, was obsessed with circular buildings, and this is well illustrated here, and at Ickworth in Suffolk (see page 118). Perched on the very edge of a cliff on a bleak headland overlooking Lough Foyle with superb views along the Donegal and Antrim coasts is the domed rotunda of the Mussenden Temple.

Built in ashlar and deriving from the Temple of Vesta at Tivoli, the Temple was originally furnished as a library. Here, in what is undoubtedly the most romantic setting for a building of its purpose in the British Isles, the Earl-Bishop could study his classical and scientific books. For company he had the waves crashing on the rocks below, the ceaseless wind and seabirds demonstrating their mastery of the elements. Included in the Trust's ownership are the ruins of Downhill Castle, probably designed by James Wyatt for the Earl-Bishop, a mausoleum to the Earl's brother, and woodland and coastal walks. The neo-classical Bishop's Gate, once the main entrance to the demesne, opens into a steep wooded valley leading to the remains of the castle, and the temple.

Open April to end Sept (glen at all times). 1m W of Castlerock.

Exquisite examples of 18th- and 19th-century costume are kept in the old laundry at Springhill. The first room is distinctly masculine; here are colonial and military uniforms, and a wide selection of headgear. Outstanding is an 18th-century gentleman's court suit – its delightful embroidery was designed here but executed in China. The other two rooms are decidedly feminine, displaying beautiful gowns of velvet, brocade, satin, silk, and taffeta, and all the accessories of a lady's dressing room.

ROWALLANE GARDEN

Co Down   *J45*

Rowallane lies upon whinstone rock which is always just protruding through or barely concealed by the turf. The rock gives the garden its character; massive outcrops have been utilised for massed plantings of azaleas and rhododendrons.

The garden was begun by the Reverend John Moore, who bought the land in 1860, but it was fully developed by his nephew, Hugh Armytage Moore who had a rare gift for planning. He developed a wide knowledge of plants and converted the walled kitchen garden into a sheltered nursery for rare bulbs, plants, shrubs and trees. Among plants raised at, and bearing the name of Rowallane, are chaenomeles, viburnum, hypericum and primula.

Splendid though the entire garden is, for many visitors the spring garden will be most appealing. Maples, dogwoods, birches, magnolia and viburnum are especially well represented. The whole shape of the garden is controlled by immense groups of rhododendrons. The spring colours are outstanding, and are matched only by the breathtaking tints of autumn.

Open April to end Oct. Admission charged. Wheelchairs available. Refreshments.

SPRINGHILL

Co Londonderry   *H88*

The Conyngham family came here from Scotland in James I's reign, and bought this estate in 1658. These early settlers built the present manor house later that century. Its walls are whitewashed and roughcast and it was originally fortified, but the defensive barrier and framework have long since disappeared. In 1765 the lower wings with their bay windows which flank the entrance front were added. The interior still has much of the original panelling and contains an early 18th-century staircase, a library and the Conynghams' furniture

collection of many different dates. The laundry, brewhouse, slaughterhouse, stables, circular dovecote and turf shed survive. One hundred and fifty years ago the turf shed was stocked by tenants who were each obliged to contribute annually a cartload of turf and a day's free work, after which they received dinner at long tables set in the yard.

In one of the outbuildings is a costume collection, and in the courtyard is an interesting example of an old Irish cottage kitchen. Beyond the outbuildings lie the garden and the two-storeyed barn, one of the first buildings erected at Springhill.

Open April to end Sept. Admission charged. Wheelchair access. Refreshments in Moneymore. 1m from Moneymore on B18.

STRANGFORD LOUGH WILDLIFE SCHEME

Co Down　　　　　　　　　　*J56*

The great island-studded inlet of Strangford Lough runs for upwards of 20 miles into the heart of the beautiful County Down countryside. The Lough and its surroundings are of interest to geologists and archaeologists, but more particularly to naturalists. Enormous flocks of wild duck, tern, waders, swans and geese gather on its waters.

For centuries the wildlife of the Lough remained largely undisturbed, but the growth of industry and the greater mobility of town-dwellers in the twenty or so years following World War II began seriously to threaten the birds. In 1966 a scheme was initiated whereby the whole of the Lough's foreshore is protected. Seven refuges have been established where the birds can be watched undisturbed. Originally developed for the protection of wildfowl, the scheme has been extended to cover all aspects of outstanding natural interest. In addition to the land leased to it under this scheme, the Trust owns about 200 acres – mostly islands – of particular scientific or ornithological interest on and around the Lough.

Visitors are particularly requested to use hides, viewpoints and car parks where provided, and to avoid disturbing the birds.

WELLBROOK BEETLING MILL

Co Tyrone　　　　　　　　　　*H77*

The Irish linen industry is remarkable in that it was successfully established, in the late 17th and early 18th centuries, in an as yet under-developed country, and has thrived ever since. Both the Irish and English governments supported the new industry by removing the duty on Irish linen entering England, and by encouraging foreign exports.

Beetling, the final process in linen manufacture, uses wooden hammers to smooth

The Founding of Wellbrook

Government aid to industry is not a new idea, for in the early 18th century it was directly responsible for the establishment of the Irish linen industry. Although linen had been spun and woven for centuries in Ireland, there was no organised industry, and the standard of the cloth was well below that of European linen. To provide a substitute for Continental imports a Linen Board was created in 1711 to superintend the growth of the industry, and the duty on Irish linen entering England was lifted.

One of those who took advantage of government help was Hugh Faulkner, a draper who desired his own bleaching and beetling mill. He was only 23 years old, but his elder brother, a well-established land agent in Dublin, put up the money. He set about finding a suitable site, pretending to be a fisherman as he wandered along the river banks of Northern Ireland. He eventually settled on a site on the Kildress River, and bought the lease for the land in 1764.

It took three years to complete the first mill at Wellbrook, but in May 1765, Hugh Faulkner wrote an amusing account of the completion of the mill-race and the impounding of the river:

'Finish'd the whole at 8 o'clock at night, turn'd the river into its usual course and let it down the race, which went very cleverly home amidst several shouts and aclamations. From 8 to 9 o'clock we drank whiskey and from 9 to near 11 fought yet by my management, no blood drawn, but several shirts and weastcoats torn. The Mountain Men when they got drunk fell out. Thus you have the compleat history of the wyer making, which took 110 men and 20 hours and 15 gallons of whiskey.'

The wheelshaft arrived by carriage a few days later, but it was not until September 1767 that all was complete.

However, Hugh Faulkner, for some unknown reason, failed to prosper, and he sold his share to his brother as early as 1771. The mill continued to work, and indeed another five were built, including the present one restored by the Trust, which dates from about 1830.

Traditional Irish linen was finished at Wellbrook Beetling Mill until 1961. 'Beetling' was the final stage of the linen-making process. The cloth was beaten with 32 wooden hammers or 'beetles' to give it a smooth, slightly shiny finish. Pictured here are the beetles (the vertical wooden beams on the right), the wiper beam and the wheel which powered the operation

the surface of the cloth and impart a slight gloss to it. This process was originally carried out in the home by women using heavy wooden mallets. Later it was often carried out independently of the other processes in small water-powered mills. Wellbrook had also been used for bleaching until the mid 18th century and it continued as a beetling mill until 1961. The National Trust was subsequently able to acquire and restore the mill to working order. It is a two-storeyed whitewashed building in an attractive glen and stands at right angles to the stream from which it derives its power.

Open April to end Sept. Admission charged. 3m from Cookstown on Cookstown–Omagh road (A505).

WHITE PARK BAY

Co Antrim   *D04*

Around this beautiful white sand bay some of Ireland's first inhabitants made their homes 5,000–6,000 years ago. Excavations have produced large amounts of Neolithic flints and pottery, including a clay figurine 4ins high. Although crudely made, it was a find of considerable importance, the only 'Mother Goddess' (an early deity of nature) figure to be found in Ireland. On the flower-clad grassy slopes fringing the bay the floors of round huts, rubbish tips and a burial cairn can all be traced.

1½m W of Ballintoy, 7m NW of Ballycastle (A2).

OTHER PROPERTIES

COUNTY ANTRIM

Collin Glen. *J27*
A glen which runs from Glen Road, 1m SW of the Falls Road boundary of Belfast to the foot of Collin mountain.

Glenoe. *J39*
Glen with waterfall next to Glenoe village.

Layde. *D22*
A small beach on the Antrim coastal path, 2m N of Cushendall. Access by footpath from car park, passing the ruins of Layde Church, thought to be 12th-century.

North Antrim Cliff Path. *C94*
A ten-mile footpath from Runkerry to White Park Bay.

Portstewart Strand. *C73*
Duneland, with a three-mile strand W of Portstewart. Car access at low tide.

Templetown Mausoleum, Templepatrick. *J28*
Robert Adam mausoleum in Castle Upton graveyard.

Torr Head to Coolranny Path. *D23*
Land acquired for a coastal path; access by right of way off Torr to Cushendun road.

COUNTY ARMAGH

Ballymoyer. *H93*
Wooded glen 4m NE of Newtownhamilton.

Coney Island, Lough Neagh. *H96*
A wooded island probably once linked to the mainland by a causeway; Neolithic and Bronze Age remains.

Derrymore House. *J02*
Thatched 18th-century manor house, the home of Isaac Corry, Speaker of the Irish House of Commons. Park. Open

on application to the NT Regional Office, Rowallane.

COUNTY DOWN

Ballymacormick Point. *J58*
Rough land on the shore of Belfast Lough. Also Cockle Island; ½ acre with no access during nesting season from May to end July.

Clough Castle. *J44*
A Norman motte and bailey, 5m NE of Dundrum.

Kearney and Knockinelder. *J65*
Foreshore and part of Kearney village with part of Knockinelder beach and adjoining land. 3m E of Portaferry.

Killynether. *J47*
Woodland 1m SW of Newtownards.

Lighthouse Island, Copeland Islands. *J58*

Managed by Copeland Island Bird Observatory: visiting by arrangement with the Boat Officer (tel. Belfast 655081).

COUNTY FERMANAGH

Tonregee Island. *H32*
Part of the Belle Isle Estate.

COUNTY LONDONDERRY

Bar Mouth. *C73*
Wildlife sanctuary at the mouth of the river Bann; observation hide.

Hezlett House. *C73*
Thatched cottage with unusual roof construction. Open April to end Sept.

Rough Fort. *C62*
An unexcavated rath or ring fort surrounded by Scots firs, oaks and beeches. 1m W of Limavady.

GLOSSARY

ARCADE
Range of arches supported by piers or columns.

ASHLAR
Masonry of large blocks with even faces and square edges.

BAILEY
Courtyard of a stone-built castle.

BALUSTER
Small shaped pillar or column.

BALUSTRADE
Series of balusters supporting a rail.

BAROQUE
Exuberant style of art and architecture distinguished by flowing lines and curves, which originated in 17th-century Italy.

BARREL VAULT
Simplest kind of vault, a continuous arch either semi-circular or pointed.

BARROW
A grave-mound.

BATTLEMENT
Parapet with indentations and raised portions called merlons. Also called crenellation.

BAYS
Internal compartments of a building divided from each other by a division on the side walls such as pillars or columns, or externally, division by windows.

BEAKER FOLK
New Stone Age tribe from the Continent who arrived in about 3,000 BC and introduced first metal tools and weapons. Buried their dead in round barrows.

BOSS
A projection usually covering the point where the ribs of a vault join.

BRONZE AGE
Between about 1800 and 600 BC.

BUTTRESS
A mass of brickwork or masonry built against a wall to give additional support.

CAIRN
Mound of stones covering a burial site.

CAPITAL
Top part of a column.

CASTELLATED
Surmounted with battlements or turrets.

CHAMBERED TOMB
New Stone Age burial mound with a stone-built chamber covered by a barrow of earth or a cairn.

CHINOISERIE
European imitation of Chinese art popular in the 18th century.

CLASSICAL
Term used for Greek and Roman architecture and later styles inspired by it.

CORBEL
A projection on a wall supporting something, a beam or some other horizontal member.

CRENELLATION
See battlement.

CRUCK
Big carved beam supporting walls and roof of a cottage.

CUPOLA
A small polygonal or circular dome crowning a roof.

CURTAIN WALL
A wall connecting the towers of a castle.

DRESSINGS
Moulded stonework round a window or other feature of a building.

FENESTRATION
Arrangement of the windows in a building.

FINIAL
Top of a canopy or gable.

FRIEZE
Part of building immediately above a column, or the decoration of a band of wall in the interior immediately below the ceiling.

GABLE
Triangular upper part of a wall supporting a pitched roof.

GARDEROBE
Medieval name for a lavatory.

GOTHIC, NEO-GOTHIC
Medieval style of architecture and the version of this which became popular after 1750 and continued into the 19th century.

HILL-FORT
Iron Age earthwork enclosed by a ditch and bank system.

HIPPED ROOF
A roof with sloped rather than vertical ends.

IRON AGE
Between about 600 BC and the Roman invasion.

KEEP
Massive tower of a Norman castle.

LANTERN
A small circular or polygonal turret with windows all round which crowns a roof.

LINENFOLD
Tudor wooden panelling carved to represent a piece of linen laid in vertical folds.

MACHICOLATION
A gallery projecting from an outside castle wall with holes in the floor which enabled defenders to drop missiles on the enemy.

MEGALITHIC TOMB
Stone-built burial chamber of the New Stone Age.

MESOLITHIC
Middle Stone Age from about 8,000 BC to 3,500 BC.

MOTTE AND BAILEY
Norman defence system consisting of an earthen mound (motte) in an enclosed area (bailey).

MULLIONS
Uprights dividing a window.

NEO-CLASSICAL
Architectural style based on Roman and Greek buildings popular in the second half of the 18th century.

NEOLITHIC
New Stone Age, between about 3,500 BC and 1,800 BC.

ORIEL
A bay window on an upper storey.

PALLADIAN
Architecture developed from work of Andrea Palladio, a 16th-century Italian architect. Used in England in 17th and 18th centuries.

PARAPET
A low wall placed for safety where there is a sudden drop.

PARGETING
Plasterwork with patterns engraved on it or in relief.

PARTERRE
A flat open space decorated with flower beds arranged ornamentally.

PELE TOWER
A small defensible keep or tower peculiar to houses and castles around the Scottish border.

PORTICO
A roofed space, open or partly enclosed forming the entrance and centre-piece of a house.

RAMPART
Stone or earthen wall around a castle, fort or fortified city.

ROCOCO
Late phase of the Baroque style, current between about 1720 and 1760.

ROMANESQUE
Architectural style of the 11th and 12th centuries.

ROMANO-BRITISH
Applied to culture and features of Britain affected by the Roman occupation of the first to fifth centuries.

ROSE WINDOW
Circular window with pattern radiating from its centre.

ROTUNDA
A circular building.

RUBBLE
Building stones laid in courses but not shaped.

SCREENS PASSAGE
Passage between kitchen etc., and the screen which separates these from the hall of a medieval house.

SOLAR
Living room in upper storey of a medieval house or castle.

WATTLE AND DAUB
Simple wall construction where thin branches or laths of wood are roughly plastered over with mud or clay between uprights of a timber-framed building.

WEATHERBOARDING
Overlapping horizontal boards on the exterior of a building.

The two National Trusts between them administer nearly 250 of Britain's outstanding historic houses and over 500,000 acres of land.

The National Trust for Places of Historic Interest or Natural Beauty (to give it its full title) protects historic buildings, gardens, countryside and coastline in England, Wales and Northern Ireland. The National Trust for Scotland has in its care a rich variety of castles, gardens, scenic areas, little houses, historic places and islands.

The two National Trusts enjoy the support of more than 8,000,000 visitors each year. The National Trust has more than 1,000,000 members in England, Wales and Northern Ireland and its Scottish counterpart 110,000 members – all of whom are admitted free to the properties of both Trusts.

Detailed information on their work, and how to join, can be obtained from the National Trust for Places of Historic Interest or Natural Beauty, Freepost, Beckenham, Kent BR3 4UN (no stamp needed), and from the National Trust for Scotland, 5 Charlotte Square, Edinburgh EH2 4DU.

ACKNOWLEDGEMENTS

Valuable help in the preparation of material for the book has been given by **Valerie and Peter Wenham**; by **National Trust** staff in the following regional offices: Cornwall, Devon, East Anglia, East Midlands, Kent & East Sussex, Mercia, Northumbria, North West, Severn, Southern, Thames & Chilterns, Wessex, Yorkshire, Northern Ireland, North Wales and South Wales; and by the staff of the **National Trust for Scotland.**

The publishers gratefully acknowledge the following for the use of photographs:

Title page: Shalford Mill by S. & O. Mathews
Contents page: Soar Mill Cove from the National Trust; Sheffield Park Garden by S. & O. Mathews; St Elvis from the National Trust; Tattershall Castle by Richard Surman; Wasdale by Derek Forss; Glenfinnan Monument from the National Trust for Scotland; White Park Bay from the National Trust.
Pages 4–5: Lanhydrock House by Harry Williams

THE WEST COUNTRY
All photographs by **Harry Williams** except the Cerne Giant (p. 16) and Killerton (p. 25) from the AA Publications Division Photographic Library; Drake's Drum (p. 15) from the British Tourist Authority; Castle Drogo (p. 15) and Zennor (p. 38) by S. & O. Mathews; Soar Mill Cove (pp. 8–9), Clevedon Court (p. 17), and Trelissick (p. 37) from the National Trust.

SOUTH & SOUTH-EAST ENGLAND
All photographs by **S. & O. Mathews** except Buscot Park (p. 50) and Sandham Memorial Chapel (p. 70) from the AA Publications Division Photographic Library; Alfriston Clergy House (p. 44), Ascott (p. 45), Chartwell (p. 51), George Inn (p. 57), Disraeli statue (p. 60), Shaw's Corner (p. 73), and Waddesdon Manor (p. 76) from the National Trust; Chedworth (p. 52), Hidcote Manor Garden (p. 61), Lacock (p. 65), and Snowshill Manor (p. 74) by Richard Surman; Hailes Abbey (pp. 58–9) and Mompesson House (pp. 66–7) by Harry Williams.

WALES & THE MARCHER LANDS
All photographs supplied by the **Wales Tourist Board** except Powis Castle (p. 98) from the AA Publications Division Photographic Library; St Elvis (pp. 82–3) from the National Trust; Hawford Dovecote (p. 93), Lower Brockhampton (p. 94), Middle Littleton Tithe Barn (p. 95), and Wilderhope Manor (p. 103) by Richard Surman; Dolmelynllyn (p. 90) and Gower (p. 92) by Harry Williams.

CENTRAL & EASTERN ENGLAND
All photographs by **Richard Surman** except Blickling Hall (pp. 108–9) from the AA Publications Division Photographic Library; Burnham Overy Mill (pp. 110–11), Felbrigg Hall (p. 114), Flatford Mill (p. 115), Lavenham Guildhall (p. 116), Scolt Head (p. 124), and Wimpole Hall (p. 130) by S. & O. Mathews; Anglesey Abbey (p. 108), Little Moreton Hall (p. 118–19), Melford Hall (pp. 120–1), Packwood House (p. 122), Shugborough (p. 125), and Upton House (p. 128) from the National Trust.

THE NORTH COUNTRY
All photographs by **Richard Surman** except Housesteads (pp. 142–3) from the AA Publications Division Photographic Library; Wastwater (pp. 132–3) and Ullswater (p. 149) by Derek Forss.

SCOTLAND
All photographs supplied by the **National Trust for Scotland.**

NORTHERN IRELAND
All photographs supplied by the **National Trust.**

Page 192 Boscastle Harbour by Harry Williams.

The publishers would also like to thank the following for the use of artwork and black-and-white photographs:

Dovecote (p. 14), Humphrey Gilbert (p. 18), Turner (p. 68), Shugborough (pp. 124–5), Hadrian's Wall (p. 142), Peter Pan (p. 156), Gannets (p. 171) and Women Spinning Irish Linen (p. 186) from the Mary Evans Picture Library; Glastonbury Tor (pp. 22–3), Jack the Giant Killer (p. 33), Shakespeare (p. 110), Bess of Hardwick (p. 117), William Morris decorations (p. 129) and Fighting at Culloden (pp. 160–1) from the Mansell Collection; photograph of Churchill at Chartwell (p. 51) from the Keystone Press; detail from the Rex Whistler Mural at Plas Newydd (p. 97) from the National Trust.